Sustainable Development
Theoretical Approaches

STUDIES IN POLITICS, SECURITY AND SOCIETY
Edited by Stanisław Sulowski
Faculty of Political Science and International Studies
University of Warsaw

VOLUME 62

Katarzyna Stachurska-Szczesiak

# Sustainable Development

## Theoretical Approaches

PETER LANG

Berlin · Bruxelles · Chennai · Lausanne · New York · Oxford

**Bibliographic Information published by the Deutsche Nationalbibliothek**
The Deutsche Nationalbibliothek lists this publication in the Deutsche Nationalbibliografie; detailed bibliographic data is available online at http://dnb.d-nb.de.

**Library of Congress Cataloging-in-Publication Data**
Names: Stachurska-Szczesiak, Katarzyna, 1976- author
Title: Sustainable development : theoretical approach / Katarzyna Stachurska-Szczesiak.
Other titles: Rozwój samopodtrzymujący. English
Description: Oxford ; New York : Peter Lang, [2025] | Series: Studies in politics, security and society, 2199-028X | Originally published in Polish as 2021 as: Rozwój samopodtrzymujący : ujęcie teoretyczne. | Includes bibliographical references and index.
Identifiers: LCCN 2025004128 (print) | LCCN 2025004129 (ebook) |
ISBN 9783631930120 hardback | ISBN 9783631930168 ebook |
ISBN 9783631935811 epub
Subjects: LCSH: Sustainable development
Classification: LCC HC79.E5 S668913 2025 (print) | LCC HC79.E5 (ebook) |
DDC 338.9/27--dc23/eng/20250721
LC record available at https://lccn.loc.gov/2025004128
LC ebook record available at https://lccn.loc.gov/2025004129

The cover image courtesy of Benjamin Ben Chaim.

UMCS
INSTITUTE OF INTERNATIONAL RELATIONS

This publication was financially supported by Maria Curie-Skłodowska University, Lublin, Poland.

ISSN 2199-028X
ISBN 978-3-631-93012-0 (Print)
ISBN 978-3-631-93016-8 (EPDF)
ISBN 978-3-631-93581-1 (EPUB)
DOI 10.3726/b22775


Published by Peter Lang GmbH, Berlin (Germany)

info@peterlang.com



This publication has been peer reviewed.
www.peterlang.com

*To my children*
*Ania and Macius*

# Contents

# List of Abbreviations

| | |
|---|---|
| Agenda 2030 | Global development strategy based on the concept on the World Bank |
| MB | Mediterranean Basin |
| COVID-19 | Respiratory disease caused by the coronavirus |
| CGDDfr | General Commissioner's Office for Sustainable Development (GCSD) |
| CSR | Corporate Social Responsibility |
| EE | Ecological Economics |
| DE | Deep Ecology |
| EC | Economy of Convention |
| EM | Ecological Modernization |
| EPA | United States Environmental Protection Agency |
| ESICs | Education for a Sustainable and Inclusive Society |
| IE | Industrial Economics |
| ITE | Industrial and Territorial Ecology |
| ESD | Education for Sustainable Development |
| FME | Free Market Environmentalism |
| FFU | Berlin School of Environmental Politics |
| CE | Circular Economy |
| GGGI | Global Green Growth Institute |
| GMO | Genetically Modified Organisms |
| GPI | Genuine Progress Indicator postępu |
| HCFC | Hydrochlorofluorocarbons |
| HDI | Human Development Index |
| HEP | Human Exceptionalism Paradigm |
| ICREI | International Centre for Research on Environmental Issues |
| IEC | Institute for Circular Economy |
| ISEW | Index of Sustainable Economic Welfare |
| IDDRI | Institute for Sustainable Development and International Relations |
| IHU | Méditerranée Infection – Mediterranean Institute for Infection |
| ISEE | International Society for Ecological Economics |
| IPCC | Intergovernmental Panel on Climate Change |
| IPBES | Intergovernmental Science-Policy Platform on Biodiversity and Ecosystem Services |

| | |
|---|---|
| LIER | French interdisciplinary laboratory for reflexivity research |
| NEP | New Ecological Paradigm |
| OECD | Organisation for Economic Cooperation and Development |
| PERC | Property and Environment Research Center |
| SD | Sustainable Development |
| SARS-CoV-2 | Severe Acute Respiratory Syndrome Coronavirus 2 |
| SCBA | Social Cost-Benefit Analysis |
| SDGs | Sustainable Development Goals |
| RT | Regulation Theory |
| EU | European Union |
| UNEP | United Nations Environment Programme |
| UNRISD | United Nations Research Institute for Social Development |

*Sustainable development is an attempt to meet the needs of the present generation without compromising the ability to meet the needs of future generations.*

Brundtland Report (1987)

# Introduction

We live in very uncertain times. The SARS-CoV-2/COVID-19 virus has "shocked the systems" we have relied on, marking the beginning of a decade of extreme turbulence. We are poised for extensive changes and transitions – both positive and negative. Numerous theoretical researchers and practitioners are currently asking questions that are crucial in the perspective of the not-so-distant future, specifically in the context of 2030. These questions assume multiple answers: will we, by that time, find ourselves in a just, resilient, and sustainable (for many years) world, or one where we witness increasingly destabilizing shocks? The possible answer to these questions may be found in the report "From System Shock to System Change – time to transform. The Future for Sustainability" from 2020, published by the Forum for the Future of Sustainability. The report analyses five key dynamics underlying these changes[1]. It takes into account the interconnected nature of human health and the planet, revealing four trajectories emerging from the COVID-19 crisis. Among them, only one ensures a just transformation, urgently needed to prevent the worst social, climate, and biodiversity crises. According to the 2021 IPCC report from the Intergovernmental Panel on Climate Change (IPCC), titled "Climate Change 2021: The Physical Science Basis," is also of significance. The aim of this report was to present world leaders with directions for action ahead of the UN Climate Summit scheduled to take place in Glasgow in November 2022[2]. This report highlights numerous negative consequences of climate change resulting from human activities, emphasizing the urgent need to immediately limit CO2 emissions. Analysts from the IPCC suggest that even the immediate cessation of carbon dioxide emissions would still result in adverse effects. However, there is hope that such actions can prevent further changes by the end of the current century[3].

The only viable proposal to halt these profound changes is the implementation of the principles of sustainable development, as formulated in the document *Our Common Future* by the World Commission on Environment and Development, also known as the Brundtland Report from 1987. It defined it as "development

---

1 See. *From System Shock to System Change – time to transform. The Future for Sustainability, Forum for the Future*, London–New York–Singapore–Mumbai 2020, pp. 3–56.

2 See more: *Sixth Assessment Report (AR6)*, Climate Change. The Physical Science Basis, https://www.ipcc.ch/report/ar6/wg1/ (18.08.2021).

3 *Ibidem*, p. 37.

that meets the needs of the present without compromising the ability of future generations to meet their own needs"[4]. Such development, as articulated, entails striving for the sustainability of human economic development while maintaining social and environmental balance. Therefore, the essence of such development is durable and dynamic socio-economic growth that does not lead to changes in the environment (its disruption) where it is already in good condition.

In areas where the environmental state is poor (areas degraded by human activity), this development aims to bring about improvementy[5]. Such an approach to sustainable development (SD) allows for associating it with a process of continuous changes and evolution in various scopes (dimensions), flexibly adapting to new challenges, rather than being associated with a state of equilibrium or a pursuit of balance[6].

Therefore, it is not surprising that the concept of sustainable development (SD), starting from the Earth Summit in Rio de Janeiro in 1992, has gained widespread political acceptance. It has become a constitutional norm in many countries worldwide, including Poland, principle governing the functioning of international organizations, including the European Union, and a reference point for development strategies. The latest comprehensive version of the Brundtland concept is reflected in the *Sustainable Development Goals* – SDGs.

In the context of the significance of the sustainable development (SD) concept itself, as well as attempts at its full and complementary application, as represented by the SDGs, this monograph is an attempt to reconstruct the scientific discourse on what sustainable development is. It considers various analytical perspectives. The main motivation behind the creation of this publication is, firstly, to encourage everyone, not just researchers in the field, to deepen their knowledge about the ways of understanding the concept of sustainable development and its evolution. Secondly, it aims to facilitate the choice of an effective path, perhaps in the face of various theoretical approaches to sustainable development, one that sets the course for just and sustainable development of human societies without compromising natural resources or opportunities for the development of both the current and future generations. This choice should be collective across different levels of activity in these societies (states, territorial units, citizens). Thirdly, the

4 *Our Common Future (Brundtland Report)*, United Nations 1987, https://www.are.ad-min.ch/are/en/home/media/publications/sustainable-development/brundtland-report.html (9.09.2019).

5 K. Stachurska-Szczesiak, *Rozwój samopodtrzymujący w polityce Unii Europejskiej wobec państw Maghrebu*, Lublin 2019, p. 50.

6 *Ibidem*.

goal is to initiate interdisciplinary discussions at the level of European science, including Polish science.

Sustainable development[7], often referred to as balanced (in Polish literature) or enduring, is a central challenge for contemporary market economies and reinforces the need to restore conditions for sustainable growth oriented towards long-term development. The existing growth model, inherited from the 20th century, has shown that it is not sustainable (balanced). Indeed, it is not only responsible for excessive greenhouse gas emissions that disrupt the climate but has also been marked by a sharp increase in inequality and numerous crises. The quantity of pollution and waste, whose gradual growth can be traced back to the beginnings of the industrial revolution, has made maintaining global life support systems more difficult due to the rapid and continuous changes in the natural environment caused by humans. L. Shi, L. Han, F. Yang, and L. Gao, in their article titled *The Evolution of Sustainable Development Theory: Types, Goals, and Research Prospects* from 2019, drew attention to eight serious pollution incidents affecting the Earth in the 20th century, indicating that humanity is facing serious problems intensifying an "ecological crisis"[8]. Challenges such as food shortages, energy crises, climate change, the rise of local unrest (such as the Arab Spring and its aftermath), or the SARS-CoV-2/COVID-19 pandemic, force humanity to re-examine its position in the ecosystem and seek a new path for long-term survival and development. In this context, the concept of sustainable development becomes an opportunity to understand and address these problems. However, the lack of understanding of the essence of the sustainable development concept remains a challenge that people need to confront at the levels of science, government agencies, and civil society. Currently, most definitions and interpretations of sustainable development do not refer to the comprehensive concept outlined in the Brundtland Report from 1987. Instead, they are often shaped by the rules of specific groups or organizations accepting the principles of sustainable development, often reducing it to a simple process of change that can continue indefinitely. L Shi, L Han, F Yang, and L Gao[9] emphasize that in this context, it would be justified to reformulate the definition of sustainable development.

7 *Why isn't sustainable development balanced*? See. K. Stachurska-Szczesiak, *Rozwój samopodtrzymujący…*, chapter 1.

8 L. Shi, L. Han, F. Yang, L. Gao, *The Evolution of Sustainable Development Theory: Types, Goals, and Research Prospects*, „Sustainability" 2019, no. 11(7158), p. 2.

9 These researchers analysed the state of the literature on SD, which showed that research they focus mainly on the area of SD practice, not its theory.

The pursuit of implementing the principles of the timeless, universally accepted concept of sustainable development signifies the emergence of a multidimensional problem. Understanding and solving this problem can benefit from the combination of various university disciplines. Social sciences, such as economics, business management, political science, economic history, sociology, psychology – all have something to contribute. In the context of the ecological crisis characterizing the recent decades and the SARS-CoV-2/COVID-19 pandemic, barriers between disciplines become less significant[10]. Science does not set barriers; on the contrary, it gradually builds a body of knowledge through specific methods, thereby developing theories, establishing laws, devising concepts, and discovering mechanisms. This set is refined through confrontation with newly acquired facts, often in connection with technological evolution. Scientific knowledge in the field of sustainable development is a collective construction that already has its own history. It is based on rational reasoning (sometimes evolving in contradiction to initial research intuitions) and the search for material causes of phenomena and processes whose effects are observed. Understanding the history of scientific knowledge in the field of SD and the evolution of how it is constructed can enhance the effectiveness of practical scientific approaches (including in its specific dimension) and develop mental attributes that are beneficial for everyone. By participating in the process of building the "science of SD" and advancing education for SD, each individual develops their intelligence, curiosity, understanding, humility in the face of facts and ideas to enrich their knowledge[11].

According to the principle of relational dialectics, the foundation of the theory is practice[12]. To better guide the practice of SD, a reorganization of the evolutionary process is necessary not only for sustainable development itself but also for the theoretical layer of the concept. Therefore, analysing ways of understanding the concept of sustainable development is crucial for its implementation. Hence, conducting research into theoretical approaches as an attempt to strengthen the theory of SD appears highly justified.

Research indicates that the theory of SD has gone through three periods: the embryonic period (before 1972), the formative period (1972–1987), and the

---

10 P. Söderbaum, *Toward sustainable development: from neoclassical monopoly to democracy – oriented economics*, „Real-world Economics Review" 2019, no. 87, p. 181.

11 Por. *Enseignement scientifique. Classe terminale, enseignement commun, voie generale, Conseil Supérieur des Programmes*, Mai 2019, p. 3–4.

12 L. Shi, L. Han, F. Yang, L. Gao, *The Evolution…*, p. 2.

development period (since 1987)[13]. These stages clearly depict the gradual implementation of the concept of SD at the global level – from an initially vague concept towards growing practical wisdom. With the widespread adoption of the SD concept and various attempts at interpretation, many researchers in the field still do not truly explain what it is all about. On the other hand, while the term is broadly defined, the meaning of the SD concept varies depending on who defines it, what issues are addressed, how it is done, and which scientific discipline is represented.

During the analysis of researchers' perspectives from various schools of thought, a crucial question arises about which of the presented perspectives will set the main trajectory for the coming years. More precisely, which assumptions of these approaches will frame the collective actions of thiscritical decade. Intentionally setting aside, in this publication, the scenarios for the application of these approaches, deepening knowledge regarding the ways of interpreting the concept of SD is crucial. As J. Gowdy and J. Erickson put it: "Even good ideas sometimes have to wait until the socio-political climate matures to blend into public consciousness"[14]. Seemingly "bad" or "unrealistic" constructs of thought may turn out to be a choice in a specific reality.

The publication of the article titled Sustainability Science in 2001 played a fundamental role in the process of understanding what SD is. This article can be considered a milestone in the field of *Sustainable Science*[15]. In this work, it was indicated that the goal of Sustainble Science is to explain the interactions between nature and society, improve the ability to manage this interaction, and choose a more sustainable trajectory. Since then, the concept of SD has become the subject of scientific inquiries, encompassing areas such as agriculture, ecological economics, forestry, and more[16]. Therefore, it's not surprising that during the "Rio + 20" summit, organized by the UN in 2012, it was indicated that cooperative global governance could resolve disputes between economic, social, and environmental

13 T. Klarin, *The Concept of Sustainable Development: From its Beginning to the Contemporary Issues*, „Zagreb International Review of Economics & Business" 2018, vol. 21, no. 1, p. 70–76.

14 J. Gowdy, J. Erickson, *Ecological economics at a crossroads*, „Ecological Economics" 2005, no. 53, p. 17.

15 R.W. Kates, W.C. Clark, R. Corell, J.M. Hall (i in.), Sustainability Science, „Science" 2001, vol. 292, no. 5517, pp. 641–642.

16 B. Zhou, Q. Ma, J. Wu, G. Hu, D. Mao, X. Zeng, J. Guo, X. Fang, Y. Liu, L. Lyu, Sustainability science revisited: Recent advances and new opportunities, „Chinese J. Appl. Ecol" 2019, no. 30, p. 325–336, quoted from: L. Shi, L. Han, F. Yang, L. Gao, The Evolution…, p. 6.

issues, effectively introducing a new dimension of governance alongside the traditional three dimensions of SD. This played a crucial role in the evolution of SD application, as evidenced by the adoption, during the SD Summit in New York in 2015, of the document *Transforming our World – The 2030 Agenda for Sustainable Development*. This program set Sustainable Development Goals (SDGs) that fundamentally changed the traditional perception of development. In addition to the pursuit of economic growth, these goals present a concept of inclusive growth and the establishment of SD, encompassing coordinated economic, social, and environmental development.

Given the above, sustainable development has become the fundamental strategy guiding global social and economic transformation. However, in the process of its implementation (practice), there are still erroneous interpretations of this concept. These manifest in the struggle between "strong" and "weak" paths of sustainable development and the confusion between intra-generational and inter-generational justice concepts.

The aim of the publication is to analyse theoretical approaches to the concept of sustainable development, considering various perspectives (with a particular emphasis on economic, ecological, and sociological perspectives) from different scientific disciplines. Firstly, the author intends to capture the process of the formation and evolution of the SD concept itself and the refinement of its goals, focusing not so much on the analysis of their origin or content but rather on the ways of thinking (arising within different scientific disciplines) that led their materialization in the form of sustainable development goals, such as the 2030 Agenda. Secondly, the goal is to enhance a comprehensive understanding of sustainable development theory, which includes selected perspectives on the reasoning of the SD concept. The publication aims not only to refer to recognized sustainable development theories presented in synthetic studies but, through an interdisciplinary approach, to present those approaches (from economists, ecologists, sociologists) that are less known but significantly influence the understanding of the essence of the SD concept.

For such a defined problem and research goal, it is essential to subject to verification the hypothesis assuming that the increased dynamics of changes in international relations affect the degree of crystallization of existing theoretical approaches to SD and the triangulation of many research perspectives. The publication adopted an analysis of literature review, applying an inductive approach and occasionally incorporating quantitative data that proved necessary in the use of the comparative method.

The presented monograph consists of four chapters. In the first chapter, titled *Theoretical Approaches to Sustainable Development*, three ways of reasoning the concept of SD (free-market environmentalism, ecological modernization, citizen participation), governing the framework for the so-called mainstream approaches, are analysed. By identifying them, the subject of individual subchapters relates to the genesis and evolution of the main thinking patterns about SD, focusing on the subjects and their roles in creating a common space for reflection to effectively achieve the goals of SD. In this context, important questions emerged, such as how to understand the assumptions of particular mainstream approaches in the context of the application of the SD concept and to what extent these approaches influence the evolution of other ways of reasoning about SD, as well as the concept of SD itself.

The key assumption of the second chapter titled *Economic Approaches to Sustainable Development* is to present those ways of reasoning within the concept of *sustainable development* that have significantly influenced its shape and the process of its evolution. This process is still in *statu nascendi*. The approaches encompass both traditional (neoclassical) understandings of the sustainable development concept (where economic phenomena are treated as if they were detached from broader social life) and perspectives of a new generation of economists, known as institutional approaches (characterized by a multi-aspect view of the lives of individuals and societies, considering both economic and non-economic factors). The ways of thinking about sustainable development within these institutional approaches extend more or less beyond the domain of economics (ecological economics, convention economics, historical-institutional approaches, or humanistic perspectives). The latter approaches attempt to avoid monetary reductionism and strive to incorporate socio-cultural and environmental aspects.

Studying "sustainability" from the perspectives of economists allows for identifying similarities and differences, indicating that various interpretations of sustainable development exist within the field of economics, illustrating the presence of "weak," "strong," and even "radical" versions. It is noteworthy that these differences arise not only between different streams within a particular scientific discipline but also within individual approaches. Some conceptual positions of SD are more idealistic, relating to moral imperatives and the direction to take, and are applicable in the long term. Others are still in the stage of crystallizing strongly orthodox positions, the realization of which would require a drastic change in societal thinking and the functioning of contemporary economies. Here, the question arises as to which economic perspective influenced the shape and content of the Sustainable Development Goals (SDGs), which set the direction for the next decade of our future development. In this context, the concept of "coevolution of sustainability" based on the principle of cumulative causation, is noteworthy. It reveals how social processes involve the interaction of many factors (both economic and non-economic), which then combine, shifting the system toward balance rather than automatic sustainability.

Entropic analysis concludes the depiction of economists' ways of thinking about sustainable development. It draws attention to the idea that the sustainability of development or growth is an illusion, arguing this based on the second law of thermodynamics. However, within the entropic framework of thinking about SD, the concept of "degrowth" emerges. It posits that every human or organism action results in a deficit for the entire system. In this approach, the goal is not to reduce growth to improve the quality of life on Earth, but rather to foster concern and awareness of the crisis, preceded by a change in worldview. This relatively radical vision of sustainable development emphasizes that the key to extending the future of human societies (though not preventing chaos and decay) on a global scale is transitioning from "colonizing" existence to "climatic" existence. This implies the most significant (conscious) change our species will have to undergo. In a low-entropy society, "less means more," where society rejects material consumption, and frugal energy use becomes the paramount imperative.

The subject of analysis in the third chapter, titled *Ecological Approaches to Sustainable Development*, is the essential ways in which ecologists perceive the concept of sustainable development, pointing out similarities and contradictions with the mainstream of SD (see Chapter 1). The construction of this chapter reflects the heterogeneous nature of the visions of SD present in ecologists' perceptions. The starting point for defining the framework of this chapter is the belief that the emergence of ecology as a science in the 1960s had a significant impact on the character and meaning of the concept of SD itself. However, ecologists' perspectives on the concept of SD strongly evolve, giving the impression of a science at a "crossroads," drawing knowledge from many other disciplines. This does not necessarily mean that this process is harmful to ecology as a distinct scientific discipline; on the contrary, these perspectives provide access to an integrative understanding of our environment and foster a collective awareness of our place in the world.

Analysing these positions has drawn attention to the paradoxical notion that the diversity of theoretical approaches among ecologists regarding Sustainable Development (SD) seems to be even greater than in the case of economists. While all of them criticize the current global economic system (capitalism), considering it the main culprit not only for the financial crisis[17], but also the ecological crisis,

---

17 See more: M. Walkowski, *Causes of the global financial crisis of 2008+. Analysis and comparison of selected opinions*, „Przegląd Strategiczny" 2013, No 2, pp. 179–196.

the ways to address it are not as clear-cut in the representation of ecological thinking, dividing them into two or more camps. Some represent a moderate stance, identifying themselves as proponents of the SD concept, showing similarities with the mainstream of SD (known as Greens or environmentalists; advocates of political ecology). Others are considered more radical than the former (Green or precursors of ecologism; eco-socialists; socio-economic branch of ecofeminism). Finally, those considered the most radical (radical eco-anarchists, so-called primitivists; advocates of deep ecology; mystical branch of ecofeminism) emphasize the need to change human-nature relations, even rejecting existing values and lifestyles.

In each case, the analysis of these ecological trends in the context of SD consists of a theoretical layer – both well-established and highly evolving – forming a platform for the emergence of new branches in the future. It is noteworthy that there is a frontal opposition between different ecological tendencies in understanding SD, which are largely irreconcilable and far from the mainstream of SD, creating uncertainty for ecologists themselves and all other analysts. One thing that unites these ecologists is awareness of environmental problems, but their diagnoses significantly differ from one another.

The fourth chapter, titled *Sociological Approach to Sustainable Development*, analyses the sociological perspective, serving as a complement to comprehensive approach to the concept of SD, which includes economic, ecological, and sociological dimensions. This chapter consists of two subchapters. The first attempts to capture the essence of the social dimension in the concept of SD, which has been neglected for decades in interpretations stemming from the Brundtland report. It also emphasizes the reasons for the revival of sociological reflection in discussions about SD. The second subchapter presents a specific "theoretical" approach of sociologists to SD, known as environmental sociology. Its roots date back to the 1970s, with full crystallization occurring in the 1990s. This approach allowed a shift from the previous paradigm of sociology, assuming the independence of people from the constraints of their environment, toward a way of thinking (aligned with SD) that considers the limited availability of natural environmental resources and their impact on shaping social phenomena.

The process of preparing the monograph was based on a wide range of sources and numerous foreign-language studies, with a particular focus on references from French-language literature. The analysis of the latter allowed for creating an objective and more comprehensive picture of the research goal, indicating that some of the "theoretical" streams of SD trace back to the thinking of French-speaking researchers. These, in turn, contributed to the evolution and development of the perception of the concept of SD visible in Anglophone literature. Especially useful, as inspiration for the author's research on sustainable development, was M. Pietras's book titled *Ecological Security in Europe* from the year (2000)[18]. In this book, firstly, the term *sustainable development* was used for the first time in Polish literature as *rozwój samopodtrzymujący* (rather than "zrównoważony," as commonly used, especially among Polish economic researchers). Secondly, international research on various aspects of ecological security was included, indicating that ecological issues and numerous security threats in Europe became a challenge for international security. However, amidst the wealth of literature on the undertaken issues, it is challenging to find a synthetic publication that includes the interpretation of all dimensions of the SD concept, illustrating its complexity. Among the foreign-language sources, particular attention is given to the synthesis of economists' perspectives on the SD concept presented by the French economist G. Destais in *Les théorisations économiques du développement durable. Proposition de décryptage critique* (2011). In the Polish-language literature, notable is the synthesis of ecological pectives on the RS concept presented by two authors, E. Rokicka and W. Woźniak, in *W kierunku zrównoważonego rozwoju. Koncepcje, interpretacje, konteksty* (2016). Despite the rapid growth of existing research on SD[19], the need for theoretical and conceptual justification persists, and significant opportunities for further analysis remain untapped. This publication is a response to this need and an attempt to fill the gap, which seems to apply not only to Poland or Europe but the entire world. The cognitive relevance of the topic and its utility for political practice, concerning the dynamics of visible changes in the economic, social, and ecological dimensions of human life and development, as well as the emergence of pluralistic thinking about the future of human development over the past decade, have been sufficient reasons for the author to write the presented monograph.

---

18 See more: M. Pietraś, *Ecological security in Europe. Studium politologiczne*, Lublin 2000, p. 8, 167–170.

19 M. Brandenburg, T. Gruchmann, N. Oelze, *Sustainable Supply Chain Management – A Conceptual Framework and Future Research Perspectives*, „Sustainability" December 2019, No. 11(24), p. 2.

# 1. Theoretical approaches to sustainable development

The emergence of theoretical approaches to Sustainable Development (SD) is associated with the publication of the World Commission on Environment and Development report, the so-called Brundtland report, in 1987, which included the definition of the concept of sustainable development. However, it is evident that this concept has intellectual predecessors, sometimes old, part of economic thought, and sometimes ecological or representing other social sciences. The issue of SD has led to the creation of significant literature from various backgrounds, characterized by controversies arising from different interpretations of certain elements of the concept. Depending on who presents them, one can distinguish moderate approaches (coming from businesses and their representatives or international institutions such as the World Bank – WB or the Organization for Economic Cooperation and Development – OECD), acknowledging possible compliance with SD principles and the dominance of economic logic. On the other hand, there are radical approaches (coming from non-governmental organizations), characterized by the search for alternative development models[20].

Given this theoretical expansion, it is possible to distinguish trends in the sciences that apply the so-called "weak sustainability" approach, initiated by the neoclassical school, or "strong sustainability," accepted by ecological economics, especially the institutional approach and proponents of the so-called absurdly strong sustainability. The common assumption of these approaches is to set contemporary societies the path of sustainability, which, in turn, requires determining the availability of resources of four types of capital and the relationships between them over a specified period. Understanding these relationships significantly influences the interpretation and assessment of sustainable development[21]. Supporters of the first approach generally uphold the hypothesis of possible substitutability among production factors (natural capital, physical capital, labour), and even between different types of goods (the environment is then treated as an economic good). If natural capital can be replaced by production capital, it implies weak sustainability. "As long as the total amount of capital increases in the

---

20 M. Maillefert, S. Rousseau, B. Zuindeau, *Lectures hétérodoxes du développement durable*, „Développement durable et territories" 2010, vol. 1, no 3, http://journals.openedition.org/developpementdurable/8681 (7.07.2018).

21 L. Shi, L. Han, F. Yang, L. Gao, *The Evolution…*, p. 7.

development process, even if natural capital degrades to an unrecoverable state, it is still sustainable"[22]. On the contrary, advocates of "strong sustainability" are critical of such an assumption and perceive the environment as a very specific variable, challenging to replace. Here, natural capital plays an irreplaceable role in production and consumption. "This concept is mainly based on the steady-state economic theory, according to which produced capital cannot be replicated without the input of natural capital. Therefore, the development process requires not only an increase in the total amount of capital but also the rationality of the capital structure and not exceeding ecological thresholds. Thus, economic development should not exceed a natural limit"[23].

The third interpretation of SD, known as "absurdly strong sustainability," is emphasized by a group of radical ecologists. They believe not only that natural capital cannot be replaced by production capital but also acknowledge the need to eliminate the exploitation and use of ecosystems. Advocates of this approach to the SD concept assume that humans and other species are equal[24].

The diverse theoretical foundations result from varied analyses and political recommendations. In the non-theoretical literature on SD from various stakeholders interested in this issue (international institutions, governmental administration, local authorities, companies and their representatives, associations, etc.), the natural environment holds a central, and even exclusive, place. However, the following theoretical approaches of the mainstream (free-market environmentalism, ecological modernization, civic participation) prioritize economic activities and their impact on the natural environment, seeking ways to limit negative effects—creating possibilities for preventive intervention, reconciling economic efficiency with environmental conservation. These approaches highlight the dilemmas of SD in terms of how to reconcile conflicting interests[25] without sacrificing SD priorities. Contradictions present in every community are mitigated through compromise-building for regulated conflict resolution. The key is to understand the complexity of these compromises: blueprints for the future

---

22 *Ibidem.*

23 *Ibidem.*

24 This way of thinking can be found in the ongoing debate between philosophers and animal ethicists regarding, among others, "species discrimination", between P. Singerem a Sh. Kaganem. See more: J. Hopster, *The Speciesism Debate: Intuition, Method, and Empirical Advances*, „Animals (Basel)" 2019, no. 9, https://www.ncbi.nlm.nih.gov/pmc/articles/PMC6940905/pdf/ani-mals-09–01054.pdf (24.07.2020).

25 For example, a conflict of interest between employees of a polluting industry and a competitive "green" industry, etc.

will not be developed overnight because what is beneficial for businesses may not necessarily apply to all other levels. There exists a whole range of theories within economics, ecology, and lately sociology that emerge, constituting alternative SD approaches.

Therefore, SD is characterized by a multitude of interpretations and theoretical approaches. Whether it concerns the representation of actors or more academic work, this issue has gained considerable diversity. The theoretical approaches to the concept of SD are developed almost simultaneously with the practice of its implementation. Practical problems undoubtedly influence the evolution of these approaches, some more or less recognized as theory. Such an approach implies considerations from various scientific disciplines. There is even a concept of a specific meta-science related to SD, creating a separate quasi-scientific discipline. However, a more realistic approach, as noted by L. Michnowski, seems to be the construction of a meta-theory of SD, which would define the fundamental goals of this developmental concept, thereby establishing a common methodological platform for research conducted within individual scientific disciplines[26].

The theory evolves through succession or surrender. It undergoes succession when one theory leads to the next transformation, signifying an update of the original theory whose foundations remain untouched. It undergoes surrender when the old theory gives way to the new by refuting a theory inconsistent with observation. J. Gowdy and J. Erickson argue that "good ideas must wait until the socio-political climate matures to blend into public consciousness"[27].

## 1.1. Free market environmentalism

In the early 21st century, pioneers of free-market environmentalism (T.L. Anderson and D.R. Leal, specifically in 2001) demonstrated that an effective way to preserve the natural environment is to extend the creativity of business owners and the principles of the free market to all natural resources[28].This requires complete privatization and the effective definition and protection of property rights. In the absence of these conditions, there are incentives for irresponsible behaviours such as unjustified consumption and pollution of many natural resources. This approach, known as Free Market Environmentalism (FME), emerged in the

26 L. Michnowski, *Jak żyć?, Ekorozwój albo…*, Białystok 1995, http://www.psl.org.pl/kte/books.htm (9.08.2019).

27 J. Gowdy, J. Erickson, *Ecological economics…*, p. 17.

28 https://mises.pl/wp-content/uploads/2012/05/Huerta-de-Soto-kilka-dodatkowych-refleksji-na-temat-kryzysu.pdf (7.06.2021).

contemporary libertarian thought[29] in the United States, focusing on the free market as the primary mechanism regulating human-nature relationships, which could contribute to solving environmental problems. Advocates of this approach, including green parties and libertarian parties, seek to reconcile two ideologies by combining the free market with ecologism[30]. Property rights and legal norms are considered the best means to establish a sustainable economy and to preserve and improve the state of the natural environment.

FME thus creates a free-market model based on property rights protection. It can be considered a specific case of the resource-based model because the mechanism of property rights protection, which forms its foundation, leads to the accurate valuation of resource values. The fundamental assumption of the model is to treat phenomena contributing to the degradation of the natural environment, such as waste, as forms of violation of private or public property[31]. In his book For a New Liberty: *The Libertarian Manifesto*, published in 1973, M.N. Rothbard advocates that "total privatization of resources and a free market will enable the protection and multiplication of resources, and do so much more quickly than government regulations"[32]. In the book *The Ethics of Liberty* from 2003, Rothbard

29 Libertarianism can be defined as a freedom-oriented and extremely individualistic socio-political ideology and the political movement inspired by its principles. It is based on the thesis that the constant and irreconcilable conflict between freedom and power is the foundation of history. Its proponents believe that every individual should have unrestricted freedom to control their own person and property—what they have produced themselves or received and acquired from others, as long as it does not limit the analogous freedom of other individuals". Quoted from: J. Bartyzel, *Geneza i próba systematyki głównych nurtów libertarianizmu* [in:] *Libertarianizm – teoria, praktyka, interpretacje*, ed. W. Bulira, W. Gogłoza, Lublin 2010, p. 15.

30 According to the PWN dictionary: "Ecologism – a philosophical movement (second half of the 20th century) addressing environmental protection issues and the place of humans in the world—mainly the mutual dependencies between humans and nature that, in a short period of time, determine the quality of life, and in the longer perspective, the conditions for the survival of human populations. It constitutes a new form of humanism shaping the ecological conscience of humans. Therefore, «ecologism» is a new political ideology based on the belief that the non-human world deserves moral consideration and should be taken into account in social, economic, and political systems. Quoted from: B. Baxter, *Ecologism. An Introduction*, Georgetown 2000.

31 See more: W. Piontek, *Gospodarowanie odpadami komunalnymi jako czynnik wzrostu gospodarczego*, Białystok 2015, chapter IV.

32 M.N. Rothbard, *For new freedom. Liberatarian Manifesto* (1973), Polish translation: W. Falkowski (2004), https://mises.pl/pliki/upload/Rothbard_manifest_libertarianski.pdf (7.09.2019).

goes further, stating "that the right to complete ownership is a principle congruent with the moral code given to every human being and that this natural right is naturally best for humans"[33]. According to him, the violation of these rights, for example, through the production of pollution, triggers interactions and actions to protect property, such as through legal proceedings. He points out that if private companies owned the rights to rivers and lakes (for example, if Lake Erie were private property), anyone who polluted them would be immediately sued for their violation. Subsequently, the court would oblige them to compensate for the damages caused and to cease similar practices[34]. Therefore, only the right to private property can put an end to the pollution of natural resources. Currently, no one can protect this natural resource from pollution because it is not owned by anyone, and there is no one to take care of its protection. In contrast, if someone caused contamination of a private lake (some small lakes are private property), they would have to stop it promptly – the owner would vigorously demand[35].

In this model, the role of the state is limited to the necessary minimum and mainly involves defining property rights within the legal framework, determining the circumstances of their violation, and ensuring the possibility of enforcing these rights.

Supporters of Free Market Environmentalism (FME) argue that free markets can be more successful than the state in solving many environmental problems. *The Property and Environment Research Center* (PERC)[36] founded 30 years ago in Bozeman, Montana, is the largest and oldest institute in the United States dedicated to improving environmental quality through markets and property rights. Originally established as a research center where experts identified state regulations and bureaucracy leading to environmental degradation, PERC simultaneously sought to explain how markets could be used to improve environmental quality. The idea of FME is a direct result of their research. R. Stroup, retired director of PERC, writing an essay on FME for the Library of Economics and Liberty, clearly pointed out that "free-market environmentalism focuses on markets as a solution to environmental problems (…) free markets can be more successful than the state – and historically – in solving many ecological problems – the private sector is often more open than the state to environmental demands. This

33 M.N. Rothbard, *The Ethics of Liberty*, New York 2003, p. 45.

34 M.N. Rothbard, *For new freedom…*, p. 152.

35 *Ibidem*.

36 https://www.perc.org/ (9.09.2019).

evidence, supported by economic theory, has led to a reconsideration of the traditional point of view"[37].

For markets to function in the environmental sphere, just as in any other, the rights to each important resource must be clearly defined, easy to defend against attack, and transferable (marketable) by owners on environmentally favourable terms: buyers and sellers. Ecological problems arise due to the lack or incompleteness of these property rights. When rights to resources are well-defined and easily defensible against invasion, all potential polluters or potential victims are interested in avoiding pollution-related problems. When air or water pollution damages private property, the owner whose wealth is at risk will think in this way – if necessary, in court – thereby minimizing the threat[38]. PERC researchers have carefully documented examples of the application of FME in practice. To transition from theory to action, PERC introduced a program allowing individuals – green entrepreneurs – to learn how to use property, contracts, and market processes to improve environmental quality. PERC's Institute of Enviropreneur attracts people from around the world who seek to implement FME principles. Currently, PERC continues to grow with its newly established university, where scientists, journalists, policymakers, and environmental protection specialists can gather, share knowledge, conduct research, and engage in impactful discussions[39]. This approach advocates for capitalist economic growth but rejects the idea of reducing it.

FME has become part of the mainstream field of environmental economics, which is a branch of economics dealing with the relationships between the economy and the environment. It examines the economics of natural resources from both sides – extraction, use, and return to the environment (waste). Many economists from the mainstream have found that well-accepted principles explaining market behaviours and contributing to prosperity also explain environmental issues and offer ways to address them. Notably, economists like M. Friedman, a free-market economist, and P. Samuelson, a leading economist of the Keynesian school, have tended to speak with one voice when discussing human behaviours with non-economic social scientists[40]. In an atmosphere of scepticism among economists (such as Samuelson and Friedman) regarding the government's role in the mainstream, new schools of economics emerged, including the Austrian

---

37 http://www.econlib.org/library/Enc/FreeMarketEnvironmentalism.html (9.09.2019).

38 Ibidem.

39 Ibidem.

40 T.L. Anderson, J.S. Shaw, Is Free-Market Environmentalism, „Mainstream"?, „The Social Studies" 2000, vol. 91, No. 5, pp. 227–228.

School, public choice economics, and new institutional economics. All these schools influenced FME. The mainstream economics is much richer now due to these insights. The main cause of environmental problems, as recognized by many economists, is not the "bankruptcy of the market," as some believed in the past, but the lack of markets – more precisely, the lack of private property, which is the foundation of markets. While economists have long acknowledged that transactions based on private property are imperfect, many now recognize that the absence of private property, and thus markets, distorts incentives even more than problems associated with incorporating costs and benefits into market transactions[41]. The problems of costs and benefits arising from decisions for economists are illustrated by "The Tragedy of the Commons" by G. Hardin[42]. Anyone who has spent a lot of time in public parks or state forests knows that people often treat them thoughtlessly, allowing trash to accumulate. Visitors to parks have little motivation to keep them clean because anyone can spoil them again at any time—there is no owner who would benefit financially. Air and water are polluted because they are also common resources. They have no owners to prevent people from degrading them. Another example of common goods is wilderness. Today, many wild animals are endangered because wilderness is a common good. Open access to natural resources leads to theiroverexploitation. Only privatization of resources and effective management will allow their preservation in the long term. The real value of resources, natural capital, and ecosystem services should be assessed through the practices of a self-regulating market, similar to the goods and services produced for sale.

Supporters of free-market environmentalism have long been aware of the problems associated with government decision-making. They propose dealing with the

41 Ibidem, p. 230.

42 In his article titled Tragedy of the Commons, published in 1968 in the journal "Science," G. Hardin described a situation in which the unlimited use of commonly available natural resources (in this case, pasturelands) leads to a social trap: complete degradation and exploitation of the pastures. When few people utilized the open space of pasturelands for grazing their animals, it served as a convenient place for their livestock. However, as villages expanded, and the number of grazed animals increased, it led to the destruction of this space. The tragedy of the commons illustrates the value of cooperation in using common goods (shared) with limited capacity. Too many users of a common good can lead to its destruction. G. Hardin, however, shows that the individual gain of one community participant results in losses for the community as a whole. An individual farmer gains by increasing the number of animals and introducing them to publicly accessible, free pasture, but this action deprives the community of that space in the longer term.

potential "tragedy of the commons" by establishing private property rights. Private ownership makes people more responsible and forces them to bear the costs of actions that reduce the value of the resources they use. At the same time, they can benefit from actions that increase the value of those resources. If they neglect what they have, the property will lose value. These facts serve as an incentive for good management. Economists are increasingly discovering examples of how the creation (or recognition) of private or quasi-private property rights can solve environmental problems[43]. Therefore, private property can be an effective remedy for the tragedy of open access that characterizes many environmental goods. Establishing property rights to such goods is certainly not technically simple[44]. In practice, this happens on land, coasts, rivers, or forests. It is more challenging to imagine in oceans or the atmosphere, but the construction of ownership and usage rights is already the subject of technical or institutional innovations[45].

There is international evidence that the protection of private property rights is closely linked to environmental quality. In a study by S. Norton, he considered countries where property rights are protected and then examined how this protection correlated with measurements of environmental quality. In countries where property rights are well protected, approximately 93% of the population has access to safe drinking water, compared to only about 60% of the population with access to water in countries with weak property rights. Norton found a similar correlation with life expectancy. He stated that the average life expectancy is 70 years in countries with strong property rights protection, but only 50 years in countries where property rights are poorly protected. Even people living in poor nations enjoy a higher quality of life if property rights are well protected[46].

Ownership is an integral part of human society, taking various forms from private ownership, where all rights belong to one person, through co-ownership (the concept of common ownership, as emphasized by Nobel laureate E. Ostrom), where a clearly defined number of right holders exercise equal or specific rights to a resource, to public ownership managed by a public entity that regulates and controls the use of the resource. While private ownership is always preferred in economic matters, the complexity of environmental management often requires

43 T.L. Anderson, J.S. Shaw, *Is Free-Market Environmentalism…*, p. 237.

44 E. Queinnec, *Réguler l'écologie au moyen de la liberté: Bref plaidoyer en faveur de „l'écolibéralisme"*, „Journaldeslibertes.fr", Été 2019, no. 5, p. 42.

45 *Ibidem.*

46 *Ibidem.*

a subtle combination of appropriation systems to adapt to specific situations[47]. Thanks to the work of E. Ostrom in 1990 titled *Governing the Commons*, it is recognized that common property ownership in various forms can be an effective way to manage resources[48].

On the other hand, K. Hansen, in his 2015 article titled *Visions of Environmentalism*, points out that all environmental problems stem from conflicting demands for limited natural resources[49]. When human demands are small compared to the resource base, conflicts between competing users are less visible. Environmental conflicts inevitably arise when scarcity dictates that one use excludes another. However, if access to usable resources is open to all, the tragedy of the commons becomes unavoidable. Eliminating the "tragedy of the commons" requires limiting and clarifying who uses and benefits from limited natural resources. This raises several questions not only about who decides which uses will dominate but also about the government's role in determining who decides. Are these decisions made by the local population directly connected to the resource? Are they democratically resolved?

Regardless of who decides, it is important to realize that solving environmental problems creates rights to access and derive value from the environment. Therefore, it is not surprising that this division is controversial. Governmental authorities at the state and local levels may impose rules for access to resources and dictate conditions for their use. K. Hansen emphasizes that if public choices take place in the political arena, it can be considered political environmentalism. On the other hand, if an individual or a group of people (resource owners) can control access to the resource and benefit from it in a private or market setting, they should be seen as proponents of Free Market Environmentalism (FME)[50].

The effectiveness of these approaches in maximizing the net value of limited resources depends on decision-makers' ability to assess the value of alternative ways of using resources and their motivation to weigh one value against another[51]. Taking the example of fisheries management, the difference between political environmentalism and FME can be highlighted. Political environmentalism relies

47 M. Falque, *Les droits de propriété dans la problématique*, „La revue foncière" 2018, no. 22, pp. 27–28.

48 See more: E. Ostrom, *Governing the commons. The Evolution of Institutions for Collective Action*, Cambridge 1990, https://wtf.tw/ref/ostrom_1990.pdf (6.11.2019).

49 K. Hansen, *Visions of Environmentalism* [in:] *Free Market Environmentalism for the Next Generation*, ed. T. L. Anderson, D.R. Leal, New York 2015, p. 1.

50 *Ibidem*, p. 4.

51 *Ibidem*, p. 2.

on regulations and permits to prevent overfishing. If too many fish are caught, regulations may limit their catch. If monitoring the total catch is too challenging, regulatory authorities may impose seasonal restrictions, thereby slowing down the harvest. In contrast, Free Market Environmentalism relies on well-defined and enforced property rights to fisheries to prevent overfishing. If fishermen are allocated a share in sustainable harvesting, they are encouraged to accumulate surplus fish rather than catching as many as possible in a short period. Neither policy nor property rights operate in isolation. Most resource management requires interaction between individual resource owners, business owners, local authorities, and governments. Social organizations increasingly act as intermediaries between markets and governments in allocating rights to resources. Collective groups, such as co-owned associations, can regulate and control access, kinship-based groups can establish rules for resource use, and private property owners can determine their utilization. The ideas of free-market environmentalism are applied in various creative ways, including the establishment of institutional agreements to generate information about values and provide incentives for individuals to act in accordance with these values. S. Regan and T. Watkins share their research findings on adopted solutions aimed at changing people's approach to natural environmental resources, particularly in the context of open access. Their article, published in August 2020 in the Property and Environment Research Center (PERC) journal, discusses the effectiveness of these solutions, pointing out their applicability and success in the United States[52].

Therefore, according to Free Market Environmentalism (FME), property rights form the foundation of environmental thinking. However, everything indicates that in Europe, especially in France, they are largely ignored, and regulations and taxes are considered the best, if not the only, tools for resource management. M. Falque, a French advocate of FME, emphasizes that such an approach "will not solve problems and will contribute to weakening or even eliminating property, and thus freedom"[53]. At the same time, he gives an example of the contemporary thinking of French decision-makers, referring to the decision of the mayor of Grambois[54] on January 24, 2018, to create a communal fruit garden (where figs

52 See more: S. Regan, T. Watkins, *The Trumps Administration Takes a Step toward Better Protecting Endangered Species*, PERC 17 August 2020, https://www.perc.org/2020/08/17/the-trump-administration-takes-a-step-toward-better-protecting-endangered-species/ (1.07.2021).

53 M. Falque, *Les droits de propriété…*, p. 30.

54 Grambois – a French commune located in the Vaucluse department, in the Provence-Alpes-Côte d'Azur region.

grow) accessible to everyone according to the principle of the "common good" advocated today. Referring to this example, M. Falque recalls the "tragedy of the commons" by G. Hardin and outlines the scenario and actions of the mayor of this French municipality in the future: "In the future, the mayor's choice will be to limit access by regulation and hire a 'common good management agent' to avoid inevitable conflicts between rights holders and preserving collections. Most likely, the orchard will be abandoned and sold to a farmer who will restrict free access and sell his fruits"[55]. The author points out that a better solution would be "common good management," a concept advocated by E. Ostrom. This example illustrates the principle that unrestricted access to a limited resource (in this case, figs) can only lead to ruin and conflict[56]. M. Falque, as a representative of French Free Market Environmentalism (FME), also points out the reasons for the lack or "absence of France in the global discussion on the rediscovery of the central role of property rights in economic development and environmental resource management"[57].

This fact is explained by the relatively new area of research in the relationship between property and the natural environment among French scientists. The author refers to three main works that have influenced the evolution of France's thinking towards FME. The first book published in 1984 by G. Berthu titled *La propriété c'est l'envol* did not directly relate to the natural environment. The second position, released a year later by H. Lepage titled *Pourquoi la propriété (Why there is property)*, focused on the use of property rights to manage environmental resources. The text ends with a political note: "Our environment suffers less from an excess of property and capitalism than the other way around. The anger that ecological movements show towards market economy institutions suggests that their leaders are driven not so much by concern for the actual protection of nature and the environment but by their ideological hatred of everything that is private property, reminiscent of capitalism. A splendid example of collective blindness cleverly exploited by all those who have set themselves the goal of weakening Western societies"[58]. The third book, published in 1991 by G. Bramoullé in a pamphlet titled *La peste verte (The Green Plague)*, mentioned the limits and perverse effects of violating property rights. However, M. Falque points out that a crucial element in France's joining the ongoing discussion was the establishment of the

55 M. Falque, *Les droits de propriété…*, p. 30.

56 *Ibidem.*

57 *Ibidem*, p. 28.

58 H. Lepage, *Pourquoi la propriété*, Paris 1985, pp. 325–352, cited in: https://www.icrei.fr/en/2019/10/02/did-you-say-freedom/ (7.11.2019).

International Center for Research on Environmental Issues (ICREI) founded in Paris in 1992 by a group of French economists and lawyers. Its goal is to disseminate publications and conduct research on the new economics of resources, namely the use of property rights and market transactions, the net impact assessment of social regulations, the application of the principle of responsibility, and the promotion of institutional solutions for a free societ[59].

* * *

Free Market Environmentalism (FME) combines self-interest with resource management by establishing private property rights to environmental resources. These rights require owners to consider the costs and benefits of their actions and facilitate business transactions that generate business profits, improving efficiency. Property rights and markets can provide appropriate incentives without relying on human altruism or good intentions towards the natural environment (which can be unreliable). Markets based on secure property rights provide a decentralized system for valuing resources and price information, giving decision-makers and suppliers objective measures of subjective values. Resource management should occur as long as private owners are rewarded for the benefits they generate through resource utilization and are simultaneously held responsible for all associated costs. Governments play a significant role in determining and recording property claims, establishing liability rules, and adjudicating disputed property rights. Therefore, well-defined and enforced property rights impose discipline on resource owners, compelling them to be responsible for the harm they cause to others and rewarding them for improving resource utilization. Thus, property rights motivate owners to protect the value of their environmental assets. Market forces based on the demand and supply of environmental goods and services stimulate human ingenuity to find ways to cope with natural resource constraints. Producers increase productivity and find substitutes, effectively economizing in the face of resource scarcity, while consumers reduce consumption and redirect their purchases in response to changing prices[60].

In the ongoing debate since the 1990s regarding whether the expansion of private property rights and market transactions is sufficient to address environmental issues, the critical approach of T. Smith in the "Journal of Agricultural and Environmental Ethics" (1995) stands out. He lists arguments both "for" and "against" the effectiveness of T. Anderson and D. Leal's assumptions when

59 https://www.icrei.fr/en/about_us/ (7.11.2019).

60 K. Hansen, *Visions of Environmentalism…*, p. 4.

confronted with reality, addressing human nature (questioning the assumption that property owners refrain from degrading their property), market specifics (questioning the assertion that market prices constitute an "objective measure" of environmental costs and benefits), and the role of the state (allegedly limited to defining and enforcing tradable property rights), ultimately concluding that FME is not acceptable[61]. In this context, the question arises whether companies are genuinely interested in the voluntary constraints imposed by the natural environment. While the motivations of business owners are diverse and challenging to pinpoint, it is essential to note that since the mid-1990s, international corporations have initiated an intensive process of implementing environmental standards, adhering to a variety of SD principles (management systems, e.g., ISO).

## 1.2. Ecological modernization

The theory of ecological modernization (EM)[62] was developed in the early 1980s by a small group of researchers from Western European countries, particularly Germany and the Netherlands. In the German group of social scientists were M. Jänicke, J. Huber, V. von Prittwitz, U. Simonis, and K. Zimmermann. Among the Dutch contributors were G. Spaargaren, M. Hajer, and A. P. J. Mol[63]. However, the term "ecological modernization" is commonly attributed to two German political scientists (J. Huber and M. Jänicke), who are pioneers in the sociological approach to "environmental reform"[64]. It was initially embraced within the Berlin school of environmental policy research (Environmental Policy Research Centre – FFU)[65], and later by other authors influencing the German political debate before becoming a political formula of the red-green federal government in Germany

61 T. Smith, *The case against Pee market environmentalism*, „Journal of Agricultural and Environmental Ethics" 1995, no. 8(2), pp. 126–144.

62 Currently, there are several synonyms or similar concepts, such as "eco-innovation", "green development", "green growth" or the transition towards a "green economy".

63 A.P.J. Mol, D.A. Sonnenfeld, *Ecological modernization around the world: an introduction*, „Environmental Politics" 2000, vol. 9, no. 1, p. 4.

64 F.H. Buttel, *Environmental Sociology and the Explanation of Environmental Reform*, „Organization and Environment" 2003, vol. 16, No. 3, pp. 306–344.

65 https://www.polsoz.fu-berlin.de/en/polwiss/forschung/systeme/ffu/index.html (13.07.2021).

(1998–2005)[66]. While authors like A. P. J. Mol and G. Spaargaren discussed EM in the context of sociological theories of modernity, the German discourse had a stronger political orientation, focusing on political advisory aspects[67]. Ecological modernization, as presented by J. Huber in the 1980s, served both as an analytical theory and a political program oriented towards environmental policy. As an analytical theory, it suggested that industrial society should "flip the ecological switch," meaning it should undergo ecological restructuring of its production and consumption processes. The "eco-social transition" from polluting to clean production processes would be possible through intelligent technology, leading to an ecological reform of both economies and societies[68]. EM can result in a structural change that reduces the share of sectors requiring large amounts of natural resources.

Ecological modernization aims to preserve or restore environmental quality through innovations that efficiently utilize resources[69]. According to this premise, environmental research should not be limited to analysing environmental degradation or its treatment but should instead focus on how public and private entities construct environmental issues for understanding.

At the level of public actions, Ecological Modernization (EM) is a concept that expresses the idea of re-conceptualizing environmental problems and their treatment. The status of the natural environment in political agendas is strengthened. Concern for the natural environment is a result of recognizing the structural nature of the environmental problem, and its "treatment" is "modernized" through its integration with the dynamics of the market environment. This approach to

66 M. Jänicke, *Ecological Modernization – a Paradise of Feasibility but no General Solution* [in:] *The Ecological Modernization Capacity of Japan and Germany. Comparing Nuclear Energy, Renewables, Automobility and Rare Earth Policy*, ed. L. Mez, L. Okamura, H. Weidner, Berlin– Tokyo 2020, p. 14.

67 Ibidem.

68 J. Huber, *The lost Innocence of Ecology: New Technologies & Superindustrial Development*, Frankfurt 1982; idem, The Rainbow Society: Ecology & Social Policy, Frankfurt 1985, cited in: K. Crowley, *Jobs and environment: the „double dividend" of ecological modernisation?*, „International Journal of Social Economics" 1999, vol. 26, No. 7–9, p. 1015.

69 M. Jänicke, *Ecological Modernization…*, p. 13.

environmental policy has become a well-established strategy and has stimulated a true global industrial revolution.

In light of the above, humans and the natural environment in which they live seem to be entangled in an unprecedented wave of changes affecting all dimensions of their functioning (see table 1). At the policy level, the natural environment, according to the EM approach, has ceased to be just a problem but has become an opportunity. As an example, not only for Europe but for the whole world, one can point to France. The General Commissioner's Office for Sustainable Development (Le commissariat général au développement durable – CGDD)[70] recently, in 2013, included in the national strategy for sustainable development the need to "export" French *know-how* in environmental technologies internationally[71]. France, as one of the first EU countries, initiated an ecological transformation of its economic model towards a more environmentally friendly and equitable economy. This transformation aligns with the UNEP definition from 2011, characterizing it as an economy that aims to improve the well-being of people and social justice through significant reduction of environmental threats and resource scarcity"[72]

---

70 The CGDD (Commissariat général au développement durable) was established on July 9, 2008, to invigorate and monitor the national sustainable development strategy in France and contribute to its implementation. Its primary goal is to organize interdepartmental activities for sustainable development. For instance, it organized the Grenelle de l'environnement. The summary report, coordinated by CGDD in collaboration with various departments, provides a comprehensive overview of the main changes observed over the last three years in 19 strategic sectors of the ecological economy. These sectors contribute to economic growth and employment while positioning French actors internationally. The second part includes a description of these sectors, their key points, opportunities, threats, and challenges.

71 *Rapport CGDD. Les filières industrielles stratégiques de l'économie verte: enjeux et perspectives*, „References" Marc 2013, pp. 5–249; http://www.teebourgogne.com/pages_contenu/ informer/etudes/files/32.pdf (10.09.2018).

72 *PNUE: Vers une économie verte: pour un développement durable et une éradication de la pauvreté – Synthèse à l'intention des décideurs*, Rapport PNUE 2011, www.natures-paul-keirn.com/article-pnue-vers-une-economie-verte-pour-un-developpement-durable-et-une-eradication-de-la-pauvrete-107304026.html (10.09.2018).

*Table 1: Advantages and disadvantages of EM*

| Dimention | Advantages | Disadvantages |
|---|---|---|
| Technological | • EM has gained significant momentum and a global dimension in technological changes, particularly in the United States (especially in California), China, Sweden, and Germany. | • EM is not an effective alternative if it only adds cleaner technology to existing "dirty" industry structures. |
| Ecological | • EM has achieved significant success in areas such as the use of renewable energy in power generation, waste recycling, and environmentally efficient water supply. | • The effectiveness of ecological modernization (EM) is often selective and limited to market-based solutions. |
| Economic | • additional employment<br>• reduced production costs<br>• innovations<br>• a more environmentally friendly economy | |
| Social | • improvement of people's well-being<br>• reduction of environmental threats and resource shortages | • problems with justice arise when it comes to assigning costs or the global distribution of benefits |
| Political | • the above-mentioned benefits have given the political process particularly high feasibility;<br>• EM is a process (based on environmental policy) of transitioning from traditional pollution control to "green industrial policy," emphasizing innovation. | • uncritical trust of decision-making centers in technological innovations |

Source: own study.

The concept of EM, discussed on international research platforms in the field of environmental sociology (see section 4.2) and political science, also gains rapid success in the political-administrative sphere. Proposing an approach to environmental protection that aligns with economic and technological development, this concept gained recognition in the 90s among decision-makers who perceived it as a theoretical justification for implementing the emerging concept of SD. The linkage of ecological modernization with the influential sociological work *Risk Society: Towards a New Modernity* by U. Beck, published in 1992[73], ultimately strengthened its scientific credibility and ensured its dissemination. V. Béal listed six characteristics constituting the concept of EM:

1. The increasing role of science and technology in public actions related to the natural environment. EM assigns a crucial role to technologies in addressing the environmental crisis, as it believes that the latter, through participation in the ecological reorientation of production systems, can serve as the basis for a profound transformation of capitalism. In this sense, it is the opposite of the criticism by ecologists in the 70s, driven by new social movements, who condemned scientific and technological development, pointing to it as one of the main causes of deepening the ecological crisis.
2. EM attributes new significance to market regulations in addressing environmental issues. It acknowledges that resolving the environmental crisis can only occur within the capitalist system. This involves a dual movement: the greening of the economy and the economization of ecology, aiming to reconcile economic growth with the protection of the natural environment.
3. Transformation of public entities into environmental public actions. Proponents of EM believe that the hierarchical modes of action introduced by states during the glorious 30s "Trente Glorieuses" have failed and should be replaced by flexible actions accompanying changes. On the one hand, this would mean an increase in the power of private entities (economic entities, the third sector, citizens, etc.) oriented towards environmental protection. On the other, EM recognizes that environmental issues cannot be addressed solely at the national level and, therefore, the multitude of levels should be taken into account: local, supranational, transnational.

   Ecological modernization is accompanied by political modernization in the form of adapting ways of action and the emergence of a less interventionist and more regulatory state[74].

73 U. Beck introduced the term "risk society" to describe the consequences of the development of industrial society caused by civilizational progress and technology. He emphasized the irreversibility of changes, including those in the natural environment, over which control cannot be regained. Functioning in such a society raises the question of how to tame and domesticate these threats. The answer to this question is provided by the assumptions of EM.

74 V. Béal, *La modernisation écologique: Quelle théorie pour quel changement social?* [in:] *Guide des humanités environnementales*, ed. A. Choné, I. Hajek, P. Hamman, Lille 2016, pp. 225–227.

4. The shift from a "curative" to a "proactive" approach to environmental issues involves anticipating and preventing the emergence of environmental problems, which is currently more cost-effective for businesses.
5. EM should be accompanied by the "desectorization" of public environmental actions. This involves implementing an interdisciplinary approach to the environment and incorporating environmental issues into all sectors of public activities (industry, planning, health, etc.). An integrated environmental approach conducive to managing complex and systemic issues, such as climate change or biodiversity, has been favoured at the European level (since the 1990s) in the context of implementing the concept of SD.
6. Modernization occurs in a movement towards the depoliticization of an action-oriented environment. This involves a pragmatic position that can create space for dialogue between the environmental movement, society, and other stakeholders. One of the main characteristics of EM is, therefore, the aim to replace the climate of distrust that characterized the relationship between public authorities and environmental movements in the 1960s and 1970s through collaboration between actors[75].

The growing role of science and technology, the rise of market logic, the emergence of horizontal and multi-level modes of operation, and ecological de-ideologization have largely been confirmed, serving as evidence of the effectiveness of Ecological Modernization (EM), as exemplified by the European Union (EU), among other instances. However, it would be a mistake to perceive these processes as the sole driving force behind ecological transformation. Their place has become much stronger in the "haze" of environmental policies and practices. This raises the question of how ecological modernization impacts SD. EM did not originate in the "corridors" of the United Nations or Anglo-Saxon universities but in the Netherlands and Germany. Similar to SD, it is likely an oxymoron – a combination of two concepts that are a priori opposed or contradictory. It is also a turning point in many streams of thought, various approaches led in different disciplines: from industrial ecology developed mainly by engineers to the latest research by political scientists on the crisis of the state or public actions[76]. This spans analyses by economists on current transformations in capitalism or works by sociologists on modernity and theorists of reflexive actions such as A. Giddens

75 Ibidem.

76 See more: Z. Bauman, *The crisis of the nation state in contemporary Europe*, „Przegląd Zachodni"1994, no 4, pp. 9–21; *A state in times of change*, ed. M. Pietraś, I. Hofman, S. Michałowski, Lublin 2018.

or the aforementioned U. Beck. In a sense, the concept of EM takes into account a major turning point that occurred in the years 1985–1995: a techno-economic shift accompanied by a change in the technical system and the globalization of exchanges, as well as an ideological shift following the emergence of new concepts such as management, SD, risk society, industrial ecology, the precautionary principle, marketable pollution permits, and others. The environment, which was initially at the periphery of the economic system, was gradually incorporated into the system to become one of the main dimensions of SD[77].

This leads to the question of whether the concept of EM will ultimately replace SD. F.H. Buttel, considered one of the pioneers of EM, would wish for this or at least imagine it[78]. Moreover, he argued that "ecological modernization became attractive as a concept because it provides an alternative to the pessimistic connotations of other forms of ecologism"[79]. The conceptual combination of ecological modernization and SD gives the impression that this is already happening. According to A. Blowers, ecological modernization, at best, can be seen as a "weak" expression of SD[80]. In his view, "EM seems to be more a description of how business and governments have adapted to the need to incorporate environmental issues into production and political processes than an explanation of the development of environmental policy." EM also serves an ideological purpose to the extent that it supports dominant power structures based on a liberal market economy. Its main belief is the tendency that environmental protection and economic development are not only compatible but mutually supportive"[81].

On the other hand, J. Theys points out that SD concept includes three "virtues" partially removed in the Ecological Modernization (EM) concept: firstly, a fundamental emphasis on timeless environmental management; secondly, maintaining a certain critical distance from the transformation of the economic system; and

---

77 J. Theys, *Après le „développement durable", la „modernisation écologique"?*, https://www.nss-journal.org/articles/nss/pdf/2000/01/nss20000801p13.pdf (12.09.2018).

78 F.H. Buttel did not fully agree with Beck's concept of reflective modernization. The latter placed emphasis on sub-politics and social movements in the restructuring of the state, while F.H. Buttel believed that environmental benefits could be achieved without radical structural changes in the state and civil society. Quoted in: F.H. Buttel, *Ecological Modernization as Social Theory*, „Geoforum" 2000, no. 31 (1), p. 62.

79 *Ibidem*, p. 63.

80 A. Blowers, *Power, Participation and Partnership. The limits of co-operative environmental management* [in:] *Co-operative Environmental Governance. Public-Private Agreements as a Policy Strategy*, ed. P. Glasbergen, Dordrecht 1998, p. 230.

81 *Ibidem*, p. 245.

thirdly, SD does not forget the social dimension of environmental issues[82]. It is worth noting, however, that many researchers attempt to shift the thinking of ecological modernists, labeling this trend as "towards the EM"[83]. In 2000, O. Langhelle presented a contrasting view on the convergence of EM with SD in the "Journal of Environmental Policy & Planning." The author pointed out differences between EM and SD and the ways in which these approaches frame environmental policy. The first difference concerns the "nature" of global environmental problems. The second relates to the scale of changes perceived as necessary. The third involves the goals and tasks emerging from the combination of environmental and developmental issues. In all three issues mentioned above, the noted differences have significant consequences for environmental policy. Through a comprehensive comparative analysis between the two approaches, O. Langhelle suggests that EM should be seen as a necessary but not necessarily sufficient strategy for SD, and these two concepts should not be conflated[84]. Therefore, the above considerations indicate that EM can be seen as a means to conduct socio-political discussions about institutional changes necessary to overcome the ecological crisis.

* * *

Ecological Modernization (EM) is based on the challenge of building a relationship between ecology and economy. It primarily focuses on scientific and technological innovations to address and overcome the environmental crisis. While this program can be considered partially realized, it also reveals its limitations. It adopts a technocratic approach that recognizes the need for continued economic growth, albeit within technological limits, involving planning, management, and human interaction with the environment. In this context, the state plays a major role in regulating the market. According to ecological modernists, economic policy should provide a framework for environmental regulations. These frameworks require a new type of partnership between the state and private enterprises, based on market incentives and voluntary cooperation. Ulrich Beck argues that the "risk society" emerges due to autonomous modernization processes that remain

82 J. Theys, *Après le „développement durable"...*

83 See more: P. Boudes, *Changement social et écologie: où en est la modernization écologique?*, „Socio-logos. Revue de l'association française de sociologie" 2017, no. 12, p. 13.

84 O. Langhelle, *Why Ecological Modernization and Sustainable Development Should Not Be Conflated*, „Journal of Environmental Policy & Planning" 2000, no. 2, pp. 303–322.

blind and deaf to the consequences and threats they bring"[85]. As pointed out by M Jänicke, a rigorous goal-oriented approach, increasing feasibility through capacity building, and innovative management seem crucial to harness the full potential of EM"[86].

It is important to emphasize that this theory weakly or not at all addressed the issues of modernization in developing countries or Third World countries, but in practice, it seems that the practice is ahead of the theory. L Zhang, A.P.J. Mol, and D Sonnenfeld point out that Ecological Modernization, at the beginning of the 21st century, expanded its scope to include Southern states, which are very dynamic spaces for the transformation of environmental issues[87].

## 1.3. Citizen participation

The third theoretical approach within the mainstream of SD relates to the idea of civil society, discursive democracy[88], and processes of political modernization. In the SD context, "participation" is an increasingly valued concept, used as a formula for consensus-building and making the best decisions regarding major environmental dilemmas. Hence, the concept of "participation" leads many researchers to consider it a strategy that encompasses the learning process itself and, as such,

---

85 U. Beck, *Rediscovering politics: a contribution to the theory of reflexive modernization* [in:] *Reflective modernization. Politics, tradition and aesthetics in the social order of modernity*, ed. U. Beck, A. Giddens, S. Lash, Warsaw 2009, p. 17.

86 M. Jänicke, *Ecological Modernization...*, p. 13.

87 L. Zhang, A.P.J. Mol, D. Sonnenfeld, *The interpretation of ecological modernisation in China*, „Environmental Politics" 2007, vol. 16, no. 4, s. 649–658, Cited in: V. Béal. La modernisation écologique..., p. 224.

88 The essence of deliberative democracy lies in the need to build individual and collective awareness at a higher level, one that enables the recognition of the surrounding social and natural reality. The evolution of perspectives on perceiving the world (from anthropocentric to ecocentric) indicates the direction, even the necessity, of conducting discourse that serves as an arena for presenting opposing theses but also creates opportunities for generating significant arguments in favour of their acceptance. Discourse thus allows the emergence of a new quality. In this sense, social development tends to be uplifting, especially in the moral aspect, providing opportunities for growth. It involves greater citizen participation in the legislative process through the organization of debates that complement the informal formation of public opinion. Deliberative democracy, sometimes called discursive, not only creates opportunities for active participation of every member of society in the legislative process but also broader involvement of people in culture. Quoted from: S. Zyborowicz, *Discursive democracy in political thinking*, „Przegląd Politologiczny" 2010, no 3, pp. 141–148.

should be included in the higher education curriculum because "participatory processes involve the engagement and interaction of various social actors with different knowledge and perceptions of environmental issues"[89]. Collaborative decision-making and taking responsibility for the global SD mean promoting just, inclusive, and fair societies and involve creating citizen participation processes[90].

A "sustainable" society is an active society in which democratic participation plays a crucial role. It does not only refer to elections to parliament but signifies a principle guiding decision-making in all areas of life[91].

All environmental issues that directly or indirectly impact the lives of citizens, the context of the places where these citizens live and work, as well as the products they commonly use or consume, form the backdrop for civic activity and the development of democracy in its various aspects. They also represent an inexhaustible source for testing new forms of democracy and civic participation[92].

Therefore, a comprehensive approach arising from the concept of SD emphasizes the crucial importance of the participatory process as a strategy to achieve the goals outlined in the roadmap of Agenda 2030[93]. Based on this premise, M.F. de Poza-Vilches, J. Gutiérrez-Pérez, and A. López-Alcarria propose research around the appropriateness and possibilities of combining both concepts by supporting the construction of a comprehensive definition. Such a definition would help incorporate SD as a cross-cutting subject into higher education curricula. The significance of this way of thinking "is the result of the dynamics of the participation concept itself, which has undergone continuous modifications corresponding to different historical stages of a given country. This evolution ranges from centralistic models, based on exclusive government involvement, to much more open and flexible models, in which citizen participation makes sense, challenging representative democracy models and seeking a more participatory model"[94].

---

89 M.F. de Poza-Vilches, J. Gutiérrez-Pérez, A. López-Alcarria, *Participation and Sustainable Development* [in:] *Encyclopedia of Sustainability in Higher Education*, ed. W. Leal Filho, Hamburg 2019, https://doi.org/10.1007/978-3-319-63951-2_57-1, p. 2.

90 T. Ouariachi, Ch.-Y. Li, W.J.L. Elving, *Gamification Approaches for Education and Engagement on Pro-Environmental Behaviors: Searching for Best Practices*, „Sustainability" 3 June 2020, p. 2.

91 H. Rogall, *Economics of sustainable development - the need to reform traditional economics* [in:] *Economics of sustainable development. Outline of research problems and teaching*, ed. B. Poskrobko, Białystok 2010, p. 19.

92 M.F. de Poza-Vilches, J. Gutiérrez-Pérez, A. López-Alcarria, *Participation and Sustainable…*, p. 1.

93 *Ibidem.*

94 *Ibidem.*

The concept of participation, also known as civic participation, although old, continues to inspire many legal texts and is abundant in scholarly literature, both in the field of social policy and ecology. Despite differences in the interpretation of this concept, its repetitive use is well-explained as it sets out possible ways to achieve the democratic ideal and the principle of equality for citizens, emphasizing that «people from below» can influence decisions that affect them. M. Bresson understands this concept as "the idea that 'people from below,' groups in economic, social, and cultural life, and even individuals can gain decision-making power at the collective level in which they are involved"[95]. Starting from this thread, three typical ideal models can be distinguished: participation as public action is a prelude to the implementation of projects decided by selected public authorities; participation as collective action, which often contributes to the emergence of spontaneous, autonomous social movements; finally, participation as mobilization, which is based on the idea of co-producing projects between decision-makers, professionals, and "people from below," but with the impetus given by the former and limited ambition to what is close[96].

The idea of civic participation emerged in the 1970s in Western Europe as a response to the search for the so-called third way between the state and the market. It involves the concept of the third sector, which includes citizen organizations working for the common good and not for profit[97]. It originated and evolved due to the inconveniences of representative democracy, or in other words, the crisis of parliamentary democracy. The increasing lack of trust among citizens in the effective decision-making process by decision-makers (on their behalf) led to the concept of participatory democracy, which, while maintaining its representative character, significantly increases citizen participation in decision-making processes that concern them[98]. The main challenge of civic participation is for both parties (authorities and citizens) to be willing to use it. At first glance, it seems that public authorities are interested (for various reasons) in society having an impact on the decision-making process. On the other hand, citizens should be interested in improving the environment in which they function. However, the success of these relationships depends on the willingness of both parties to change for the better and, above all, mutual trust. A common problem in implementing this concept is that public authorities must make decisions, taking into account

95 M. Bresson, *La participation: un concept constamment réinventé*, „*Socio-logos*" 2014, no. 9, http://journals.openedition.org/socio-logos/2817 (22.08.2018).

96 *Ibidem*.

97 T. Schimanek, *Partycypacja obywatelska w społeczności lokalnej*, Warszawa 2015, p. 3.

98 *Ibidem*, p. 4.

various, sometimes conflicting social interests. This requires additional financial resources or the activity of state officials, such as social consultations[99]. Similarly, a problem may arise on the part of the citizen, whose civic activity can be explained by the desire to achieve individual interests at the expense of the general good. In this context, the natural environment, being a shared living space for humans on Earth, minimizes such behaviours. Although there will always be people lacking not only a sense of solidarity regarding common actions but also broader, perspective thinking about themselves and humanity. The crucial role of civil society should be to exclude such behaviours regardless of the material or social status of individuals who exhibit them.

Part of the problems with civic participation results from not adhering to the basic conditions of effective participation[100]. Non-compliance with these conditions causes both parties to get lost in their mutual relationships, feeling unfulfilled in their expectations, and coming to the conclusion that what they are participating in is of little significance[101].

SD requires the involvement of citizens individually or collectively. Participation is an inherent element of SD, as it requires significant changes in citizens' behaviour, awareness, and their participation in the decision-making process through participatory democracy. This form of democracy, aimed at "good governance," transparent, responsible, involves the participation of citizens and organized civil society in a given issue. Participation of this kind characterized by a diversity of forms, actors, levels, and degrees of involvement[102]. There are two main dynamic principles that characterize participation according to its origin: either participation originates from citizen initiatives, then it is called *bottom-up*, or it originates from public authorities, then it is called *top-down*. Top-down

99 *Ibidem*, p. 10.

100 The basic conditions for effective participation include: the involvement of civic partners in all stages of the decision-making process (from planning to the implementation of public decisions); adherence by all participants in the dialogue to binding laws; clear definition of goals, rules, and roles of the parties in their mutual relations; equality of partners; belief in the good intentions of all partners; recognition of the legitimacy of public authorities to make laws and responsibility for the decisions made; responsibility for expressed opinions and views; preparation of partners for conducting dialogue; representation; transparency in actions. Quoted from: *Ibidem*, p. 11.

101 *Ibidem*.

102 M. Hurard, *La participation citoyenne au développement durable à l'échelle locale en Europe*, http://www.pourlasolidarite.eu/sites/default/files/publications/files/working_paper_-_ participation_citoyenne_26.08.11_0.pdf (18.11.2019), p. 4.

participation results from initiatives by public authorities, which organize activities such as providing information to citizens, consultations, or public consultations[103]. In such cases, the aim is to persuade citizens or involve them in a project (organizing public meetings, explanations, publications, exhibitions, etc.) or verify their affiliation through, for example, surveys. Public authorities may also organize a co-production process. On the other hand, citizen participation can be initiated by citizens according to the "top-up" logic. In such cases, it takes the form of citizens' demands, events, or assemblies to defend their interests, among other things. This can happen in an organized way, such as through associations, or in a more disorganized manner, where bottom-up participants can experience or provoke state decision-makers[104].

In Europe, citizen participation is fundamental, on the one hand through representative democracy and the exercise of "classic" citizenship, i.e., the right to vote and run for office in elections, and on the other hand, through participatory democracy situated between direct democracy and representative democracy. Participatory democracy is, therefore, a third democratic way, combining certain aspects of representative democracy and direct democracy. It involves giving citizens a voice through various forms of participation, more or less formal. Citizens can speak at different levels on issues directly affecting them. Quoting the words of D. P. Decoster, it is about "placing the human being at the center of decisions, that concern them"[105], indicating that participatory democracy is undoubtedly closer to the local level in accordance with the principle of subsidiarity. In essence, this means that a decision must be made at the appropriate administrative level to be considered effective. However, the local scale is the most suitable and effective in addressing local problems that directly impact citizens. Citizen participation

---

103 At the end of the 20th century, dialogue, then called "environmental dialogue," gradually became a principle of public action in the field of the environment, planning, land management, and more broadly – public and collective resource management. Its development is closely linked to the principle of participation inspired by the World Charter for Nature (1982) and international conventions such as the Rio Declaration on Environment and Development in principle 10 (1992) or the Aarhus Convention (1998). These texts encouraged governments to incorporate the imperative of consultation into the law.

104 A significant example of such a grassroots initiative from civil society, without the involvement of political parties or trade unions, was the "yellow vests" protest that paralyzed the existing governance system in France (November-December 2018). See more: https://wiadomosci.radiozet.pl/Swiat/Zamieszki-w-Paryzu.-Protest-zoltych-kamizelek (18.11.2019).

105 M. Hurard, *La participation citoyenne…*, p. 5.

legitimises decisions made at the local level, and citizens then implement these decisions. It is about a way of governance in which authorities in a given area manage their resources (economic, social, and environmental).

In fact, some elements of "good governance" are particularly important for Sustainable Development, including the integration of the economy, society, and the environment in policies, cooperation between different levels of decision-making (local, regional, national, European), and citizen participation. Good governance is "the exercise of power by its various levels in an effective, fair, transparent, and responsible manner"[106]. In the White Paper on European Governance from 2001, the EU defines five fundamental principles of *good governance: openness, participation, accountability, effectiveness, and coherence.* Participation, as one of these principles, largely depends on the member states' governments, which co-create and then implement EU policies within their countries. The document recommends a shift away from hierarchical governance within the European Union and supplementing the existing set of tools with the so-called soft law instrumentsgo[107]. *Good governance* plays a "crucial role" in achieving SD[108], co as confirmed in the 2009 report on the EU Sustainable Development[109]. Management for Sustainable Development has become an ideal strategy for participatory public management, ensuring socio-political interactions between governments, civil societies, and markets[110]. In this context, Sustainable Development appears as an area for applying various new management forms for dialogue, collective reflection, and consensus-seeking, addressing socio-ecological issues not only based on individual expectations but also from a global perspective. This socio-political approach requires the identification of the most appropriate participation strategies, resulting in the education (social, economic, and environmental) of

106 *Ibidem.*

107 The White Paper on *European Governance (European Governance a White Paper),* Commission of the European Communities, Brussels 2001, quoted in: W. Rudolf, The concept of Governance and its application - from international institutions to lower levels of government, „Acta Universitatis Lodziensis. Folia Oeconomica" 2010, no 245, p. 79.

108 H. Combe, *La gouvernance, une impérieuse nécessité pour le développement durable,* „Développement durable et territories" 2015, vol. 6, no. 2, http://journals.openedition.org/ developpementdurable/10852 (29.08.2018).

109 https://ec.europa.eu/eurostat/documents/3217494/5704439/865-FR-FR.PDF/c99a8ad6-23bf-4bdf-9021-bfdcda583857 (25.11.2019).

110 M.F. de Poza-Vilches, J. Gutiérrez-Pérez, A. López-Alcarria, *Participation and Sustainable…*, p. 6.

citizens aimed at providing information about sustainable management models and actions[111].

SD is a participatory development process that establishes a "virtuous circle" between the environment, economy, and society, connecting these three spheres. It is a form of development that respects the environment (natural resources, ecosystems), ensuring economic growth conducive to social inclusion[112]. The 10th principle of the Rio Declaration from 1992 states that "the best way to solve environmental problems is to ensure the participation of all concerned citizens at the appropriate level"[113]. Every individual must have the opportunity to participate in decision-making processes, and the signatory states of this declaration commit to providing citizens with the necessary information for their awareness and participation. Challenges related to citizen participation at the local level are numerous, including engaging citizens in the development of their living environment, managing cities, their redevelopment through renovation and renewal processes, and sustainable management of local authorities. It is essential for residents to be regarded as experts in their living environment and to be involved in decisions that affect them, aiming to improve and take responsibility for their territory. Decisions are more justified when developed by citizens or when consulted with technicians or experts during the decision-making process regarding their shared space. Both decision-makers and technicians (experts) have an interest in listening to residents, who are the "users" of the territory and, therefore, possess empirical knowledge about it. This is an important combination of consulting residents with experts who have technical knowledge to make decisions effectively. However, citizens' conclusions are sometimes challenging to achieve, as they may not consider legal and technical constraints. Projects must be practical. Even if residents do not have spatial planning or planning skills, they have their experiences. This knowledge should be more appreciated by decision-makers.

Therefore, citizen participation (a concept involving societal involvement, participation in social life, and participation in elections) is a key principle of SD, recorded and recognized as essential in many international treaties and organizations. A particular mechanism for implementing the concept of civil society is Agenda 21, which literally means what needs to be done in the 21st century. This international action program for sustainable development consists of 40 chapters, with Chapter 28 titled *Local Authorities' Initiatives in Support of Agenda 21* placing

111 *Ibidem.*

112 M. Hurard, *La participation citoyenne…*, p. 6.

113 P. Pieczyński, *Earth Summit in Rio* [in:] *Eco-development and Agenda 21*. Interdisciplinary education model, ed. P. Pieczyński, Szczecin 2007, p. 210.

local entities in a decisive position for implementing the principles of this document[114]. In essence, the local scale allows for capturing the economic, social, and environmental specificity of the territory while ensuring proximity to residents and local entities[115]. This tool enables addressing SD issues at the local level in relevant areas (district, city, neighbourhood, village, etc.). Actors of this territory, including its residents, are mobilized to implement the local Agenda 21, which can be initiated by both local authorities and citizens themselves. Considering the above, citizen participation is at the very heart of Agenda 21 and must occur at every stage[116] through information dissemination, public consultations, citizen engagement in SD, and utilizing their expertise. Some participating bodies are exclusively dedicated to Agenda 21, such as Forums 21[117].

Citizen participation at the local level is a crucial element in renewing democracy, both in European Union countries and neighbouring states. The forms of this participation also vary depending on the traditions of the countries, their specificities, and local conditions. In all cases, there are limitations on participation, often relating to the right to speak rather than the right to decide. In this context, it is essential to develop an increasing number of participatory mechanisms to achieve genuine involvement, especially by combining both top-down and bottom-up dynamics. The boundaries of participation in terms of representativeness raise questions about whether the created bodies are merely reproducing representative democracy. Practices related to empowerment and co-production must, therefore, proliferate to establish something more than just the right to express oneself, moving towards the right to decide and thus real active citizen participation[118].

* * *

---

114 The Agenda 21, adopted in Rio de Janeiro in 1992 by 150 countries, has become a tool for implementing Sustainable Development. During the European Conference on Sustainable Cities in 1994 in Aalborg, Denmark, after signing the Aalborg Charter, cities committed to implementing local Agenda 21. The Earth Summit held in Johannesburg in 2002 reaffirmed the need to strengthen actions at the local level through the implementation of local Agenda 21.

115 M. Hurard, *La participation citoyenne…*, p. 16.

116 The Local Agenda 21 is divided into several stages: ensuring political engagement, creating a public forum to determine citizen participation, conducting a diagnosis, establishing priorities and goals (developing an action plan), and finally, implementing, monitoring, and evaluating the project.

117 „Fora 21" are public meetings for residents, representatives of associated economic entities, and all members of civil society worldwide. These forums provide the broadest possible consultation with residents.

118 M. Hurard, *La participation citoyenne…*, p. 25.

The concept of SD, strongly promoted by environmental policies, requires transformation not only at the political level but also at the economic and social levels, supporting a participation model that fosters civic discussion to seek consensus and define the most appropriate course of action, taking into account the needs of the context[119]. This entails a model of democracy closely linked to participation in its fullest sense, rather than representation by political groups. The consolidation of governance must occur, considering socio-political structures, to make participation effective. Therefore, governments should support new forms of management that make citizens' decisions binding and require implementation. A necessary redefinition process of the frameworks of contemporary democracies is crucial, with SD as a global goal serving as a reference point in this transformative journey.

SD emerges as an area for the application of new management forms aimed at fostering dialogue, collective reflection (towards consensus-building), addressing socio-environmental issues not only at the individual level but also collectively. This new approach requires the establishment of participation strategies that result in social, economic, and environmental educational processes to provide information about action models aligned with SD principles. Significant in this context are the experiences of the decade of Education for Sustainable Development (ESD) conducted from 2005 to 2014. This decade resulted in the incorporation of values inseparably linked to SD into all aspects of learning to encourage behavioural changes that, would lead to a more sustainable and just society for all[120]. In this context, SD can be a common ground for agreement among people from different backgrounds, breaking prejudices and intolerance within communities of countries at various stages of development. Hence, the currently strongly promoted project of Education for Sustainable and Inclusive Civil Societies (ESICS) is directed towards developing countries[121]. This project, initiated in 2018 by Japanese scientists K. Taniguchi and E. Nakano, aims to develop students in today's pluralistic society into citizens willing to understand people of different social and economic statuses. ESICS addresses the weaknesses of ESD, emphasizing the need for education based on society, culture, and the "individual life of the state"[122].

---

119 M.F. de Poza-Vilches, J. Gutiérrez-Pérez, A. López-Alcarria, *Participation and Sustainable…*, p. 6.

120 J. Huckle, A.E.J. Wals, *The UN Decade of Education for Sustainable Development: business as usual in the end*, „Environmental Education Research" 2015, no. 3, vol. 21, p. 491.

121 K. Taniguchi, E. Nakano, *Citizenship Education for Sustainable Development: Theoretical and Practical Approaches for Project ESICS*, „International Journal of Information and Education Technology" 2017, no. 10, vol. 7, p. 765–766.

122 *Ibidem*.

# 2. Economic approaches to sustainable development

Sustainable development is the result of a combination of reflections on many complementary yet conflicting levels. R. Costanza emphasizes that debates on sustainable development require having a precise vision of the world before designing tools or implementing policies[123]. Therefore, for the better implementation of *sustainable development* principles, it is necessary to create relatively precise conceptual frameworks. Nevertheless, these frameworks, defining the content of the sustainable development concept and the way it is understood, are formulated in various ways. Below, economists' considerations on SD will be presented.

In economic literature, there are already systematized presentations of theoretical approaches to understanding the concept of SD, particularly those carried out by O. Godard in 1994[124] and F.-D. Vivien in 2004 and then in 2010[125]. The intention of this chapter is not to reiterate recommendations but to present on the economic stage the approaches (schools) that continue to have a significant influence on how SD is understood. Following G. Destais, we can identify nine currents of thought among economic trends regarding SD[126]:

- neoclassical model of growth with natural capital,
- ecological economics (London school),
- ecological economics (industrial ecology with a strong emphasis on the development of the French school, known as industrial and territorial economics),
- ecological economics (American school),
- analysis in terms of scientific controversies in an uncertain world,
- conventionalist analysis (at the level of conventions) in terms of moral controversies,

---

123 Quoted in: L. Abdelmalki, P. Mundler, *Économie de l'environnement et du développement durable*, Paris 2010, p. 69.

124 O. Godard, *Le développement durable: paysage intellectuel*, „Natures, Sciences, Sociétés" 1994, vol. 2, no. 4, pp. 309–322.

125 See more: F.-D. Vivien, *Le développement soutenable: un objet économique controversé* [in:] *Stratégies de développement durable. Développement, environnement ou justice sociales?*, ed. A. de Heering, S. Leyens, Namur 2010.

126 G. Destais, *Les théorisations économiques du développement durable. Proposition de décryptage critique*, Colloque international francophone, „Le développement durable: débats et controversies", 15 et 16 décembre Clermont-Ferrand 2011, p. 3.

- humanistic approach to the three pillars of the concept,
- historical-institutional analysis,
- entropic analysis.

It's worth noting that economists of all schools have long operated as if the natural environment did not exist. Everything began to change in the 1970s when certain theories started to integrate the natural environment with the economy (rather than the other way around) without questioning growth or the market. Simultaneously, the beliefs of critical economists, the so-called heterodox economists, who had long been "captives" of a technicist vision of progress, partially evolved and resulted in the emergence of political ecology and ecological economics, which combine social criticism with ecological criticism. A new generation of economists, or even socio-economists, is currently attempting to propose an alternative way of thinking for both the sought-after "sustainability" and the current growth model. It seems that the battle of ideas has not been decisively settled yet.

## 2.1. Neoclassical approach

The neoclassical understanding of the relationship between the economy and the natural environment dates back to the late 18th century, significantly earlier than is generally suggested in the environmental economics literature[127]. These relationships can be clearly found in the discussions of J.S. Mill and D. Ricardo[128]. These economists, despite acknowledging the limited nature of natural resources, primarily sought solutions to this problem through technological development rather than the necessity of limiting the pace of economic growth or changing the way of managing the economy. For representatives of this school, the natural environment is a source of resources and is considered an external element to the economy. "According to neoclassicals, environmental destruction is a result of a market failure - a 'market failure' that arises not from the flaws in its operation

127 A. Sandmo, *The Early History of Environmental Economics*, „*Review of Environmental Economics and Policy*" 2015, vol. 9, no. 1, p. 45.

128 This topic was mainly addressed in the context of the theories of distribution and factor production, developed in subsequent centuries. The theories of distribution focused on the issue of income distribution among the owners of production factors, including land (and, therefore, the hidden natural resources within it), labor, and capital. Within the theories of factor production, the emphasis was on their productivity and remuneration, paying particular attention to the scarcity of essential production factors, especially natural resources. Quoted from: A. Świstak, *Opodatkowanie wydobycia surowców naturalnych w* Polsce, Warsaw 2018, p. 13.

but from the undervaluation of the price of nature's resources. Here, resources are traditionally perceived as so-called *common goods*, available for free or at a low price"[129].

The neoclassical growth theory initiated by R.M. Solow has been expanded to include natural capital (endogenous growth). Both R.M. Solow and J. Stiglitz introduced the natural environment into standard economic theory. Nature was assigned a monetary value, and time was also taken into account for the calculation of future prices through the use of a discount rate[130]. Unfortunately, the discount rate applied by economists often minimizes the future values of natural resources or the costs of environmental changes, as presented in the Stern Review on the Economics of Climate Change from 2006[131].

In this approach, the hypothesis of perfect substitutability between different factors of production is maintained: technical capital can, if necessary, replace natural capital. This is a matter of "weak sustainability." Not only R.M. Solow but also J. Hartwick extends the concept of capital to encompass the entire environment[132]. According to them, the economy relies on three types of capital: material capital (machines, infrastructure), human capital (people and their skills), and natural capital (all natural resources). In this context, growth and development are somewhat blended, and we speak more about sustainable growth/self-sustaining growth rather than sustainable development[133]. This concept is linked to the (optimal) growth trajectory, in which total capital remains constant. There is an exchange that takes place over time: the current generation consumes "natural capital" but, in return, passes on greater productive capacity in the form of a stock of equipment, knowledge, and skills to future generations[134]. Therefore,

---

129 Quoted in: J Zrałek, *Ecological economics. Revision of economic theory in the light of the concept of sustainable economic development go*, „Studia Ekonomiczne. Zeszyty Naukowe Uniwersytetu Ekonomicznego w Katowicach – Ekonomia 7" 2016, no 303, p. 73.

130 The discount rate is the interest rate that determines the present value of future cash flows one must forego to have resources today. It is a computational technique aimed at comparing the prices of resources at different times.

131 See more: N. Stern, *The Economics of Climate Change*, Cambridge 2007; S. Dietz, Ch. Hope, N. Patmore, *Some economics of „dangerous" climate change: reflections on the Stern Review*, „Global Environmental Change" 2008, vol. 17, no. 3–4, pp. 311–325.

132 A. Lalucq, *Economistes et écologie: des physiocrates à Stiglitz, „Alternatives économiques"* 2013, vol. 2, no. 58, pp. 44–45.

133 *Ibidem.*

134 See more: R.M. *Solow, An Almost Practical Step toward Sustainability*, „Resources Policy" 1993, vol. 19, no. 3, p. 162–172, http://pinguet.free.fr/solow1992.pdf (11.08.2020).

if natural resources are depleted, it is possible to balance the losses by investing in substitute resources. For example, if there is a shortage of oil, it is sufficient to invest appropriately in alternative energy sources.

On the other hand, the growth of the relative price of non-renewable natural resources allows for balancing the gradual depletion of these resources according to the optimal pattern of H. Hotelling[135], This induces technological progress leading to the development of substitutes. Proponents of this approach believe that growth can last indefinitely and is sustainable. E. Laurent and J. P. Fitoussi acknowledge "that we can decide on growth as strong as we want (…) but on condition that there is a sufficient level of knowledge to ensure the sustainability of the system"[136].

## 2.2. Ecological economics

*Ecological economics* emerged in the context of criticism (of the assumptions of environmental economics)[137] particularly the postulate of total substitutability between "natural capital and technical capital," without departing from other

---

135 Hotelling's principle from 1931 states that prices of non-renewable resources should increase at the rate of interest. This assumption was based on a time distribution of resource exploitation to maximize the benefits derived from consumption. The rule assumes that depleted resources should be subject to the same economic laws as other capital assets. For more details, refer to S. Śmiech, Economic theories of valuing energy resources" in Modeling and Forecasting Energy Resource Prices: S. Śmiech, *Economic theories of valuing energy resources" in Modeling and Forecasting Energy Resource Price*, ed. M. Papież, S. Śmiech, Warsaw 2015, pp. 21–25.

136 J.-P. Fitoussi, E. Laurent, *La nouvelle écologie politique. Économie et développement humain*, Paris 2008, p. 54.

137 This criticism initially focused on consumption, as evidenced in the discussions of economist and sociologist T. Veblen. In the early 20th century, Veblen described how the elite (leisure class) squandered time and money to distinguish themselves from other classes through conspicuous consumption. J. Galbraith continued this critique of consumption, evident in his 1958 book *The Affluent Society*, where he illustrates how entrepreneurs, through the constant creation of new needs, generate their own demand, reducing citizens to the status of consumers. It wasn't until B. Commoner's 1971 book, *The Closing Circle: Nature, Man, and Technology*, that a critique emerged against the scientific and technological drift of American society, which he held responsible for the socio-environmental crisis.

postulates of the previous analysis. This school of thought developed in the early 1980s in response to the emergence of the so-called era of sustainable development, crystallized after the publication of the Brundtland Report in 1987[138]. The members of the association Resources for the Future[139] founded in 1952 by W. Paley, played a role in this development. It was the first think tank exclusively focused on environmental issues, gathering "certain free and wandering minds that easily move between disciplines," including N. Georgescu-Roegen, K. Boulding, and H. Daly[140].

In 1989, R. B. Norgaard, in an article titled *The case for methodological pluralism*, called for a pluralistic approach to economic theory and policy in the first issue of "Ecological Economics"[141]. He believed that "ecology and economics have the same Greek root. Both fields of knowledge deal with complex systems. The former consists of many approaches to understanding natural systems, such as energy, population biology, food web models, hierarchy theory, etc. Ecology also highly values field knowledge and reporting new observations. In contrast, economics is dominated by a single pattern of thinking and a standard 'proof,' market models, and econometrics, while field knowledge and observations as such are not highly valued"[142].

The goal of ecological economics (EE) is to go beyond both environmental economics, understood narrowly as the application of neoclassical analysis to environmental issues, and ecology, understood narrowly as the science of the natural world[143]. Ecological economics adopts the principle based on the concept of absolute scarcity[144], stating that natural resources are so fundamental to human survival (satisfying basic needs) that they cannot be replaced. Thinkers in this new

138 É. Laurent, *La transition juste. Un nouvel âge de l'économie et de l'environnement*, „Revue de l'OFCE" 2020, no. 165, p. 9.

139 See more: https://www.rff.org/ (13.12.2020).

140 *Ibidem*.

141 R.B. Norgaard, *The case for methodological pluralism*, „Ecological Economics" 1989, vol. 1, pp. 37–58.

142 *Ibidem*.

143 É. Laurent, *La transition juste...*, p. 9.

144 See more: S. Baumgärtner, Ch. Becker, M. Faber, R. Manstetten, *Relative and absolute scarcity of nature. Assessing the roles of economics and ecology for biodiversity conversation*, „Ecological Economics" 2006, no. 59(4), pp. 487–498.

discipline seek to understand the existing inconsistencies between the ecological system and the economic system, where the latter is completely detached from the former, by reembedding the economy in ecology as the only formula capable of establishing sustainable growth. According to them, a "sustainable economy" is an economy capable of maintaining constant stocks of natural resources, both renewable and non-renewable[145].

The concept of "strong sustainability" is thus associated with this new discipline, which encompasses three schools: the London school, the industrial ecology school, and the American school.

### 2.2.1. Ecological economics (London school)

In this school, the possibility of substitutes is acknowledged, but they are considered limited by the existence of critical natural capital, for which there is no substitute, citing biodiversity as an example. D.W. Pearce (thanks to his work in 1989 and 1993)[146] is recognized as a representative of the London school of ecological economics. This approach takes into account that nature provides not only resources for other productive activities but also for final goods, questioning the benefits of the Kuznets curve[147] concerning environmental protection. However, this approach limits ecological considerations in the economy, maintaining the monetary valuation of "natural capital." This leads to normative implications

145 A. Lalucq, *Economistes et écologie…*, p. 51.

146 See more: D.W. Pearce, A. Markandya, E. Barbier, *Blueprint for a Green Economy, London* 1989; D.W. Pearce, G.D. Atkinson, *Capital theory and the measurement of sustainable development: an indicator of „weak" sustainability*, „Ecological Economics" 1993, vol. 8, no. 2, pp. 103–108.

147 Environmental Kuznets Curve postulates a relationship between environmental pollution and the economic development of a country. This means that industrialization leads to an increase in the negative impact of economic activities on the environment until a certain point, after which this impact decreases with further economic growth. The source of this proposed change is the shift in the structure of consumer needs (more services and increased demand for a clean environment by households) as well as technological progress. See more: J.L. Van Zanden, *Tracing the beginning of the Kuznets curie: western Europe during the early modern period*, „The Economic History Review" 1995, vol. 48, no. 4, pp. 643–664.

deviating from the *laissez-faire*[148] approach in neoclassical justifications for public intervention[149].

The London School is the source of the distinction between "weak" and "strong" sustainability, aiming to affirm the commitment of these researchers to SD and to demonstrate that they have rejected a return to traditional economics while also dismissing more radical proposals[150]. D.W. Pearce believed that "according to the «strong sustainability» paradigm, sustainability is achieved by protecting certain components of the natural capital and ensuring no overall decline in this capital"[151].

Striving to achieve a constant value of natural capital per person, ecological economists recognize the need to limit demand, which can be achieved by controlling population growth and reducing per capita consumption[152].

This approach significantly influences the definition of sustainable consumption, especially in determining what behaviours can be considered appropriate. Advocating for the adoption of the criterion of "strong SD" aims to ensure that natural capital is not entirely replaceable by produced capital. Emphasizing the irreplaceable nature of certain elements or aspects of the natural environment implies accepting the hypothesis of a "critical natural capital threshold," below which one should not go. „Strong sustainability" does not imply the complete absence of substitution between different forms of capital but rather the recognition of limits

---

148 Laissez-faireism is a philosophical-economic view advocating individual freedom in the socio-economic sphere. The role of the state is limited to that of a night watchman, whose task is to guard fundamental principles: the freedom to manage and private property. The reasoning of laissez-faireists is not limited to perceiving humans guided solely by the principle of material benefit but also considers other manifestations of needs, including non-material ones.

149 B. Billaudot, G. Destais, *Les analyses de la durabilité en économie. Fondements theorique et implications normatives*, Grenoble 2009, p. 10.

150 V. Boisvert, L. Carnoye, R. Petitimber, *La durabilité forte: enjeux épistémologiques et politiques, de l'économie écologique aux autres sciences sociales*, „Développement durable et territoires" 2019, vol. 10, no. 1, p. 3.

151 D.W. Pearce, G. Atkinson, K. Hamilton, *The measurement of sustainability development* [in:] *Theory and Implementation of Economic Models for Sustainable Development*, ed. J.C.J.M. von den Bergh, M.W. HoLes, „Economy & Environment" 1998, vol. 15, p. 176.

152 L. Voget-Kleschin, *Large-Scale Land Acquisition: Evaluating its Environmental Aspects Against the Background of Strong Sustainability*, „Journal of Agricultural and Environmental Ethics" 2013, no. 26, pp. 1105–1126, quoted from: J. Zrałek, Ekonomia ekologiczna…, p. 78.

to substitutability. From this perspective, economic activities should be conceived under ecological pressure and within ecological limits. It is precisely the concept of "limited substitutability" that forms the foundation of ecological economics[153].

V. Boisvert, referring to R. Passet[154] recognized as one of the founders of French ecological economics, emphasizes the need for normative management under pressure. He points out the proximity of Passet's proposals to the ideas advocated by the London school. This involves imposing ecological constraints on economic activities, essentially acknowledging the existence of growth limitations. Boisvert suggests that such an approach does not specify the height at which limits should be set, the methods for determining them, the dimensions or units in which they should be expressed, or what actions should be taken in this regard[155].

### 2.2.2. Ecological economics (Industrial school)

Industrial Ecology (IE)[156] is the second school within the field of ecological economics, contributing to the challenges of SD[157]. This school represents a method of reflection and analysis of human socicties, considered significant for the challenges of SD. IE employs a systemic analytical structure known as industrial metabolism, also referred to as territorial metabolism or material flow balance.

153 V. Boisvert, L. Carnoye, R. Petitimber, *La durabilité forte...*, p. 4

154 R. Passet, a French professor credited with creating ecological economics (EE) and the original concept of the economy known as "biogospodarka" (biogovernance). In this context, "biogospodarka" refers to an approach that opens the economy to the biosphere, considering it only as a subsystem rather than integration with *strictly* economic logic. Eight years before the Brundtland Report, R. Passet set the goal of "defining the conditions that economic activities must meet to avoid jeopardizing the fundamental changes in the natural environment, the reproduction of which imposes on everything else." Cited from: R. Passet, F.-D. Vivien, *René Passet: la quête d'une bioéconomie transdisciplinaire*, „Natures Sciences Sociétés" 2011/4, vol. 19, s. 410. See also: idem, L'économique et le vivant, Paris 1979.

155 V. Boisvert, L. Carnoye, R. Petitimber, *La durabilité forte...*, p. 6.

156 The concept of the Industrial Ecology encounters several semantic barriers as soon as its operational implementation of its principles is experienced. This expression creates a terminological contradiction (oxymoron), conveying both the idea of environmental protection and the idea of its degradation.

157 S. Dermine-Brullot, G. Junqua, B. Zuindeau, *Écologie industrielle et terrotoriale à l'heure de la transition écologique et socjale de l'économie*, „Revue d'Économie Régionale & Urbaine" 2017, no. 5, p. 775.

Its objective is to investigate the interactions between industrial activities within a specific area and the biosphere, aiming to identify imbalances and address them through industrial ecological strategies[158].

The term "Industrial Ecology" (IE) was first used[159] towards the end of the 1980s by two engineers involved in research and development at General Motors, namely R. Frosch and N. Gallopoulos, in the magazine "Scientific American"[160]. Building on the observation that the industrial system is part of a finite world, they proposed a shift from the "end-of-pipe"[161] model towards an "integrating finite natural resource availability" model. They defined IE as an organizational model aimed at decoupling growth from resource extraction, drawing inspiration from the functioning of natural ecosystems. According to them, to achieve this, four challenges must be addressed: decarbonization of energy, systematic closing of material and energy flows, dematerialization of the economy, and waste recovery[162]. In their article, they suggested the need for creating an "industrial ecosystem" where "energy and material consumption is optimized, waste and pollution are minimized, and each product in the production process has an economically viable role"[163].

158 *Ibidem.*

159 Somewhat earlier, in 1977, the meaning of this term can be traced in the works of the American geologist P. Cloud. He introduced the term "industrial ecosystem" in the sense we know today, referring to an industrial system inspired by the functioning of natural ecosystems. He proposed a radical critique of the operation of modern industrial societies (MIS). Quoted from : C. Figuière, A. Chebbi, *Écologie Industrielle (EI) et Économie Circulaire (EC). Concurrentes ou complémentaires?*, XXXIIèmes journées du développement ATM 2016, Colloque: „Catastrophes, vulnérabilités et résiliences dans les pays en développement", Université Lille, 1–3 Juin 2016, p. 5, https://halshs.archives-ouvertes.fr/halshs-01564030/document (20.07.2020).

160 R. Frosch, N. Gallopoulos, *Strategies for Manufacturing*, „Scientist American" 1989, vol. 261, no. 3, pp. 144–152, quoted from: C. Figuière, A. Chebbi, *Écologie Industrielle...*, p. 2.

161 "End-of-pipe solutions" aim to reduce pollutants generated in the production process, but they do not prevent the creation of new pollutants. Their goal is to decrease emissions in the final stage of production, hence the name.

162 C. Figuière, A. Chebbi, *Écologie Industrielle...*, p. 2.

163 *International Society for Industrial Ecology*, https://is4ie.org/about/history (5.08.2020).

S. Erkman (1998)[164] and M. E. Porter (1995)[165], recognized as pioneers of Industrial Ecology (IE), pointed out that a profound institutional change in technical procedures is necessary for growth to become self-sustaining. The challenge lies in creating the so-called "Type III"[166], ecosystem, a system where elements are constantly renewed—essentially an industrial system mimicking nature. This perspective treats industry as a human-made ecosystem that operates similarly to natural ecosystems, where waste or by-products from one process are used as input for another. Therefore, Industrial Ecology collaborates with natural ecosystems and aims to transition from a linear to a cyclic or closed system. Similar to natural ecosystems, IE undergoes continuous changes. The main assumption of this approach is to reduce environmental stress caused by industry while encouraging innovation, efficient resource management, and growth in line with SD. Advocates of this approach believe that industry will continue to operate and grow but will be "more environmentally conscious" and less burdensome on the planet. In this context, industry collaborates with nature, utilizing waste and by-products from other industrial sectors as inputs for its own processes. Industrial Ecology encompasses both purely industrial ecosystems and purely natural ecosystems, along with a variety of hybrid industrial ecosystems. By considering both industrial management and technology, IE also takes into account other concepts and tools of SD. These include material flow analysis, environmentally friendly technologies, design for disassembly, and dematerialization[167].

This approach introduces an innovative perspective by challenging traditional practices and emphasizing the necessity of interaction between the biosphere and economic activities. The term "industrial" here is understood in the Anglo-Saxon sense as "integrating the apparatus of production, distribution systems, public or private services, agriculture, communities, transportation, habitats…,

---

164 S. Erkman, *Vers une écologie industrielle*, Paris 1998, pp. 11–213, http://docs.eclm.fr/pdf_livre/285VersUneEcologieIndustrielle.pdf (13.08.2020).

165 M.E. Porter, C. van der Linde, *Towards a new conception of the environment-competitiveness relationship*, „Journal of Economic Perspectives" 1995, vol. 9, no. 4, pp. 97–118, https://pubs. aeaweb.org/doi/pdfplus/10.1257/jep.9.4.97 (14.08.2020).

166 T. E. Graedel and B. R. Allenby published a work in 1994 titled "Industrial Ecology," in which they remove the concept of the evolution of industrialized societies from a completely unsustainable type I ecosystem towards a much more sustainable type II ecosystem, ultimately leading to the establishment of a completely sustainable type III ecosystem. Quoted from: N. Buclet, *Ecologie industrielle et économie circulaire: définition et principes* [in:] *Économie circulaire et écosystèmes portuaires*, ed. Y. Alix, N. Mat, J. Cerceau, Paris 2015, p. 33.

167 C. Figuière, A. Chebbi, *Écologie Industrielle…*, p. 2.

but also consumers"[168]. This concept highlights that the industrial system can be considered a particular case of an ecosystem driven by the flow of matter, energy, and information. It cannot be reduced merely to exchanges between economic actors (production and services) valued in non-material or monetary terms by individual units[169].

H. Tibbs, in the "Technical Report" in 1993, outlined the principles of industrial ecology, indicating that, firstly, industrial ecosystems should be created – closing the loop, perceiving waste as resources, forming partnerships with other industrial sectors to trade by-products used as input for other processes; secondly, balancing inter-industry flows to natural levels – managing the environmental-industrial interface, expanding knowledge about ecosystem behaviour, capacity, and recovery time, broadening knowledge about how and when industry can interact with natural ecosystems and limitations; thirdly, dematerializing industrial production[170] – consuming fewer primary materials and energy, increasing resource utilization efficiency, reusing materials, or substituting them with more environmentally friendly ones; fourthly, improving the efficiency of industrial processes – redesigning products, processes, equipment, reusing materials to protect resources; fifthly, concerning energy use – considering energy supplies in industrial ecology, using alternative energy sources that have a smaller or no impact on the environment; sixthly, adjusting policies to the concept of industrial ecology – incorporating the environment and the economy into organizational, national, and international policies, internalizing external effects, using economic instruments to encourage a transition towards industrial ecology, applying an appropriate discount rate, using a more comprehensive index to measure the nation's wealth than GDP[171] (see Figure 1).

---

168 *E. Payre*, L'écologie industrielle: une stratégie conciliant les dimensions économique et environnemental du développement durable?, Paris 2008, p. 13.

169 *Ibidem*.

170 In 1989, G. Junne, J. Komen, and F. Tomeï already pointed out that "dematerialization of production can lead to a significant reduction in the demand for resources, especially minerals." Quoted from : G. Junne, J. Komen, F. Tomeï, *Dematerialisation of production: Impact on raw material exports of developing countries*, „Third World Quarterly" 1989, no. 11(2), p. 142, file:///C:/ Users/user/AppData/Local/Temp/Junne-Komen-Tomei-TWQ_1989-1.pdf (12.08.2020).

171 H. Tibbs, *Industrial Ecology: An Environmental Agenda for Industry*, „Technical Report" 1993, January, pp. 10–23.

*Figure 1: Main principles of industrial ecology.*

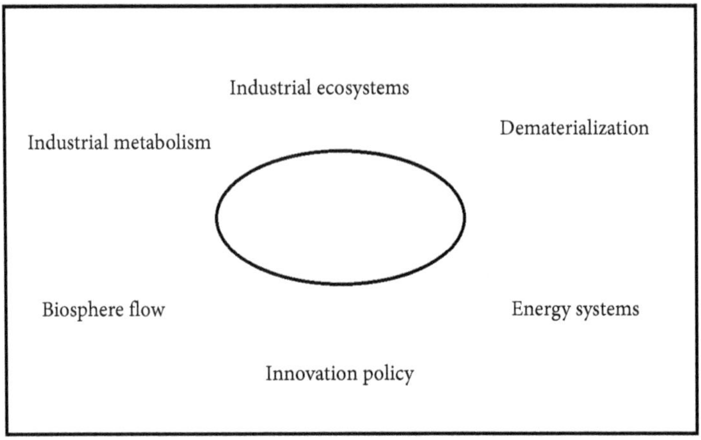


Source: H. Tibbs, *Industrial Ecology: An Environmental Agenda for Industry*, „Technical Report" 1993, January, p. 9.

Therefore, the general assumption of industrial ecology is to examine the functioning of the current system to determine changes that would enable its evolution towards a system "compatible with the normal" functioning of biological ecosystems. These changes should permit human activities that do not degrade the environment and consistently consider the limitations associated with natural resources[172]. However, there are still significant differences in dealing with substitution possibilities[173] in this approach. The specificity of this school lies in recognizing that necessary institutional changes should occur spontaneously, meaning that it does not fall within the scope of government initiative. Referring to H. Coase's assertion, this approach postulates that when information is sufficient (and transaction costs are not too high), private arrangements will enable the spontaneous realization of a goal-oriented ecosystem[174]. This challenges the automatic need for state intervention in case of market dysfunctions. It is, therefore, a self-regulating institutional change carried out by companies committed to voluntary agreements in a mutually beneficial manner[175].

172 *Ibidem.*

173 B. Billaudot, G. Destais, *Les analyses…*, p. 10.

174 See more: E. Bertrand, Ch. Destais, *Le „théorème de Coase", une réflexion sur les fondements microéconomiques de l'intervention publique*, „Reflets et Perspectives de la vie économique" 2002/2, t. XLI, pp. 111–124.

175 *Ibidem.*

IE is perceived, on the one hand, as the "science of SD" that enhances the competitiveness of businesses through environmental positioning, and on the other hand, as a radical breakthrough in the functioning of industrial societies[176]. Taking this into account, one can identify both the disadvantages and advantages resulting from adopting the assumptions of this school. Advantages include better protection of the natural environment, income generation from the sale of waste or by-products, enhanced corporate image, improved relations with other industries and organizations, and a competitive advantage. On the other hand, limitations of industrial ecology encompass a lack of support from government and industry, industry reluctance to invest in appropriate technology, absence of material markets, legal difficulties, and resistance to switching to another supplier.

#### *2.2.2.1. Industrial ecology and circular economy*

Starting from the postulate that breaking away from the prevailing linear logic (extract, produce, consume, discard) is necessary to combat the depletion of natural resources, numerous similarities between the principles of industrial ecology (IE) and the concept of a circular economy (CE) can be identified. Indeed, the proximity between the two projects is evident from the initial definitions of both concepts. As early as 1998, S. Erkman observed "that the concept of industrial ecology seems at first glance a simple tool for implementing a circular economy"[177]. The circular economy involves closing the life cycle of products, services, waste, materials, water, and energy[178]. This definition is more or less embraced by various institutions, with different emphases on one or another element of this concept[179].

However, the analysis of various works on these two concepts allows us to conclude that, apart from apparent similarities, IE and CE do indeed represent two

---

176 C. Figuière, A. Chebbi, *Écologie Industrielle…*, p. 10.

177 Quoted from: N. Buclet, *Ecologie industrielle…*, p. 29.

178 *Ibidem.*

179 During the same period, legal texts introducing the "circular economy" were emerging worldwide. For example, in Germany in 1996, the Circular Economy Act was introduced, aimed at reusing and recycling waste. This concept appeared in French institutional debates and was at the center of the *Grenelle de l'Environnement* debate conducted from 2007. Similarly, at the EU level, it can be found in the communication of July 2, 2014 (COM 398 *final*), stating that closed-loop economy systems allow for the longest possible circulation of value-added products in the economic system and eliminate the concept of waste. This document emphasizes the thorough rationalization process.

distinct projects that are not necessarily compatible with each other (see table 2). In their studies, C. Figuière and A. Chebbi identify three main elements that differentiate these two concepts: their historical foundations and theoretical origins, as well as the level of "transfers" (public-private partnerships or scientific research).

*Table 2: IE i CE – twin projects?*

| According to S. Erkmana (1998) | According to A. Geldrona (2013) |
|---|---|
| • IE is based on four main complementary axes of action | • Identified seven characteristics of the "circular economy" |
| • waste recovery<br>• emission minimization (process sealing)<br>• dematerialization of the economy (functional economy)<br>• decarbonization of energy | • sustainable supply<br>• eco-design<br>• industrial and functional ecology<br>• functional economy<br>• sustainable consumption<br>• extension of product lifespan<br>• recycling |

Source: C. Figuière, A. Chebbi, *Écologie Industrielle (EI) et Économie Circulaire (EC). Concurrentes ou complémentaires?*, XXXIIèmes journées du développement ATM 2016, Colloque: „Catastrophes, vulnéra- bilités et résiliences dans les pays en développement", Université Lille, 1–3 Juin 2016, p. 3, https://halshs. archives-ouvertes.fr/halshs-01564030/document (20.07.2020).

Given the above, at first glance, industrial ecology and the circular economy seem to describe the same reality, referring to the same goals and the desire to increase the sustainability of industrialized societies. So why the need for this new term, CE, and its blending with IE, or even the absorption of industrial ecology by the circular economy? N. Buclet points out the reasons for the emergence of these two similar concepts. The first is related to the fact that the international scientific community has organized itself around the term "industrial ecology," which is recognized in the richness of this expression, unified by numerous theoretical and empirical works. Moreover, through the prism of literature analysis, it can be observed that social science researchers (mainly from France) emphasize the desire to move from the term "industrial ecology – IE" to "industrial and territorial ecology – ITE"[180], to break free from the discipline – both from a vision limited

180 It is worth noting that, while IE treats the territory as a reality in the field—a context that needs to be understood in physical, organizational, and economic dimensions to facilitate implementation—ITE treats the territory as an independent object of study. For the latter, cultural issues related to the identity of the territory are an integral part of the reflection on what the territory is, not just how it functions.

to the industrial world and an approach mainly guided by engineering sciences. However, this branching establishes a difference between scientific work on the dynamics of industrial ecology at the local level and the public institutions' willingness to promote a circular economy on a global scale, with industrial ecology becoming one of the strategies enabling the application of the circular economy at the local level[181].

With the gradual shift towards the concept of the "circular economy," proponents of this approach have moved away from a methodological element considered central in industrial ecology, namely the application of system metabolism analysis, especially in the industrial context. In this sense, it is noteworthy that the Institute of the Circular Economy (Institut de l'Economie Circulaire)[182] founded in 2013 by F-M Lambert (France), does not even mention this method when defining the circular economyty[183].

It is important to recall that, in analyzing the system's metabolism, industrial ecology aims to measure all flows of matter and energy circulating within the system, entering it from the outside and leaving it (the cycle between the economy and the natural environment)[184]. This research allows for a quantitative inventory of interactions within and outside the system, understanding the main streams that need to be closed to increase their utilization, reduce environmental extractions, and minimize pollutant releases. System metabolism analysis is therefore the foundation of any industrial ecology approach. However, determining the boundaries of the system to be analyzed is essential, and it becomes more complex as the scale increases. Hence, methodological limitations lead to reflections in industrial ecology, emphasizing the need to position itself on a small territorial scale. One undeniable difference between industrial ecology and the circular economy is evident here, as the latter has been established without specific consideration of scale[185].

The circular economy is supported and "driven" by institutions (with the support of the business world), and this is reflected in job creation, national value-added, and profits for companies, giving the impression of overcoming underlying environmental problems (as it is primarily an economy, not ecology). There is no doubt that the environmental situation will bring additional benefits if

---

181 N. Buclet, *Ecologié industrielle…*, p. 36.

182 See more: https://institut-economie-circulaire.fr/ (20.10.2020).

183 See more: https://www.economiecirculaire.org/static/h/du-concept-a-la-pratique.Html (20.10.2020).

184 J. Kronenberg, *Sustainable production* [in:] *Challenges of sustainable development in Poland*, ed. J. Kronenberg, T. Bergier, Kraków 2010, p. 134.

185 N. Buclet, *Ecologie industrielle…*, p. 37.

economies transition to the CE model, thereby enhancing their competitiveness. Mobilization around this issue has become a playing field for companies that primarily see it as an opportunity to develop their competitiveness in a highly competitive world. On the other hand, IE is promoted primarily by the academic world (especially engineers and planners in various fields), resulting in an ongoing industrial discourse on the efficiency and rationality of industrial organization, the optimization of resource utilization, and environmental resource management[186].

Despite IE being clearly one of the pillars of the CE, C. Figuière and A. Chebbi have shown that these are, in reality, two very different projects. Work on IE is much older than that on the CE concept, and their paths and academic achievements are embedded in various reasoning approaches to SD. Research on the circular economy, mainly conducted through public-private partnerships, almost exclusively operates under the "weak sustainability" framework, even though some recent publications initiate initial proposals for a more radical CE (see Table 3 and 4).

*Table 3: Comparison of circular economy, industrial ecology and industrial and territorial ecology*

| **Industrial ecology** | **Circular economy** | **Industrial and territorial ecology (ITE)** |
|---|---|---|
| Local approach on the territorial level | Global approach at the national or European level | Local approach at the territorial level |
| Economic and participatory vision of resource management | Economic vision of resource management | Greater attention given to human-nature interactions |
| Industrial and territorial metabolism focused on quantitative aspects | Lack of clearly presented methodology | Territorial metabolism to determine socio-ecological dynamics |
| Weak sustainability | Weak sustainability | Strong sustainability |
| Environmental economics | Green growth | Social-ecological economics (Splash's concept from 2011)[187] |

Source: N. Buclet, *Ecologie industrielle et économie circulaire: définition et principes* [in:] *Économie circulaire et écosystèmes portuaires*, ed. Y. Alix, N. Mat, J. Cerceau, Paris 2015, p. 39.

186 *Ibidem*, p. 39.

187 C.L. Spash, *Social Ecological Economics. Understanding the Past to See the Future*, „American Journal of Economics and Sociology" 2011, vol. 70, no. 2, pp. 340–368, https://www. clivespash.org/wp-content/uploads/2015/04/2011_Spash_AJES_Social_Ecol_Econ1.pdf (14.08.2020).

*Table 4: Comparative analysis of C. Figuière and A. Chebbi of the circular economy concept – CE/IE (mainstream), IE (radical)*

| | **Circular economy** | **IE (mainstream)** | **IE (radical)** |
|---|---|---|---|
| Economy and natural environment | Green growth | Environmental economics | Socioecological economy (Spasha concept) |
| Procedure | Pragmatic | Objective/quantitative/pragmatic | Normative/quantitative and qualitative/theoretical |
| The use of metabolism | Location unclear | Industrial metabolism | Territorial metabolism |

Source: own study based on: C. Figuière, A. Chebbi, *Écologie Industrielle (EI) et Économie Circulaire (EC). Concurrentes ou complémentaires?*, XXXIIèmes journées du développement ATM 2016, Colloque: „Catastrophes, vulnérabilités et résiliences dans les pays en développement", Université Lille, 1–3 Juin 2016, p. 17, https://halshs.archives-ouvertes.fr/halshs-01564030/document (20.07.2020).

* * *

The circular economy has seen a significant increase in interest over the past few years and continues to gain momentum. In an effort to define a common language for the circular economy, various terms and definitions used by over 20 organizations—non-governmental organizations, government agencies, academic institutions, consulting firms, etc.—have been mapped. Working on the elements of this topic, after interpreting and grouping these different terms, seven key elements have emerged. These elements define the majority of terms related to the circular economy, thus constituting its principles[188]. They include:

Firstly, incorporating a systemic perspective during the project planning process to use appropriate materials, design with a focus on proper durability, and consider future usability (designing for the future).

Secondly, monitoring and optimizing resource utilization, and strengthening the connection between supply chain entities through digital and internet platforms, as well as technologies that provide insight (embracing digital technology).

188 https://www.circle-economy.com/circular-economy/7-key-elements (9.12.2020).

Thirdly, when resources are in use, maintaining, repairing, and upgrading to maximize their lifespan and give them a second life through take-back strategies (preserving what has been produced).

Fourthly, using non-toxic resources and utilizing them as materials and energy efficiently.

Fifthly, utilizing waste streams as a source of secondary raw materials and recovering waste for reuse and recycling.

Sixthly, adjusting incentives through business models that rely on the interaction between products and services.

Seventhly, collaboration throughout the supply chain, internally within organizations, and with the public sector to increase transparency and create shared value[189].

### 2.2.3. Ecological economics (American school)

The third element of ecological economics is the American school. Its main representatives are considered to be E. H. Daly and R. Costanza, for whom only a steady-state economy would allow the realization of SD. Conceptually, the goal is to achieve a state in which all natural, economic, and demographic quantities find themselves in a sustainable situation indefinitely. In this state, human beings only extract the flows necessary to maintain both their capital and consumption levels (in reality, into infinity), as well as accumulated resources[190].

According to E. H. Daly, this economy functions with constant consumption of natural resources at a sustainable level, allowing for the maintenance of the same consumption level in the future. This condition naturally limits the size of the economy[191]. E.H. Daly defines three criteria for preserving "natural capital": for renewable resources, the consumption level should not exceed the regeneration rate; for non-renewable resources, their use must be accompanied by appropriate investments in research to find suitable substitutes; the level of waste should not exceed the environment's capacity for assimilation[192]. Only the replacement of

189 *Ibidem.*

190 A. Verchère, *Le développement durable en question: analyses économiques autour d'un improbable compromis entre acceptions optimiste et pessimiste du rapport de l'Homme à la Nature*, „L'Actualité économique" 2011, vol. 87, no. 3, p. 345.

191 *Ibidem.*

192 Y. Verger, *L'économie stationnaire du point de vue de la production jointe: le cas des bioénergies. Écologie politique vs écologie industrielle, quelles stratégies pour le développement durable?*, Mars 2013, p. 3, Clermont-Ferrand, https://hal.archives-ouvertes.fr/hal-00804223/document (10.01.2020).

quantitative growth will ensure sustainability, leading to a call for a stationary economy[193] achieved under the pressure of intervention measures.

E.H. Daly wrote more decisively and in greater detail about the steady state than anyone else. The idea first appeared in his 1968 article On *Economics as a Life Science*[194]. He used biological and ecological analogies to formulate a more comprehensive model of the economic process, clearly demonstrating the influence of his mentor, N. Georgescu-Roegen[195]. For E.H. Daly, the need to establish a steady-state economy arose for two reasons. Firstly, the neoclassical growth paradigm assumed that "well-being" comes from both the growth of capital, especially produced capital (stock), and the growth of income generated by that capital (flow). Secondly (reflecting his desire to embed economics in biophysical realities), Earth "approaches an open-system steady state," and thus nature imposes an "inescapable general scarcity"[196]. These two ideas represented an irreconcilable internal contradiction in neoclassical economics, requiring a new paradigm – the steady-state economy. The steady state necessarily implies a constant capital

193 The idea of a steady-state economy comes from classical economics and was developed in 1857 by J.S. Mill, who referred to it as a "stationary state." The main assumption was that the population and capital resources did not grow. The sustainability of these two physical resources determined the scale of the economic subsystem. Birth rates would be equal to death rates, and the production level would be equal to the depreciation rate, so that both the population and the artifact resources (physical capital) would remain constant—not static, but in a state of dynamic equilibrium. Most classical economists were concerned that J.S. Mill's concept foreshadowed the end of progress. Quoted in: H.E. Daly, J. Farley, *Ecological Economics. Principles and Applications*, Washington 2011, pp. 55–57. Herman E. Daly's concept builds upon the one formulated by J.S. Mill but involves the analysis of the ecological flow of natural resources through the economy. It differs in that it advocates for immediate political actions to establish a steady-state economy by imposing sustainable government restrictions on any resource use. Classical economists believed that the stationary state of any economy would evolve on its own without government intervention. Quoted in: M. Blaug, *Economic Theory in retrospect*, Cambridge 1985, p. 135. The concept of a steady-state economy should not be confused with economic stagnation. The former arises from deliberate political actions, while economic stagnation is an expression of the decline (unexpected and undesirable) of a growth economy.

194 E.H. Daly, *On Economics as a Life Science*, „Journal of Political Economy" 1968, no. 76, pp. 392–406.

195 Herman E. Daly was a student of Nicholas Georgescu-Roegen at Vanderbilt University, an American private university in Nashville, Tennessee, founded in 1873.

196 M. Anderson, Economics, *Steady State*, https://umaine.edu/soe/wp-content/uploads/sites/199/2013/01/Economics-Steady-State.pdf (16.11.2020), p. 82.

stock and a constant population. However, this alone was not sufficient. Capital resources must be durable for the system to have a low pass-through coefficient[197]. The idea that we can continue to develop even when there is no more growth is a crucial feature of the steady-state economy (in this, E.H. Daly reflects the thinking of J.S. Mill). However, the possibility of development without growth challenged one of the main principles of neoclassical economic theory – that well-being is measured by the willingness to pay for goods and services and that human desires for additional consumption are limitless[198].

E.H. Daly rejected the notion that people always value more over less. He emphasized the need to perceive economic well-being as rooted more in development than in growth. According to the researcher, the "steady state (…) is defined by constant resources of physical wealth (or artifacts) and a constant population, maintained at both chosen levels desired by low flows – «meaning low birth rates, equivalent to mortality rates, and low physical production rates, equivalent to consumption rates – so that the longevity of the population and the sustainability of physical resources are high»"[199]. This requires considering the biophysical limits of economic growth[200] and contemplating the possibilities of replacing produced capital in place of resources and the capacity to absorb environmental pollutiona[201]. E.H. Daly's articles on the steady-state economy (published in the 1970s) reflect his profound knowledge that goes beyond the boundaries of economics. Ecology, physics, ethics, and evolutionary biology were integrated to address issues related to defining the steady-state economy[202].

This approach, the most radical one (non-substitutability of natural resources), asserts that it is not possible to replace "natural capital" and other components. The condition for "strong sustainability" is that "natural capital" remains constant over time, in a specific physical composition serving as the basis for determining environmental standards. Therefore, it seems that Daly's steady state is an ideal type, more related to a moral imperative and the direction to be taken than a

197 *Ibidem.*

198 *Ibidem.*

199 H.E. Daly, *The Economics of the Steady State*, „*American Economic Review*" 1974, no. 64(2), pp. 15–21, quoted from: A. Verchère, *Le développement…*, p. 346.

200 H.E. Daly, *Steady-State Economics. The Economics of Biophysical Equilibrium and Moral Growth*, San Francisco 1977, quoted from: V. Boisvert, *Des limites de la mise en marché de l'environnement. Des services écosystémiques aux „banques de conservation"*, „Écologie & politique" 2016, no. 52, p. 71.

201 *Ibidem.*

202 M. Anderson, *Economics…*, p. 81.

precise definition of a true "steady state." In any case, in this context, one must understand his hostility toward indefinite quantitative growth, which he labels as "mania," accusing many economists, especially orthodox ones[203]. According to E.H. Daly, economic decisions should focus on the scale of use (e.g., setting limits on fishing in a particular area) and resource allocation (distributing the fishing limit among potential users) or determining the overall level of permissible emissions, which in practice means establishing the scale of environmental intervention. Therefore, the question arises as to who would emit to ensure that the collectively determined level is not exceeded[204].

In the ongoing debate accompanying the emergence of ecological economics, E.H. Daly distances himself from attempts to assimilate ecology into economics and vice versa. On the contrary, he emphasizes that both disciplines have different subjects of study and methodologies. He advocates that each discipline should be utilized for what it is best suited for. Thus, ecology should indicate the extent to which humans can intervene in the environment, i.e., make decisions about the scale of nature use. Allocation decisions (regarding who should consume how much of the collectively available resources) are most competently examined by economics. In this context, the researcher also perceives the role of the market. According to him, the market is not suitable for making decisions about the scale of consumption of natural resources, but it is an excellent tool for deciding on the allocation of what the economy will take from nature. Therefore, in this perspective, "ecology" sets the framework for the consumption of natural resources, while "economics" assists in achieving the best possible benefits within those limitsy[205].

The American school does not reject development; instead, it distinguishes it from growth. For E.H. Daly, "growth" is quantitative, while "development" is qualitative. This means that while the former does not guarantee the latter, the latter is possible without growth[206]. If we use "growth" to denote quantitative change and "development" in reference to qualitative change, we can say that the steady-state economy develops but does not grow, much like the planet Earth, whose economy is a subsystem that develops but does not grow[207].

---

203 *Ibidem*, p. 347.

204 http://coin.wne.uw.edu.pl/tzylicz/0904AURA.pdf (16.11.2020)

205 *Ibidem.*

206 C. Gendron, *Le développement durable comme compromis. La modernisation écologique de l'économie a l'ère de la mondialisation*, Québec 2006, p. 35.

207 H.E. Daly, *Steady-State Economics…*, p. 17.

On the other hand, R. Costanza[208] coming from a completely different academic background, gradually established connections with economists interested in energy and environmental issues, stemming from his expertise in modeling and quantifying embodied energy in biosphere products. This led him to become a key figure in ecological economics. His publications have contributed to the development of EE, even though the conceptual foundations of R. Costanza's intellectual approach are not without their challenges.

R. Costanza i E.H. W In 1987, R. Costanza and E.H. Daly, in their article *Toward an ecological economics*, pointed out the reasons for moving beyond the existing paradigms of economics and ecology, which they considered too narrow. This article is recognized as the first step towards a true synthesis of ecology and economics, which later became known as the American school of ecological economics. This development was seen as a hope for better management of renewable and non-renewable natural resources and the future outlined by the concept of SD. According to the pioneers of this school, "the most obvious danger of ignoring nature in economics is that nature is a life-support system in the economy, and by ignoring it, one can unintentionally damage it irreversibly"[209]. Achieving a true synthesis of economics and ecology is, alongside avoiding nuclear war, the second most important task of our generation. Without such integration, we gradually deprive the Earth of the ability to sustain life on its own[210].

One of R. Costanza's consistent ambitions is to quantitatively determine the biosphere's contribution to economic activity, especially as encapsulated in the concept of ecosystem services. He assigns a central role to monetary valuation in measuring the world. In 1997, he published an article in the journal "Nature" with other researchers, estimating the total value of ecosystem services provided by the biosphere to humans at a minimum of $16–54 trillion annually, with an estimated average of $33 trillion annually[211]. These figures show that the value of natural capital is greater than the annual global GDP, which was around $18 trillion at that time. When divided among 6 billion people, these $33 trillion provide approximately $5500 per person annually for basic services "provided" by

208 He studied environmental engineering in Florida, learning about energy exchange systems.

209 R. Costanza, H.E. Daly, *Toward an ecological economics*, „Ecological Modelling" 1987, no. 38, pp. 3–4.

210 *Ibidem*, p. 7.

211 R. Costanza, R. d'Arge, R. de Groot, S. Farber, M. Grasso, B. Hannon, K. Limburg, S. Naeem, R. O'Neill, J. Paruelo, R. Raskin, P. Sutton, M. Van Den Belt, *The value of the world's ecosystem services and natural capital*, „Nature" 1997, no. 387, pp. 253–260.

ecosystems, such as regulating atmospheric composition, climate, water, resilience, water supply, erosion control, soil formation, nutrient cycling, waste processing, pollination, biological control, habitat provision, food production, raw materials, genetic resources, entertainment, and cultural support[212].

Therefore, R. Costanza proposes a reorientation of the economy towards new values: integration within the limits of nature, considering the maximum state of resources, emphasizing well-being rather than growth[213]. Following this pioneering research, economists such as N. Stern, with his study on the cost of climate change, and P. Sukhdev, with his work on the economics of ecosystems and biodiversity, have determined the values of ecosystem "services": values of direct use, indirect use values, discount rates, non-use values, or intrinsic values[214].

Similarly, research conducted by the Rockström Institute in Stockholm, Sweden, in 1997, confirmed unsustainable development, reintroducing the concept of "limits" inaugurated in the Meadows report in 1972 (Limits to Growth). According to the work of J. Rockström and his colleagues, nine sectors urgently call for defining planetary boundaries: climate change, loss of biodiversity, excessive nitrogen and phosphorus production, depletion of the ozone layer, ocean acidification, global freshwater consumption, land-use changes, air pollution, and chemical pollution. They indicated that humanity has already exceeded three of these critical thresholds: climate change, loss of biodiversity, and excessive nitrogen production. Only the "true cost" of these degradations could enable their prevention[215]. R. Costanza played a key role in raising awareness of the growing degradation of ecosystems, which can impact the economy, and that growth itself "has a negative impact on well-being, social capital, and natural capital." According to him, only replacing quantitative growth with a sense of well-being sets one of the key paths to national prosperity. This would be achieved if people

212 *Ibidem.*

213 J. Rockström, W. Steffen, K. Noone, A. Persson, F.S. Chapin, E. Lambin, T.M. Lenton, M. Scheffer, C. Folke, H. Schellnhuber, B. Nykvist, C.A. De Wit, T. Hughes, S. van der Leeuw, H. Rodhe, S. Sörlin, P.K. Snyder, R. Costanza, U. Svedin, M. Falkenmark, L. Karlberg, R.W. Corell, V.J. Fabry, J. Hansen, B. Walker, D. Liverman, K. Richardson, P. Crutzen, J. Foley, *Planetary boundaries: exploring the safe operating space for humanity*, „Ecology and Society" 2009, vol. 14, no. 2, http://www.ecologyandsociety.org/vol14/iss2/art32/ (16.12.2020).

214 *Ibidem.*

215 *Ibidem.*

consumed less, spent more time with loved ones, and took care of their mental and physical health"[216].

Therefore, nature and the biosphere, in R. Costanza's perspective, are reduced to the status of providers of what he calls natural capital. In the eyes of ecological economics as seen by him, the environment is perceived in terms of monetary appreciation. He proposes integrating non-market contributions to the economy through indicators such as the Human Development Index (HDI)[217], the Index of Sustainable Economic Welfare – (ISEW)[218] or the Genuine Progress Indicator – (GPI)[219]. The second path of economic development involves the expansion of assets necessary to support the real economy that generates prosperity: built capital, human capital, social capital, and natural capital. Built capital is created from natural capital. Recognizing this means acknowledging that natural and social capital cannot be indefinitely replaced by built and human capital. In the future, the pursuit of productivity will no longer be the leading motive. Human capital will be reinforced through a more cooperative economy and participatory democracy, but also through shorter working hours, an effective way to reduce resource consumption as it naturally limits production and consumption[220]. The third path is associated with establishing a new set of ownership regimes. The majority of natural and social capital assets constitute common goods and, therefore, cannot be effectively managed by private ownership. R. Costanza, along with other ecological economics researchers, proposes establishing a commons sector

216 A. Sinaï, *L' économie écologique déploie ses propositions*, https://www.actu-environnement.com/ae/news/economie-ecologique-robert-costanza-18443.php4 (16.12.2020).

217 The Human Development Index (HDI) is an index that measures key dimensions of social development: 1) long and healthy life – measured by life expectancy at birth; 2) access to education – assessed by the expected years of schooling for school-age children and the average years of schooling for the adult population; 3) decent standard of living – assessed by Gross National Income (GNI) per capita adjusted for purchasing power parity.

218 The Index of Sustainable Economic Welfare (ISEW) is a measure of well-being developed in 1989 by E. H. Daly and J. Cobb. They expanded the traditional measure of individual consumption by adding: unpaid household work services, services related to the use of durable consumer goods, services related to the use of roads and highways, consumption associated with education and health services, net capital growth, the balance of foreign investments in the country.

219 The Genuine Progress Indicator (GPI) emerged in 2003 as an evolution of the Index of Sustainable Economic Welfare (ISEW), representing another measure of well-being that incorporates the principles of SD.

220 A. Sinaï, *L'économie écologique*…

separate from both the public and private sectors. This would involve common ownership rights to resources held by the entire society. This sector "would be tasked with managing these resources in such a way that all citizens, as well as future generations, could equally benefit from them." Decision-makers could also transfer these rights through a common goods trust fund, overseeing their utilization and limiting their use to a level lower or equal to their renewal[221]. The fourth path involves reclaiming the power of money creation by the public sector. The state would take away the banks' right to create money by gradually transitioning to a 100% reserve requirement. Meanwhile, the public sector could create money in various ways: producing neglected public goods, investing in social and human capital to create jobs, changing state infrastructure, or restoring natural systems. The state would no longer need to borrow money or repay with interest. According to researchers, "without exponential growth of debt and interest payments, nothing would force us to choose between poverty and infinite growth". The goal is to achieve a "steady state" for the economy, a state of balance with sustainable production levels, which would likely require a significant reduction in market activity in wealthy countries and, consequently, a decrease in the overall money supply needed to support the economy[222].

In opening a conference co-organized by the Institute for Sustainable Development and International Relations (IDDRI) on April 25, 2013, in Paris, R. Costanza outlines a vision of a planet exploited by humans, entering a state of unknown instability, stating that "the world is a complex nonlinear adaptive system with thresholds, tipping points, and surprises"[223]. According to the American economist, this cannot happen in a finite world without eroding the very foundations of natural and social capital[224]. In a collective work published in 2012 by the United Nations titled *Building a Sustainable and Desented Economy-in-Society*, R. Costanza and his co-authors propose a thorough rethinking of our economic system based on the "ecological economy" defined by the American economist E.H. Daly[225].

---

221 *Ibidem.*

222 J. Farley, M. Burke, G. Flomenhoh, B. Kelly, D. Forrest Murray, S. Posner, M. Putman, A. Scanlan, A. Witham, *Monetary and Fiscal Policies for a Finite Planet*, „Sustainability" 2013, no. 5, pp. 2802–2803.

223 A. Sinaï, *L'économie écologique…*

224 *Ibidem.*

225 R. Constanza, G. Alperovitz, H.E. Daly, J. Farley, C. Franco, T. Jackson, I. Kubiszewski, J. Schor, P. Victor, *Building a Sustainable and Desirable Economy – in Society – in Nature*, New York 2012, https://sustainabledevelopment.un.org/content/documents/Building_a_Sustaina-ble_and_Desirable_Economy-in-Society-in-Nature.pdf (16.12.2020).

In his article from 2013 titled *A further critique of growth economics*, E.H. Daly posed the question of whether growth is still economic in the literal sense or has become uneconomic. This question was a response to the lack of reaction or dialogue from the authors of the *Growth Report*[226] which included 18 members from 16 countries, including Nobel laureates in economics. According to Daly, the *Growth Report* was a "political manifesto" and a "hymn to growth in the guise of objective research"[227]. E.H. Daly suggests that the authors of the report may have considered the case for "growth" to be so ironclad and obvious that any defense against criticism was unnecessary. He questions why they felt the need for such a strong defense of growth in the first place. According to E. H. Daly, this context illustrates the unfortunate state of the public debate on economic issues and the lack of seriousness among many economists engaged in such discourse. E. H. Daly, dismayed by the attitude within his field, points to examples like "The Journal of Economic Perspectives," which has a policy of not printing comments on published articles[228]. This reluctance to engage in discussion from both sides leads Daly to reflect more broadly on economics. He highlights eleven "crushing errors" made by contemporary economists dealing with growth, calling for a dialogue and an attempt to grapple with the fact that what was once economic growth may now be considered uneconomic growth. Additionally, he emphasizes that hope must involve not only a better understanding of the errors he identifies but also a greater concern for loved ones and the entire creation[229].

A genuine step forward, reflecting the mindset of researchers from the American school of EE, is the adoption of the Sustainable Development Goals (SDGs) agreed upon in the UN Agenda, the achievement of which is set for 2030. The SDGs process provides an opportunity to initiate a systemic change for building a sustainable future in an increasingly interconnected world. However, according to R. Costanza, additional efforts are required for the development of this process, including: 1) complex Interconnections between goals 2) a continuum of means and ends towards an overarching goal 3) a "narrative of change" describing the social changes and political reforms needed to achieve the SDGs and how this

226 *Commission on Growth and Development. The Growth Report : Strategies for Sustained Growth and Inclusive Development*, World Bank, Washington 2008, https://openknowledge. worldbank.org/handle/10986/6507 (17.12.2020).

227 E.H. Daly, *A further critique of growth economics*, „Ecological Economics" 2013, no. 88, p. 20.

228 *Ibidem*.

229 *Ibidem*, p. 24.

could actually occur under existing socio-economic and geopolitical conditions[230]. The SDGs necessitate the definition of an overarching goal with clear metrics to measure progress on the path directed towards the integration of sub-goals[231], In this context, the "ultimate goal" is sustainable and equitable well-being, with intermediate goals encompassing economic, social, and environmental objectives. The 17 proposed goals of SD, aligned with the three partial goals of ecological economics initially proposed by E.H. Daly in 1992, involve sustainable scale, just distribution, and efficient allocation. These goals are situated within the spectrum of "intermediate goals." The requirement for a "sustainable scale" is based on the assumption that a sustainable system cannot deplete natural capital or degrade ecosystem services beyond a certain "safe operational space." The aim is to achieve a system that is both sustainable and desirable in every aspect, considering natural, social, human, and created capital[232]. Ultimately, to properly assess SD, an integrated approach to modeling dynamic systems will be required.

The SDGs represent an important step in building global consensus on the type of world that is desirable, and SD in the sense of longevity is certainly one characteristic of the desired world, but it can only be predicted, not directly measured. The goals set in the 2030 Agenda, along with indicators, provide a detailed navigational dashboard for the transition to SD. Some argue that a cockpit-based approach is sufficient and is the only feasible option. According to researchers, both the cockpit and dashboards or aggregated indicators are not mutually exclusive—in reality, all of them are necessary[233].

The approach is based on the assumption that the best system is one that achieves the overarching goal of simultaneously ensuring a high quality of life that is fairly shared and sustainable. Figure 2 presents 17 SD goals and their contributions to each of the three categories corresponding to the three fundamental goals outlined by E. H. Daly (1990) and R. Costanza (1991 and 2014) within ecological economics, as well as the three fundamental components of SD. It is important to note that many of the sub-goals of the SDGs contribute to more than one category. Ultimately, in the short-term perspective, a pluralistic approach will be necessary to explore several options, and a consensus-building process will be required to

---

230 R. Costanza, L. Daly, L. Fioramonti, E. Giovannini, I. Kubiszewski, L.F. Mortensen, K.E. Pickett, K.V. Ragnarsdottir, R. De Vogli, R. Wilkinson, *Modelling and measuring sustainable wellbeing in connection with the UN Sustainable Development Goals*, „Ecological Economics" 2016, no. 130, p. 350.

231 *Ibidem.*

232 *Ibidem*, p. 351.

233 *Ibidem.*

narrow down these possibilities. This approach is based on the assumption that the best system is one that achieves the overarching goal of simultaneous prosperity, a high quality of life fairly shared, and sustainability. The aim is not infinite growth but rather well-being, equality, and development in line with the concept of SD.

*Figure 2: The relationship of the 17 SDGs to each other, to the EE framework and to the overarching goal of a sustainable, equitable and prosperous human system embedded in the rest of nature.*

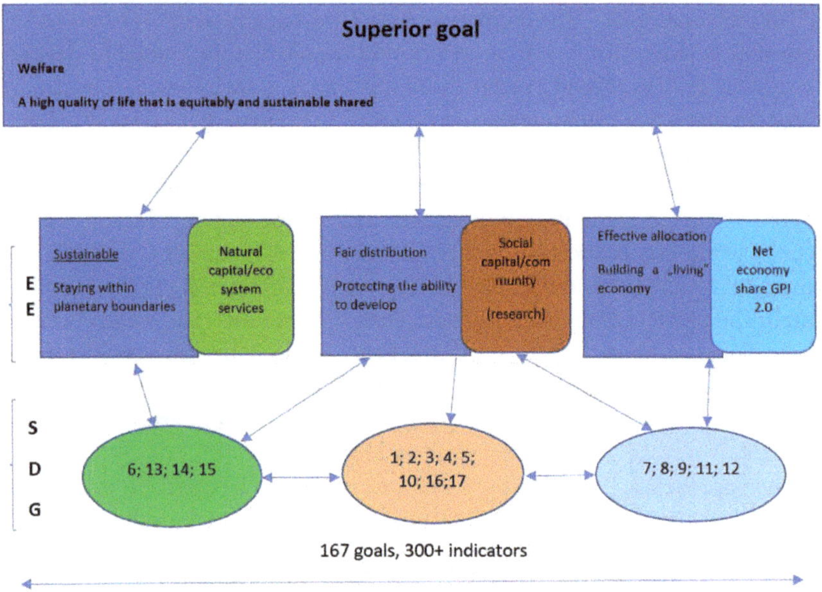


Source: own study based on: R. Costanza, L. Daly, L. Fioramonti, E. Giovannini, I. Kubiszewski, L.F. Mortensen, K.E. Pickett, K.V. Ragnarsdottir, R. De Vogli, R. Wilkinson, *Modelling and measuring sustainable wellbeing in connection with the UN Sustainable Development Goals*, „Ecological Economics" 2016, no. 130, p. 353.

The SDGs represent a major achievement in developing shared goals for all of humanity. They have been agreed upon by all United Nations member states and encompass economic, social, and environmental elements. However, they lack an effective progress indicator in their implementation. It can be argued that such an aggregated indicator is not necessary (or possible), and the pursuit of individual goals is sufficient for achieving sustainable development. This could be true if the goals were independent of each other and all equally contributed to achieving the overarching goal. According to R. Costanza, an aggregated indicator allows assessing the relative contribution of each resilience to SD gaols and their interactions to evaluate overall progress. The authors of *Modelling and measuring sustainable wellbeing in connection with the UN Sustainable Development Goals* suggested three fundamental categories that could form a hybrid indicator and how they could be combined. They also proposed developing a basic system dynamics model to assess interactions and synergies in space and time, considering both resources and flows, causes and effects. They emphasized the need for policy reforms and social changes to achieve SDGs at both national and global levels. The authors concluded that in today's interconnected world, SDGs cannot be achieved without sustainable prosperity worldwide[234].

* * *

While environmental economics, which emerged in the early 1970s, originates from economic sciences, ecological economics is not so much a discipline as a field of research. One of its goals is to establish resilience, contributing to stabilizing sustainability among its three pillars (economic, environmental, and social)[235]. Starting with the assumption that the economic process is a social phenomenon occurring in a finite biophysical world, this sets the basic direction of thinking for proponents of ecological economics and is of great importance for transforming social policy. This approach can play a leading role in ongoing efforts to reconcile economic theory and policy with the acceptance of knowledge from other disciplines. This is particularly relevant as neoclassical welfare economics still offers "wrong solutions" in dealing with some of the most pressing environmental and social issues in the 21st century, including growing income inequality, global climate change, and biodiversity loss[236].

R. Costanza, J. Erickson, J. Farley, and I. Kubiszewski, in their latest work published in 2020 titled *Sustainable Well-being Future: A Research and Action Agenda for Ecological Economics*, define ecological economics as a transdisciplinary effort aimed at understanding the complex system of humans and the rest of nature and managing them for mutual improvement of the well-being of

---

234 *Ibidem*, p. 355; R. Costanza, I. Kubiszewski, E. Giovannini, H. Lovins, J. McGlade, K.E. Pickett, K.V. Ragnarsdóttir, D. Roberts, R. De Vogli, R. Wilkinson, *Time to leave GDP behind*, „Nature" 2014, no. 505, pp. 283–285; https://www.nature.com/news/development-ti-me-to-leave-gdp-behind-1.14499 (12.11.2020).

235 https://www.fondsfmoq.com/leconomie-ecologique-un-courant-digne-dinteret/ (12.11.2020).

236 J. Gowdy, J.D. Erickson, *The approach of ecological economics*, „Cambridge Journal of Economics" 2005, no. 29, pp. 207–208.

all life[237]. According to them, the main challenge is that "ecological economics focuses on urgent problems where facts are highly uncertain, and values matter. The scale and interdependence of many of today's problems require a shared vision of the world we all desire (rich and poor, north and south, east and west). A better understanding of the current state requires collaboration among many disciplines and traditional knowledge bases. Achieving solutions will require even greater collaboration between the academic community, decision-makers, the business sector, civil society, and nations"[238].

If ecological economics is to remain a credible theoretical and practical approach, it must transcend the traditional boundaries of the academic environment and co-create research and actions. EE acknowledges that people are part of nature and do not operate outside of it. As a complex, interdependent, and constantly evolving whole system, the economy is fundamentally embedded in society, which is embedded in the remaining part of nature. It requires a better understanding of well-being and SD.

EE, instead of advocating for and defending a single discipline or paradigm, seeks to enable the representation, comparison, and synthesis of a broad, pluralistic range of perspectives and models to better understand the nature of complex systems. As such, ecological economics is an "approach" that represents a commitment of scientists and practitioners to learn from each other, discover new patterns of thinking, and facilitate the derivation and implementation of effective economic, social, and environmental policies. Advocates of this approach do not "offer a grand theory but rather a flexible approach recognizing the uniqueness of specific cultures and ecosystems"[239]. To avoid thinking in terms of a "one-world" perspective, ecological economics deliberately and consciously sought a pluralistic character in its conceptual foundations. Pluralism makes sense, as emphasized, especially since the late 1980s, by R. B. Norgaard, one of the pioneers of EE. He clearly pointed out that "ecological economics must deal with the complex interdependence of global and local economies, sophisticated technologies and human frailties, environmental systems, and social control of their use, as well as limited resources"[240]. In his view, "there is no one best perspective for understanding and managing the complexities of the problems we currently face"[241]. Therefore,

---

237 R. Costanza, J.D. Erickson, J. Farley, I. Kubiszewski, *Sustainable Wellbeing Futures: A Research and Action Agenda for Ecological Economics*, Cheltenham 2020, p. 1.

238 *Ibidem.*

239 J. Gowdy, J.D. Erickson, *The approach…*, p. 219.

240 R.B. Norgaard, *The case…*, p. 52.

241 *Ibidem.*

it is not surprising that ecological economics encompasses certain aspects of economics, ecology, environmental impact research, and other methodological approaches as components, while simultaneously questioning the uniqueness of their worldviews and the usefulness of some of their assumptions and methods. It facilitates the integration and synthesis of new and emerging fields of science, such as behavioural economics, positive psychology, Earth system science, multi-level selection theory, and many others. It is based on pluralism but recognizes that "all models are wrong – but some are useful," as famously stated by George Box. Therefore, it strives for "intelligent pluralism" in problem-solving, acknowledging the limitations of all paradigms while also recognizing which ideas and perspectives are most useful for a given task. This transdisciplinary, coevolutionary, pluralistic orientation of ecological economics has helped create a solid institutional foundation. After numerous experiments and joint meetings of economists and ecologists in 1988, the International Society for Ecological Economics (ISEE) was established. The association's journal, "Ecological Economics," published its first issue in February 1989 and currently releases twelve issues annually[242].

Supporters of ecological economics share a common way of thinking that condemns monolithic, reductionist, and one-dimensional reasoning in both traditional economics and environmental economics. They reject the dominance of neoclassical economics, which perceives the economy in terms of trade and production, and treats the environment as a collection of goods available for individual preferences. From the perspective of ecological economists, the challenges facing humanity require moving beyond simple attempts to apply economic tools to environmental issues by encouraging people to consider the externalities of their actions[243].

This age-old approach of the neoclassical school is called "internalizing externalities," involving incorporating the costs of external effects of a business's activities into its expenditures. Concerning external effects, they refer, from an environmental standpoint, to all types of pollution, degradation, or destruction of the environment caused by the same activities. Without rejecting this approach, ecological economics believes that it is not sufficient to ensure, with a focus on preserving and renewing the biosphere, compliance with the principle of strong SD (according to which the rate of consumption of renewable resources should not exceed the rate of their regeneration or the development of renewable and

242 R. Costanza, J.D. Erickson, J. Farley, I. Kubiszewski, *Sustainable Wellbeing Futures…*, p. 7.
243 *Ibidem.*

sustainable substitutes). It also contends that the volume of pollutant emissions should not exceed the environment's capacity for absorption and assimilation. In other words, it goes beyond preventing the erosion of natural capital and its components (Earth's natural resources, ecosystems) and allows for the effective combatting of various socio-ecological negative consequences (inequality, poverty, global warming, pollution, depletion of natural resources, etc.). Unlike environmental economics, ecological economics models the behaviours of actors and decision-makers and aims to develop assessment frameworks and tools that these entities can use to construct an economy while respecting the conditions and capacities of nature and communities. Asserting that the economy and the environment do not have to be in conflict, ecological economics aims to contribute to better integrating the environmental dimension—a key factor in the success of addressing climate change, global warming, and biodiversity loss[244].

Ecological economics, despite being nearly 30 years old, has not yet evolved into a coherent school of thought but stands as a leading contender among heterodox schools to become a comprehensive alternative to neoclassical orthodoxy. Despite the numerous research efforts, materialized in various theoretical approaches, sometimes overlapping and sometimes mutually exclusive, the economic discipline, as É Laurent puts it, "largely neglects the environment, and the vast majority of economists ignore environmental issues in the double sense of ignorance and indifference." When economists do take notice, they often downplay the impact of environmental issues and propose remedies that may exacerbate them, such as accelerating economic growth, monetizing ecosystem services, or minimizing values to mitigate contemporary ecological crises. There is no doubt that there are thousands of economists worldwide who, by addressing environmental issues, contribute to understanding them, (including members of the IPCC[245] and IPBES[246]). However, they constitute a small minority in the vast field of economic research and decision-making, even as humanity enters 2020"[247]. The overwhelming majority of economists are now interested in the real world, but it seems that

244 *Ibidem.*

245 The Intergovernmental Panel on Climate Change (IPCC) is a scientific and intergovernmental advisory body established in 1988 by two UN organizations: the World Meteorological Organization and the UN Environment Program.

246 The Intergovernmental Science-Policy Platform on Biodiversity and Ecosystem Services (IPBES) is an intergovernmental organization established to enhance the linkages between science and policy on issues related to biodiversity and ecosystem services.

247 É. Laurent, *La transition juste…*, p. 10.

their environment is not part of it. This lack of interest in environmental issues is all the more harmful since ecological transformation is currently a matter for the social sciences: the exact sciences have largely worked on revealing the scope and urgency of ecological crises. This is the main challenge of the upcoming decade; we must change attitudes and behaviours to prevent the self-destruction of human prosperity in the second half of the 21st century. In other words, the social sciences, including economics, are key to addressing the problems revealed by the exact sciences[248].

Representatives of the mentioned schools of ecological economics share the recognition of the limits of the biosphere and propose ways to create prosperity with minimal growth. Convinced of the need to reduce this growth, they advocate for the redefinition of wealth indicators, reduced consumption and production, decreased inequality, and a better distribution of resources. They also propose the establishment of a *Green New Deal* to restore employment and macroeconomic modelling to adjust contemporary economic policy towards genuine ecological transformation[249].

## 2.3. Analyzing scientific controversies in an uncertain universe

Unlike previous analyses, some authors consider the existence of controversies in the public space. SD is then perceived as the result of a group of entities (firms, experts, politicians, civil society) in a controversial world. Research on scientific controversies has increased in recent years, but the concept of "scientific controversies" itself has not been strictly defined[250]. L. Scotto d'Apollonia, in his work[251] makes an effort to explain and specify the subject of research on scientific controversies as accurately as possible. He does so using the example of climate controversies. He points out that scientific controversies are characterized by the persistent and public division of several members of the scientific community,

---

248 *Ibidem*, p. 14.

249 A. Lalucq, *Économistes et écologie…*, p. 52.

250 Scientific controversies can be described as a debate among personalities within the scientific community or its observers (philosophers of science, epistemologists, sociologists of science, journalists, etc.) regarding scientific theories or historical, philosophical, or factual aspects related to those theories. All scientific controversies are inherently controversial, reflecting the evolution of the history of science, accompanying the development of knowledge. See more: J.C. Baudet, *Les plus grandes controverses de l'Histoire de la science*, Paris 2015.

251 L. Scotto d'Apollonia, *Les controverses climatiques: une analyse socioépistémique*. Sociologie, Montpellier 2014.

coalition or not, who support conflicting arguments in the interpretation of a given phenomenon. Providing a definition of climate controversies, he believes they are "persistent and public discussions among researchers from different scientific disciplines who support different arguments in the interpretation of the Earth's climate system. The specificity of climate controversies lies in presenting the greatest political challenge on a global scale, as the focal point of disagreement is the impact of human activity on the climate. In this sense, they are socio-scientific controversies"[252].

One can mention, in addition to climate change, many controversies from recent years, such as GMOs (genetically modified organisms), electromagnetic waves, or nanotechnologies. Controversies are not just debates; they arise because several actors intervene in the subject: researchers, journalists, members of associations, politicians, etc. Once established, they bring scientific or technical-scientific issues into play, which are conveyed through economic, legal, or ethical issues[253].

In rare cases in the scientific field, controversies arise that have no social repercussions and remain strictly confined to scientific disciplines, such as certain controversies in mathematics. There are also scientific controversies that receive widespread attention but are not the subject of citizen mobilization or public debate (e.g., the recent reopening of the discussion about the possible exceeding of the speed of light by elementary particles called neutrinos). If these scientific controversies play out in the public sphere, even to a limited extent, they take on a social character[254].

Why study controversies? Examining controversies—both historical and current—is significant. The goal is to understand that scientific issues are complex and do not simply result in a series of linear outcomes. Controversy may generate debate or disagreements, but it doesn't simplify into one or the other. Science is a field of observation and research, and for experimental sciences, it involves experimental methodology that introduces tangible elements to hypotheses (which either confirm or invalidate them). Unfortunately, science itself is sometimes confused with its technological applications, scientific outcomes, and new knowledge used to create new applications. As a result, the public is intrigued by both science and technology. And even, as J.-M. Besnier put it: "Science has become the object of consumption, which must. That is, to heal us, to prevent aging and death, so that

252 *Ibidem*, p. 14.

253 https://theconversation.com/de-la-controverse-scientifique-au-debat-de-societe-112039 (10.07.2018).

254 L. Scotto d'Apollonia, *Les controverses climatiques…*, p. 14.

we can give birth to children correctly"[255]. Controversial topics, such as GMOs, electromagnetic waves, or nanotechnologies, most often have a possible impact, direct or indirect, on human health. In this aspect, critics and the media rely on sharing arguments with the largest possible audience through radio, television, press, etc. In reality, these topics influence the actions of decision-makers[256], and may determine priorities, potentially narrowing the scope of research topics, at least in experimental areas[257].

The health crisis related to the outbreak of the SARS-CoV-2 epidemic, which we are experiencing, brought sudden fame to Professor D. Raoult, the director of the Mediterranean Institute of Infections (IHU Infection Méditerranée). His proposal to treat people with SARS-CoV-2 with a protocol combining hydroxychloroquine and azithromycin stirred both hope and opposition. Such a direct conflict between clearly established camps (supporters and opponents of solving the epidemic problem in this way) is far from the most common configuration but tends to arise usually when controversy enters an intensification phase, often accompanied by escalating public debate[258].

However, the urgent timeframe in which the controversy surrounding D. Raoult is unfolding sheds light on an additional aspect, less visible in controversies experiencing differences in intensity and characterized by more ordinary temporality. The article that D. Raoult published on the website of the newspaper "Le Monde" on March 25, 2020, provides much information on this matter. As stated in the article: "The greatness of a doctor lies in treating his patients with all the currently available means, as if it were a matter of saving his own child"[259]. In this sense, according

255 https://www.telerama.fr/idees/climat-pesticides-ogm-les-scientifiques-font-le-buzz-ok-dom,136680.php (6.12.2020).

256 The National Research Strategy (*Strategie Nationale de Recherche* – SNR) embedded in French law has been developed in line with the EU strategy. Its purpose is to define the number of scientific and technological priorities to meet the main challenges of the coming decades. S N R is based on consultations with the scientific and academic community as well as the socio-economic world. Quoted from: https://www.enseignementsup-recherche.gouv.fr/cid86688/strategie-nationale-de-re-cherche-france-europe-2020.html (17.12.2020).

257 https://theconversation.com/de-la-controverse-scientifique-au-debat-de-societe-112039 (6.12.2020).

258 D. Linhardt, *Didier Raoult, ou la controverse scientifique dans le temps de l'urgence*, 27 mars 2020, https://www.ehess.fr/fr/carnet/coronavirus/didier-raoult-ou-controverse-scien-tifique-dans-temps-lurgence (18.12.2020).

259 https://www.lemonde.fr/idees/article/2020/03/25/didier-raoult-le-medecin-peut-et-doit-reflechir-comme-un-medecin-et-non-pas-comme-un-methodologiste_6034436_3232.html (6.12.2020).

to the perspective of the scientific worker D. Linhardt from the French Interdisciplinary Laboratory for Reflexivity Studies[260] (Laboratoire interdisciplinaire d'etudes sur les réflexivités – LIER), "the true human of medical art directly opposes what D. Raoult condescendingly calls the «methodologist», who demands that one act solely on the basis of certainties duly acquired according to objective and falsifiable procedures, as is usually the case in randomized double-blind trials"[261]. D. Linhardt raises the question: What is the source of authority if there is no evidence confirmed by the aforementioned method of seeking truth? In attempting to answer this question, the researcher points to intuitive knowledge, stating that "this kind of knowledge is absolutely not arbitrary; it takes the form of cognitive flashes[262] beyond any proper process. Similar to a detective relying on their «nose» during an investigation. Accumulated experience increases the chances of 'doing it well.' As such, it can be a source of certainty. However, this certainty, even if reinforced by positive feedback from experience, is not objective in the opposing evidentiary system; it is epistemologically embedded within a community of experts who shape it in the form of passionate conviction. There is no scientific knowledge that does not go through this phase of intuitive knowledge, this specific moment in which a preliminary hypothesis is formed, leading the researcher to continue their efforts in a specific direction without yet knowing exactly why. In the literature, this stage is sometimes referred to as the «logic of discovery». Before a discovery is recognized as such, before it becomes a universally accepted fact, a long effort is needed. However, this effort relies on an entirely different modality, on the «logic of justification» Typically, scientific controversies focus precisely on these justifications. It is their resistance to criticism that ultimately gives the discovery the quality of a fact. If this coherence is flawed, the discovery may add to the already long list of forgotten artefacts. What we call this method is nothing more than expecting the logic of justification in the logic of discovery"[263]. The uniqueness of the controversy surrounding the treatment promoted by D. Raoult in the fight against the COVID-19 epidemic lay in the fact that it was already too late for humanity to wait for the discovery to be justified or refuted. The rush at that time led to the politicization of the question of whether to rely on the intuitive

---

260 See more on the concept of reflexivity: M. Krotoszyński, *Reflectivity and research on transactional justice*, „Archiwum Filozofii Prawa i Filozofii Społecznej" 2015, no. 2(11), pp. 59–68.

261 D. Linhardt, *Didier Raoult…*

262 See more: J. Pleszczyński, *Evolutionary theory of knowledge and cognitive science*, „Roczniki Filozoficzne" 2006, no. 2, t. LIV, pp. 175–195.

263 D. Linhardt, *Didier Raoult…*

knowledge of the scientist and his teams. Social sciences are unable to resolve this hopeless dilemma. What they can draw attention to is that it is unlikely that D. Raoult could long escape the logic of justification if that is the significance of the challenge he threw to the "methodologists." Social sciences may even add that it would be ill-advised because in diversified societies like ours, tensions between the protocolization of "evidence-based medicine" and the clinical optimization of care provided to each patient individually—what D. Raoult calls the "method of Tom"—can and should be examined and potentially resolved within the medical environment and institutions after the period of threat has passed[264].

Some researchers adhere to the first source of scientific controversies related to the radical, impossible-to-probabilize uncertainty in which we find ourselves regarding future states of nature due to human actions' consequences for ecological balance. There is also uncertainty about the preferences of future generations. Advocates of this approach support legitimizing public intervention to reconcile the economy with the preservation of nature for future generations. Incorporating the precautionary principle into the French constitution was one of the recommendations of this approach[265]. The stakes for actors here involve taking advantage of the situation of scientific controversy to try to impose a "worldview" that better suits their interests[266].

J.J. Ch Hourcade, J. M Salles, D. Théry in their 1992 article titled Ecological economics and scientific controversies. Lessons from some recent policy-making in the EEC[267] conclude that scientific controversies about certain environmental issues (effects, causes, solutions) open the way for some entities to exploit them for their own technical-industrial strategies, entirely unrelated to ecological constraints. In the case of very high uncertainty about the impact, the application of social cost-benefit analysis – SCBA)[268] becomes impossible as an optimizing tool. These authors developed their economic analysis as a way to improve the quality of life in the future[269].

---

264 https://www.ehess.fr/fr/carnet/coronavirus/didier-raoult-ou-controverse-scientifique-dans-temps-lurgence (18.12.2020).

265 G. Destais, *Les théorisations économiques…*, p. 5.

266 O. Godard, *Une approche méta-économique*, Paris 2015, pp. 101.

267 J.Ch. Hourcade, J.M. Salles, D. *Théry, Ecological economics and scientific controversies. Lessons Pom some recent policy making in the EEC*, „Ecological Economics" 1992, vol. 6, no. 3, pp. 211–233.

268 See more: G. Lissowski, *Społeczne aspekty analizy kosztów i korzyści*, „Decyzje" 2015, no 23, pp. 47–69

269 J.Ch. Hourcade, J.M. Salles, D. *Théry, Ecological economics…*

## 2.4. Convention analysis (Economics of convention)

In the early 1990s, a new research trend[270] called the Economics of Convention (EC) emerged, emphasizing the analysis of the role of rules and conventions in economic coordination. In the context of the genesis of this theory[271] one can speak of a significant contribution from French researchers (J. P. Dupuy, F. Eymard

---

270 This trend, however, refers to the thought that emerged in the 1980s under the influence of economists (mainly from the French National Institute of Statistics and Economic Studies - INSEE) and sociologists (questioning the actors' ability to assess what is valuable and what is not). They were contemplating forms of work organization, behaviors in financial markets, and standards regulating relationships between companies.

271 The theory of conventions has its roots, on the one hand, in the foundational works of D. Lewis and, on the other hand, in the research programs initiated by both the French convention school and the American convention school. The so-called standard theory includes the "theory of contracts" and the "American convention," while the "regulation school" and the "French convention" are associated with the so-called non-standard theory. The Extended Standard Theory is based on the criterion of individual rationality in relation to organizational coordination phenomena. The Non-Standard Theory is linked to the work of H. Simon, who analyzes organizations based on a procedural and non-material concept of rationality. The non-standard theory is an alternative to Lewis's convention, departing from the postulate of individual rationality. In this context, the regulatory theory approach has also proven useful, allowing the understanding of conventions as implicit collective agreements. The French convention school emphasizes the possibility of complementing the convention as a means of coordination in the market. The institution for contractors is an exogenous concept; it allows the existence of conventions. For American convention theorists, whose theoretical basis is game theory, the institution is endogenous to the posed problem of the game; the institution corresponds to the convention. While standard theory ignored rules, the extended standard theory reveals them by endogenizing them in the form of an optimal contractual agreement between at least two individuals. The rule emanating from individuals boils down to an externally imposed agreement (comes down to coercion). D. Lewis starts from the idea that agents in relation to each other are typically confronted with coordination problems that can be solved favorably or not. However, according to Lewis, these problems can be rationally resolved through a system of mutual expectations regarding the actions and preferences of the parties. According to D. Lewis, the existence of a convention is based on the concept of regularities in the behavior of entities and a system of preferences and mutual expectations. However, he suggests supplementing this definition with hypotheses related to both the concepts of rationality and arbitrariness. An agent should always be rational. Even in the context of imperfect information, the rationality of agents is not threatened if they manage to agree on "common knowledge": they can ignore things, but they know what they know, and they know that everyone is aware of it.

Duvernay, O. Favereau, A. Orléan, R. Salais, L. Thévenot), who led to the emergence of the innovative concept of conventions[272]. The authors' project, (mainly led by O. Favereau)[273] aimed "not so much to offer a better theory but to reopen the language of economic theory," which gives too much weight to rationality and too little to institutions[274].

The term "convention" refers to a tool that constitutes an agreement of will, as well as its product, endowed with normative binding power. Agreement is understood as the result of individual actions and as binding frameworks for the entities involved[275]. Researchers in this trend, outlined in the "Revue économique" in March 1989, aimed to develop partially original analytical frameworks without, however, criticizing the market economy. The central hypothesis of the Economics of Convention (EC) asserts that "an agreement between individuals, even limited to a trade exchange, is not possible without common frameworks, i.e., without

---

Coordination, therefore, exists through the convergence of interests of both players. If they agree and accept cooperation, the benefits are for each of them. They are greater than in the case of non-cooperation. Everyone manages coordination with others because there is knowledge that others are interested in coordinating with the rest. This unlimited mirroring, i.e., putting oneself in another's place, is synonymous with order and stability because it tends to strengthen the belief in and respect for the convention rather than doubting it. According to D. Lewis, the convention solves the coordination problem and is by definition a norm based on the assumption of the obligation to comply with it. These are regularities to which we must adapt, a set of common opinions, etc. In his opinion, most conventions can be called rules (unwritten rules, known rules), but not all rules are conventions. In turn, the extended convention approach integrates contract theories and the American approach to conventions. According to A. Schotter, a convention is "a regularity of behaviour to which all members of the community adhere and which determines the behaviour to be followed in certain recurring situations. In this approach, the existence of pressure favours conformist behaviours, and the benefits of conformity outweigh individual preferences a priori". See more: L.M. Miller, *Two notions of conventions: an experimental analysis*, „Journal of Institutional Economics" 2008, vol. 4, no. 3, pp. 327–349.

272 N. Postel, *L'économie des conventions. Une approche instrumentale de la rationalité individuelle?*, „Revue économique" 1998, vol. 49, no. 6, p. 1473.

273 O. Favereau, *Marchés internes, marchés externes*, „Revue économique" 1989, vol. 40, no. 2, p. 277–282, https://www.persee.fr/doc/reco_00352764_1989_num_40_2_409141 (13.01.2021).

274 https://conventions.hypotheses.org/the-economics-of-convention (13.01.2021).

275 O. Favereau, *Marchés internes...*, p. 143.

a constitutive convention"[276]. Here, a convention can be defined as a "system of mutual expectations regarding competences and behaviours taken for granted"[277].

The starting point of the theory of conventions is to understand how individuals manage to establish rules of cooperation and behaviour in situations of uncertainty, assuming that individuals have limited rationality. Following the precursor of this economic trend, J. P. Dupuy, "without the help of collectively irreducible objects to individual rationality, such as conventions or interactions between rational individual actors, it would not be possible to independently develop a specific social reality"[278]. Conventions are thus a solution to the coordination problem, which tends to repeat itself regularly. It is a principle of behaviour that originates in social interactions but appears to actors in objectivized form. Importantly, conventions systematically compete with other rules of behaviour that could also enable coordination but evoke behaviours and social interactions. Actors always retain the possibility of criticizing and changing rules when they cease to meet coordination needs. Conventions correspond to both individual and collective representations, common references that solve coordination problems in an uncertain environment[279]. These representations are conventional in the sense that they constitute one of several possible solutions and can always be questioned[280].

Unlike a contract where every detail is specified, when there is a convention, expected behaviours do not have to be known in advance, written down, and then mandated for execution (the convention creates spatial frameworks for compromise). Thus, it allows for the temporary removal of "lower forces of suspicion" and mistrust. A convention is an announcement of a solution to the coordination problem of decisions between entities.

The goal of the economics of convention is to "reconcile a certain social autonomy, going as far as recognizing its own rights, with the idea that it is always individuals, and not supraindividual entities, that act and bear collective intentions (individual and/or collective)"[281]. The rule or convention discussed in the

---

276 *Ibidem.*

277 *Ibidem.*

278 J.P. Dupuy, *Convention et common knowledge*, „Revue économique" 1989, vol. 40, no. 2 p. 361.

279 There are many fields where we deal with uncertainty and the need for conventions to cope with it, such as production activities (quality conventions for goods and business models), the healthcare system, etc.

280 https://conventions.hypotheses.org/the-economics-of-convention (13.01.2021).

281 Ch. Bessy, O. Favereau, *Institutions et économie des conventions*, „Cahiers d'économie politique" 2003/1, no. 44, p. 121.

economics of convention supports a "worldview" understood in ethical terms. This is an important element of the theory. Alongside the necessity to expand hypotheses about instrumental rationality, this theory integrates ideas of rationality or ethical reasons, relying on the choice of actions independent of their effectiveness[282].

Other authors emphasize the second source of controversy, the pluralism of moral views regarding the principle of a higher common good that would allow people to coordinate their relationships with nature. They address the issue within the framework of the economics of convention, according to which rationality is not a reference point but is created for each individual in relation to others, and thus in solving the coordination problem that needs to be found. Such an approach, taking into account the diversity of environmental conventions, i.e., ways of representing relationships with the environment, profoundly renews politics, namely democratic debate. Here, nothing specific is defined to establish new norms to achieve SD, but these controversies concern the sense[283]. According to O. Godard[284] in the context of SD, "we are dealing with a compromise in which participants give up the idea of explaining the principle of their agreement but try In contemporary terms, this "common good" is the realization of the principles of *sustainable development*.

## 2.5. Humanistic issues

In this approach, SD is the result of normative conditions determined at the intersection of three spheres (economy, environment, society), necessitating not only institutional changes. The foundation of this issue lies in the prior consideration of the ecological question. This perspective draws inspiration from the field of development economics (especially from F. Perroux and A. Sen). Development, which is not limited to the economic dimension, is defined as a normative concept. It refers to a change that can be considered a good or progress, qualified as social or human, in relation to various criteria that cannot be summed up in economic terms alone. While development implies economic growth, economic growth does not necessarily lead to development. With the introduction of ecological issues, the environmental (or ecological) dimension has been added to the social and economic dimensions, forming the three pillars of SD. This concept refers

282 Ibidem.

283 G. Destais, *Les théorisations économiques…*, p. 5.

284 O. Godard, *Sustainable development and the process of justifying choices in a controversial universe* [in:] *Sustainable Development: Concepts*, Rationalities and Strategies, ed. S. Faucheux, M. O'Connor, J. der Straaten, „Environment Series" 1998, p. 316.

to the diagram of three dimensions proposed in 1979 by the French economist R. Passeta[285] (see fig. 3).

*Figure 3: Diagram of three dimensions of R. Passeta.*[286]

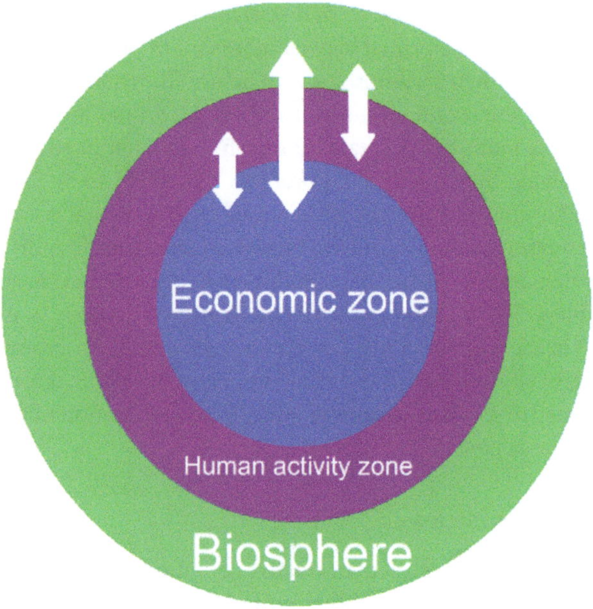


Source: own study based on: https://www.alternatives-economiques.fr/schema-trois-sphe-res-de-rene-passet-0103201366859.html (17.12.2020).

Sustainability means that development must be both fair (economically viable and socially acceptable), sustaining (economically viable while preserving nature, species, and natural and energy resources), and survivable (its impact on the environment must not threaten humanity). This requires a different kind of development than what we have experienced so far because the current development

285 A. Lalucq, *Comment l'économie est venue à l'écologie*, „Alternatives Economiques" 2013, no. 061, https://www.alternatives-economiques.fr/leconomie-venue-a-lecologie/00066861 (13.01.2021).

286 R. Passet is recognized in the scientific community as a specialist in new interdisciplinary approaches. He created a schematic system consisting of three dimensions, where the biosphere (ecological system) encompasses the social system, and the social system, in turn, encompasses the economic system.

is not sustainable. It is neither fair (deepening inequalities within each country and between the North and the South), nor sustaining (depletion of non-renewable natural resources), nor survivable (climate changes related to greenhouse gas emissions emissions, pollution, etc.). Therefore, SD remains a challenge as it must be fair, as advocated by proponents of so-called just economics[287] (J. M. Harribey, L. Sachs, E. Laurent), primarily guided by the protection of the natural environment (known as ecological development) or socio-ecological issues, emphasizing the role of social inequalities in ecological crises. Establishing SD requires many institutional changes, but the nature of the changes that need to be implemented varies depending on the author.

J. Sachs emphasizes the importance of supporting the implementation of SD based on values that give humans a central role in this process and do not reduce them to a means to achieve economic growth or environmental respect. This observation aligns with the ideas of M. Weber[288]. According to Weber, ideas and beliefs can form the basis for the economy (which in many theoretical approaches to SD is considered a superstructure for the functioning of human societies), hence the need to emphasize values based on human rights. J. Rockström[289] explains that humanity has entered the Anthropocene era[290], where there is an evolution from perceiving SD as a concept based on three pillars towards a more

---

287 M. Décaillot, Favoriser *l'émergence de l'économie equitable*, „Variations. Revue internationale de théorie critique" 2007, no. 9/10.

288 V. Munongo, *Un nouveau courant de pensées pour le développement durable*, 21 avril 2020, https://isnad-africa.org/2020/04/21/un-nouveau-courant-depensees-pour-le-developpement-durable/ (9.02.2021).

289 J. Rockström is a globally recognized scientist who focuses on global sustainability issues. He played a key role in leading a team of scientists that presented the concept of planetary boundaries, first published in 2009 with an update in 2015. Following these studies, it was acknowledged that nine planetary boundaries are crucial for maintaining a "safe operating space for humanity." These frameworks have been adopted as an approach to sustainability and used as guidelines for governments, international organizations, NGOs, and businesses considering SD.

290 Anthropocene is a new geological epoch characterized by the emergence of humans as the primary force of change on Earth, surpassing geophysical forces. It is the age of humans! This unprecedented planetary disturbance. The concept of the Anthropocene can also be seen as an attempt to depoliticize the entities it reveals and the phenomena it triggers. Here, all people united in a common endeavor of destruction are equally responsible for the transformations taking place on the planet. Quoted from: F. Gemenne, M. Denis, *Qu'est-ce que l'Anthropocène?*, https:// www.vie-publique.fr/parole-dexpert/271086-terre-climat-quest-ce-que-lanthropocene-ere-geo-logique (9.02.2021).

integrated and inclusive approach that treats economic growth through development within the limits set by nature. This allows for ensuring the planet's resilience to climate change[291].

Similarly, L.J. Kotzé notes that the Anthropocene requires a new vision of sustainable development, which is essential for reforming current visions of human rights in an environmental context, while also radically departing from existing orthodox concepts of SD through which people justify and rationalize their environmental claims"[292]. He points out that the biggest mistake among various SD paradigms is the recognition of "weak sustainability," emphasizing its insincerity and the satisfying promise of sufficient resources during global ecological shocks[293]. There may be an opportunity for greater "humanization" (a human rights lens)[294] of SD challenges, such as climate change[295]. This means that "human rights" can play a "humanizing" role in the Anthropocene, as they have the ability to go beyond purely scientific fields. In this way, human rights could bring the ecological crises of the Anthropocene closer to human understanding by presenting a human perspective on anthropogenic changes and their ecological consequences. This can also be done at the level of science (systemic and social) and at the level of policy and governance by developing laws, including human rights, that take into account and are sensitive to evidence and Earth system forecasts, aiming to set boundaries for human behaviour based on scientifically determined ecosystem limits[296].

According to M. Limon, "human rights can be used to create ethical imperatives that can later be translated into legal obligations, creating specific duties

291 V. Munongo, *Un nouveau courant…*

292 L.J. Kotzé, *Human rights and the environment in the Anthropocene*, „The Anthropocene Review" 2014, vol. 1(3), p. 265.

293 *Ibidem*, p. 266.

294 This perspective allows for shifting the focus of the international climate change debate directly onto individuals, resulting in the impact of climate change on their lives. This, in turn, has significant potential consequences for how they perceive it.

295 The humanistic perspective (through the lens of human rights) on climate change creates an ethical imperative for action, which over time may translate into legal commitments. Emphasizing human rights puts pressure on decision-makers to look beyond their own circles and recognize the human and global consequences of their actions.

296 L.J. Kotzé, *Human rights…*, p. 262.

and corresponding rights to address the ecological and socio-economic whims of the Anthropocene"[297].

One function of rights in the environmental context is that they should provide people with the rights and moral authority to seek specific benefits that mainly arise from human interaction with the ecosystem, goods, and services. However, in the Anthropocene, the possibilities for unrestricted exploitation of the Earth by humans are limited. Similarly, these limitations will have to be imposed on the rights to ecological goods and services, which may mean that traditional rights to environmental resources may need to be transformed towards limited anthropocentrism and an increased emphasis on the natural environment. Transforming human rights in this way will have to occur through the paradigm of "strong sustainable development," which aims to reconnect people with the environment[298].

SD also touches upon the ontological and axiological spheres, as evidenced by the engagement of philosophers, especially ecological philosophers, in the debate over the concept. SD can be seen as a new global philosophy of development that defines a new way of thinking, taking into account changing contextst[299]. This new way of thinking is transposed onto the levels of scientific disciplines. The philosophy of development thus denotes a change in the model of human activity in nature by seeking alternative rules of governance and functioning in the future that are more acceptable to humanity as a whole. The integration of the three areas of human activity (economic, social, and ecological) in the concept of SD requires, firstly, a reconsideration of the relationships that should occur between these areas. Secondly, it involves changing the value system to one that promotes the formation of preferred social attitudes and behaviours (between humans and species). The main subject of these objective and subjective actions is human beings, who are part of the biosphere and should take care of it "here and now," as well as in the future. Thus, the era of the Anthropocene marks the beginning of the ecological era, in which humans become agents of action but also, perhaps primarily, express a willingness to harmoniously coexist with nature.

297 M. Limon, *Human rights and climate change: Constructing a case for political action*, „Harvard Environmental Law Review" 2009, no. 33, pp. 450–451, quoted in: L.J. Kotzé, *Human rights...*, p. 262.

298 L.J. Kotzé, *Human rights...*, p. 267.

299 W. Tyburski, *Introduction* [in:] *Principles of shaping attitudes conducive to the implementation of sustainable development*, ed. W. Tyburski, Toruń 2011, p. 7.

This involves accepting principles such as justice (within and between generations), responsibility (mainly linked to realizing values and making choices), the common good (understood as the totality of material and spiritual factors conditioning the achievement of prosperity and harmonious development), and a catalogue of values that define a new order. Respecting these values will create possibilities for realizing the assumptions of the SD concept[300].

## 2.6. Historical and institutional analyses

In economics, there are two research approaches[301], that currently influence the emergence and evolution of understanding the concept of Sustainable Development (SD). The first approach is the traditional (classical) approach, where the analysis of economic phenomena is conducted as if they were not part of a broader societal life shaping over generations (ahistorical)[302]. The second approach, institutional, involves a multi-aspect view of life, considering both individual human and societal perspectives (historical). In this latter approach, it is recognized that economic decision-making involves both economic and non-economic factors[303].

Furthermore, among economists who separate *development* from economic *growth*, some refrain from expressing opinions on how development should be perceived: whether as a good or progress. Instead of normalizing different concepts, they seek to understand their emergence. SD is thus seen as a compromise between centers of economic power and forces—collective actors or social movements—that bring with them requirements for nature protection while adhering to the principle of justice. However, such a compromise only emerges, as emphasized by G. Destais[304]. This approach cannot lead to precise normative recommendations, except that businesses themselves can contribute to embarking on the path of SD. This position aligns with institutional environmental economics[305], which

300 A. Podsiad, *Dictionary of philosophical terms and concepts*, Warsaw 2000, p. 183.
301 R. Bartkowiak, *Ekonomia rozwoju*, Warszawa 2013, p. 21.
302 *Ibidem*.
303 *Ibidem*, p. 22.
304 G. Destais, *Les théorisations économiques…*, p. 6.
305 C.L. Spash, H.G. Villena, *Exploring the Approach of Institutional Economics to the Environment*, Cambridge 1999, pp. 6–37.

is based on the open nature of the economic system. This means that economic activities are in constant relation to the social system and the natural environment. According to this perspective, the principles of interaction between the economic system and its eco-social context are determined by a set of social parameters, which institutional economics combines under the term "institutions"[306].

P. Söderbaum, in several publications from the early 1990s, argued that adopting theoretical frameworks based on institutional economics[307] is a better approach than the neoclassical approach because it can take into account the complex nature of current environmental problems (multidimensional, interdisciplinary, financial, and non-financial in character). Inspired by the works of G. Myrdal from the 1970s, he addresses the concern for the role of values and ideology in economic analyses and the impossibility of conducting economic sciences without them[308]. In the "Real-World Economics Review" in 2019, he explicitly emphasized being "skeptical about formulations of the sufficiency of neoclassical theory and methods. Something more is needed"[309]. He strongly states that the time has come to open university economics departments to alternative schools of thought, such as institutional economics and ecological economics[310].

306 This school of thought, by "institutions," understands various social processes that sustain society over time: customs, values, social and legal principles, ways of thinking and acting, etc. The set of institutional arrangements existing in a given society at a particular time creates institutional frameworks. These frameworks, in turn, determine the kind of social relationships that can be achieved through numerous rights and obligations, also associated with access, use, and exploitation of natural resources.

307 Institutional economics is often equated with evolutionary economics. Both emerged as alternatives to neoclassical economics. According to W. Stankiewicz, the term "evolutionary economics" is associated with an attempt to integrate old and new institutionalism and is used to describe many often conflicting approaches to describing economic phenomena. A characteristic of this approach is the treatment of economic phenomena and processes as never reaching a state of equilibrium, only being observed in the process of striving towards that state. Quoted from: T. Zalega, *Evolutionary economics as one of the trends in contemporary economics – outline of the issues*, „Studia i Materiały" 2015/2, no 19, pp. 160–161, 171.

308 P. Söderbaum, *Ecological Economics*, London 2000, pp. 42–44.

309 P. Söderbaum, *Toward sustainable development…*, p. 182.

310 *Ibidem*.

In his opinion, "because the dominant market ideology does not align with SD, the role of economists must be to argue for pluralism and democracy"[311]. Consequently, the evaluation of sustainable investment projects in society will differ from the previous technocratic approach (such as neoclassical cost-benefit analysis[312]) in favour of a democracy-oriented approach (position analysis)[313]. P. Söderbaum redefines economics in a new way. According to him, for economics to constructively contribute to SD, the first step is to eliminate the neoclassical monopoly in education and research in university economics departments and open the doors to competitive schools of thought. In a democratic society, this kind of dialogue between schools of thought based on partially different ideological orientations[314], is highly necessary. Therefore, the role of economists is to articulate alternative visions, narratives, and ideological orientations that appear crucial for policymakers and other actors, discussing their advantages and possible weaknesses. According to the researcher, the above arguments support

---

311 *Ibidem*, p. 186.

312 Cost-Benefit Analysis (CBA) is a method for assessing the efficiency of investments and projects, taking into account the entirety of anticipated costs and benefits (both quantitative and qualitative elements). It allows determining the degree of investment efficiency in a complex environment. The theoretical foundation of CBA lies in welfare economics. In this approach, socio-cultural and environmental aspects are considered in the form of external costs. See more: J. Dyduch, *Using cost-benefit analysis to evaluate investment projects*, „Managerial Economics" 2011, no. 10, pp. 95–108.

313 Positional Analysis (PA) is associated with institutional ecological economics. It is an attempt to avoid "monetary reductionism" in cost-benefit analysis by separating monetary and non-monetary impacts. Particularly on the non-monetary side, issues of inertia and irreversibility of effects are observed. While Cost-Benefit Analysis (CBA) has a specific ideological orientation with an emphasis on markets, PA seeks to identify more than one ideological orientation or narrative as significant among actors involved in a particular issue. It is part of an effort to conduct a multi-aspect analysis. Quoted from: P. Söderbaum, *Positional Analysis: A Multidimensional and Democracy-Oriented Approach to Decision-Making and Sustainability*, „Sustainability" 2020, no.12,https://www.researchgate.net/publication/342859681_Positional_Analysis_A_Multidimensional_and_Democracy-Oriented_Approach_to_Decision-Making_and_Sustainability (23.02.2021).

314 Here „ideological orientation" as a useful and accurate term to describe the differences between thinking and motives among actors.

introducing democracy into the definition of economics: "I suggest that economics should be defined as the multidimensional management of (limited) resources in a democratic society"[315]. P. Söderbaum, as a representative of the institutional approach, points out the possibility of changing or modifying institutions by individual actors or groups of actors (who have their ideological orientation), who can use their position to facilitate or hinder certain types of institutional changes[316]. The researcher emphasizes that institutions can be deliberately changed at the policy level to better support SD.

Supporters of this approach have contributed to the development of the concept of "coevolution[317] of sustainability," exemplified by R.B. Norgaard[318]. Institutional economists, in their evolutionary approach, proposed the principle of

315 P. Söderbaum, *Toward sustainable development…*, p. 187.

316 *Ibidem*, p. 192.

317 The term "coevolution" originates from P. R. Ehrlich and P. H. Raven, who in 1964 described the mutual relationship between plants and butterflies that shapes the evolution of both. Since then, this term has been widely used in ecology. It has also been applied in other disciplines that have developed theories based on generalized forms of Darwinian evolution. Originally used in reference to relationships between species, it has later been applied to complex units or systems that mutually interact. This concept has been employed in computer science, economics, history, anthropology, geography, sociology, and environmental sciences. Quated from: H. Weisz, E. Clark, *Society-Nature Coevolution: Interdisciplinary Concept for Sustainability*, „Geografiska Annaler: Series B, Human Geography" 2011, no. 93(4), p. 281. In economics, this concept was first used by K Polanyi in his 2001 publication entitled *The Great Transformation: The Political and Economic Origins of Our Time*, where the economic system is portrayed as an element of human culture, and, like our culture, it constantly evolves. In essence, our ability to adapt to changing environmental conditions through cultural evolution is what sets us apart from other animals. Economic, social, and political systems, as well as technological progress, are manifestations of cultural adaptations. All these systems have adapted in response to changes in the environment, and these adaptations trigger environmental changes to which we must once again adapt in a coevolutionary process.

318 R.B. Norgaard, *Sustainable development: A co-evolutionary view*, „Futures" 1988, vol. 20, no. 6, pp. 606–620.

"cumulative causation"[319]. The first to introduce this concept was K.W. Kapp, who in 1965 defined it to reveal how social processes involve the interaction of multiple factors, both economic and non-economic. These factors combine (cumulate) to shift the system towards a position of balance rather than automatic self-stabilization[320]. Recognizing the importance of physical factors in causation, K.W. Kapp also emphasized the significance of social factors. He argued that the fundamental issue for environmental economics should be the identification of random processes causing "disturbances" for both the physical and social environment. He places particular emphasis on socio-economic and legal relations in contemporary society, and their analysis is crucial for understanding the processes contributing to disruptions in the natural environment[321]. According to him, natural-physical systems and social systems are interdependent, so human actions impact both systems in an evolutionary process. J.A. Swaney and R.B. Norgaard argue that a comprehensive systemic approach to environmental issues must begin by recognizing that social systems coexist with natural systems.

According to J.A. Swaney, the principle of coevolution of sustainability can be understood as an extension of the principle of institutional adaptation created in 1981 by J.F. Foster[322] and adherence to the environmental compliance criteria recommended by M. Tool[323]. The second representation fitting into the historical-institutional approach is associated with researchers connected to the Regulation

---

319 The "cumulative causation theory" refers to the "principle of circular and cumulative causation." It explains underdevelopment in certain areas through the hypothesis of the circular accumulation of growth stimuli (demand, income, investment, production). In a system based on circular causation, a change in one variable triggers a change in another variable, transforming in the same direction. Feedback mechanisms intensify mutual influences, initiating a cumulative process of transformations and the emergence of spread effects. Positive changes lead to a cumulative growth process, while negative changes result in a cumulative contraction (decrease) process. Simultaneously presenting backwash effects and spreading effects, it emphasizes non-economic factors that determine development (technical infrastructure: road system, electrical network, information technology network; social infrastructure: education, healthcare), as well as sociocultural factors (especially religions). Quoted from: M. Zajdel, *Wybrane teorie rozwoju regionalnego oraz lokalnego a rynek pracy*, „Studia Prawno-Ekonomiczne" 2011, t. LXXXIII, p. 405.

320 C.L. Spash, H.G. Villena, *Exploring the Approach…*, p. 19.

321 *Ibidem.*

322 See more: J.F. Foster, *The Theory of Institutional Adjustment*, „Journal of Economic Issues" 1981, vol. 15, no. 4, pp. 923–928.

323 C.L. Spash, H.G. Villena, *Exploring the Approach…*, p. 20.

School. The beginning of the regulatory approach is marked by the publication of M. Aglietta's *Régulation et crises du capitalisme* from 1976, considered a cornerstone of regulatory theory. However, key figures in this line of thinking also include B. Billaudot, R. Boyer, and A. Lipietz. Regulators are interested in the destabilizing factors during crises. They start their analysis with the examination of the concept of accumulation regime and modes of regulation. Representatives of this school point to phenomena that explain the problems of capitalism, manifested in crises[324]. The starting point for the Regulation Theory (RT) analysis is Fordism[325] which represents another stage in the development of economies. Regulators posit that severe crises cause disturbances and imbalances between key macroeconomic variables (consumption, investment, production). The market cannot spontaneously restore equilibrium, so society must introduce appropriate regulations. Similar to institutionalists, regulationists propose an economic analysis that starts with institutions understood as social rules referring to customs, beliefs, convictions, rights, and state regulations. These institutions shape the behaviours of economic entities, thus ensuring the regulation of conflicts[326].

The regulation school is a theory that seeks to explain the dynamics of accumulation, its characteristics, entry into crisis, individual stages, and their sequence. For this school, SD is not a theory but an analytical reference system focusing on the triple register of interdependence: domains (economic, social, ecological, institutional), time, and space. On the other hand, regulationists consider SD as

---

324 R. Pęciak, *Geneza podejścia regulacyjnego we Pancuskiej teorii ekonomicznej*, „Prace Naukowe Uniwersytetu Ekonomicznego we Wrocławiu - Ekonomia" 2015, no 401, pp. 373–382.

325 Fordism derives its name from Henry Ford, the creator of the model of organization and development for enterprises, established and implemented in 1908 in the United States. Along with its principles for organizing the production process, it is based on intensive accumulation resulting from mass production. Simultaneously, structural forms appear that guarantee mass consumption. It also signifies a compromise between the management and wage laborers. This compromise, resulting from intensive accumulation, mass production, and consumption, allowed for the generation of economies of scale, thereby increasing production profits and leading to the growing role of the state. Numerous regulations were proposed in the areas of social, cyclical, and industrial policies. The new regulations favoured increased demand and the institutionalization of the Fordist growth system.

326 R. Boyer, *Les institutions dans la théorie de la regulation*, „CEPREMAP" 2003, no. 8, p. 5, quoted from: R. Pęciak, *Problemy kapitalizmu we Pancuskiej teorii regulacji*, „Studia Ekonomiczne. Zeszyty Naukowe Uniwersytetu Ekonomicznego w Katowicach" 2014, no. 176, p. 31.

a normative repository of public and private actions with the most fundamental purpose of connecting intergenerational capital with intragenerational capital. So, what are the connections between the regulation theory and self-sustaining development? In 2007, S. Rousseau and B. Zuindeau conducted a comparative analysis of RT and SD, identifying mutual common elements (see table 5).

*Table 5: SD and RT: common features and differences*

| Criteria | SD | RT |
|---|---|---|
| Conceptualization of the economic system | Global: emphasizing the productive dimension | Detailed: accumulation regimes and variable regulation modes |
| Attitude towards institutions | Vague or *ad hoc* | Precise: five institutional forms |
| Environmental awareness | Fundamental to this approach | Unclear[327] |
| Attitude to time | Long term | The historical dimension of time |
| Crack analysis | Irreversibility, uncertainty, etc | Big and small crises |
| Privileging spatial frames | Global level | (Mostly) national level |

Source: S Rousseau, B Zuindeau, *Théorie de la régulation et développement durable*, „Revue de la regulation" 2007, http://journals openedition org/regulation/1298 (25.07.2018).

327 RT should focus more on the role of the natural environment in economic dynamics. In the mid-1990s, A. Lipietz observed that RT had long ignored the ecological issue. According to this author, this apparent indifference was all the more surprising since other regulationists were often involved as activists in environmental protection. To explain this paradox, A. Lipietz presented two reasons for this situation. On the one hand, these actors are specifically "political ecologists," not ecologists. For them, the environment is merely an artificial production in which social relations materialize. Therefore, there is a greater interest in the urban and built environment than in the natural environment in the strict sense. On the other hand, the regulationist approach traditionally focuses on Fordism and its questioning. Until this point, "it is difficult to argue that Fordism has undergone a crisis in terms of the relationship between society and the environment.". See mroe: A. Lipietz, *Écologie politique régulationniste ou économie de l'environnement?* [in:] *Théorie de la régulation:* l'état des savoirs, ed. R. Boyer, Y. Saillard, Paris 1995, p. 351.

These authors conducted an analysis of capitalism (Fordism, Post-Fordism), considering how this particular economic and social system can be consistent with the logic of sustainable development. According to their research, certain forms of capitalism, especially those classified as Post-Fordism, appear to be part of the logic, even if they are not entirely consistent, they are not antagonistic to SD. The role of public authorities, and more broadly, all entities, would be to support this kind of continuous evolution. According to these authors, Fordism, which led to an increase in income levels and a reduction in economic inequalities in society, to some extent realized one of the goals of SD: intragenerational justice. However, only to some extent, as inequalities persist and even deepen, (especially in the context of North-South relations)[328].

While points of reference to the social dimension of SD can be found in the Fordist version of capitalism, it is challenging to identify manifestations of environmental protection, which is one of the goals of SD, in the functioning of this system. The accumulation system of Fordists, and thus economic growth in the post-war years, largely relied on easy and relatively low-cost access to natural resources, essentially involving a certain tolerance for the exploitation and degradation of the natural environment, such as the discharge of industrial wastewater into the environment. The authors explain this negative impact of production on the natural environment through the existence of a real "productivity compromise" involving major actors (companies, labor unions, the state) "playing" against the environment.

The concept of progress in the Fordist regime, therefore, has a material and technical character, where environmental degradation is ignored, and at best, one could argue that a "weak sustainability" approach is applied to the natural environment. Fordism tends to assign a particular role to the state in the area of this production compromise concerning the natural environment. Consequently, public authorities gradually participate in the management of the natural environment, including the mentioned industrial wastewater or household waste. However, state actions remained limited in this regard until the 1970s when the Environmental Protection Agency (EPA)[329] was established in the United States.

Nevertheless, proponents of the RT are increasingly acknowledging its alignment with the goals of SD, evident in the focus on so-called immaterial

328 S. Rousseau, B. Zuindeau, *Théorie de la regulation…*

329 *Ibidem.*

accumulation, contributed to by factors such as the servicization of economies[330]. In a sense, post-Fordism allows more room for non-material elements in competitive forms. This facilitates the growth of knowledge and new technologies that are less labor-intensive and generate fewer pollutants. One consequence is the emergence and strengthening, in the 1990s, of new environmental regulation tools: environmental management, assessment tools (environmental auditing, life cycle analysis), environmental labeling, and standardization (especially ISO 14000). These new elements and others, such as reporting, were articulated within the framework of Corporate Social Responsibility (CSR) – a movement that significantly influenced large companies.

However, increasing costs of environmental protection regulations, insurance premiums, and heightened costs of access to natural resources highlight what J. O'Connor refers to as the "second contradiction of capitalism"[331]. Companies may seek to limit environmental regulations, viewing them as a factor contributing to cost increases[332]. Therefore, decisions regarding environmental protection depend on estimates of economic burden. Over the past 30 years, economists have developed and applied various tools to measure this burden. Hence, many economists conduct research to better understand cost measurements for improved application of existing methods[333].

In conclusion, two forms of capitalism (Fordism and Post-Fordism) are not entirely aligned with the logic inherent in SD. Nonetheless, RT conducts research in the field of SD, pondering whether it represents a new form of capitalism or challenges it. Ultimately, these researchers focus on identifying characteristics of capitalism to find clues about its compatibility with the concept of SD.

330 The process of servitization - the flourishing of the service civilization. Quoted in: E. Szymańska, *Serwicyzacja gospodarki jako źródło jej transformacji*, „Optimum. Studia Ekonomiczne" 2015, no. 1(73), p. 98.

331 See more: *James O'Connor secondo contradiction of capitalism*, https://libcom.org/blog/james-oconnors-second-contradiction-capitalism-25042014 (15.08.2018).

332 See more: J. Kulawik, Regulacje środowiskowe i innowacje a konkurencyjnośi, „Zagadnienia Ekonomiki Rolnej" 2016, no. 1(346), pp. 3–21.

333 See more: W.A. Pizer, R. Kopp, *Calculating the Cost of Environmental Regulation*, Resources for the Future: Discussion Paper: 03–06, https://media.rff.org/documents/RFF-DP-03-06.pdf (2.02.2021).

One fundamental characteristic of capitalism is that it is a mode of production aimed at capital accumulation. While SD is undoubtedly related to human needs, including those treated in material and quantitative terms, the pursuit of capital growth does not necessarily align with meeting human needs. In Southern countries, the pursuit of capital growth, including economic profit, does not ensure the satisfaction of needs and perpetuates income inequalities. Similarly, the second characteristic of capitalism emphasizes a potential contradiction with SD. According to the theory of "fictitious commodities" by K. Polanyi, the author of *The Great Transformation* published in 1944[334] (see more in the *Sociological Perspective section*), alongside currency and labor, nature constitutes a fictitious commodity. This is because the market system is unable to ensure the sustainability of natural resources, and the process of value accumulation may go hand in hand with the process of depleting natural capital[335]. K. Polanyi, in his examination of the causes of the capitalist crisis, particularly in the context of efforts to establish "self-regulating markets" for land, labor, and money, argued that the transformation of these three fundamental bases of social life into "fictitious commodities" led to the plundering of nature and the breakdown of communities[336]. According to

334 *The Great Transformation* is also an extremely accurate analysis of the situation that occurred during the 1920s to 1940s (starting from market fundamentalism after World War I, the Great Depression, fascist and socialist attempts to create an economic-social order after World War II), exploring what happened and could happen in the history of capitalism if the economy and society are organized according to the liberal vision of a self-regulating market, and if society becomes a "market society" driven by the mechanisms of demand, supply, prices, and profit-oriented market dynamics. In such a system, where "human society has become an accessory to the economic system," even elements that were never produced or supplied for sale—land (nature), labor, and money—have become "fictional commodities." However, labor and land are not different from human beings, who constitute every society and the natural environment in which it exists. Including them in the market mechanism means subjecting the essence of society itself to the laws of the market and leads to its disruption. Quoted in : B. Aulenbacher, *75 lat Wielkiej transformacji*, „Globalny Dialog" 2019, v. IX, p. 10.

335 S. Rousseau, B. Zuindeau, *Théorie de la régulation…*

336 N. Fraser, *Can society be commodities all the way down? Polanyian reflections on capitalist crisis*, „FMSH-WP" 2012, no. 18, pp. 4–5.

the researcher, the development of capitalist societies should be accompanied by improvements, economic progress, and socio-cultural security. Civilizations that focus solely on improving their economic situation in the long term may collapse, as was the case with liberal civilizations in the 1930s.[337]

In the face of these contradictory features of capitalism with regard to SD, authors pose the question of whether specific characteristics of regulatory approaches or accumulation regimes can reduce the strength of these contradictions. The fundamental question for regulationists in the context of SD is: in which direction is capitalism evolving? Capitalism is variable over time and space, and SD currently contributes to thinking about the future. Regulationists may seek factors that limit environmental problems indicating that the natural environment is gaining increasing importance in their agenda. It might even be recognized as one of the foundations of accumulation. In this context, one can speculate that there are currently searches for new social compromises conducive to SD[338].

The regulation school also points to the need to build new alliances and new power relations, evolving from the national level to the international level, to achieve sufficient effectiveness. This would ultimately lead to the creation of "new global regulations," which, indeed, was the main "dream" of regulationists. Therefore, the implementation of SD forces not only profound changes in capitalism to keep it "alive" but also until the system in place is no longer capitalism[339].

## 2.7. Entropic analysis encourages reduced growth (degrowth[340])

Another type of analysis developed by economists in the context of SD relates to the pioneering work of the American researcher of Romanian origin, N. Georgescu-Roegen, who applied the second law of thermodynamics[341], to the

337 A. Novy, Trwale dziedzictwo Karla Polanyiego, „Globalny Dialog" 2019, vol. IX, p. 24.

338 S. Rousseau, B. Zuindeau, *Théorie de la regulation…*

339 *Ibidem.*

340 *Décroissance*(fr.) and *degrowth* (eng.).

341 The first law of thermodynamics states that the amount of mass-energy in the universe is constant, and it cannot be created or destroyed. It can only change its form, but its essence remains unchanged.

economy, known as the law of entropy[342]. Maintaining that the Earth resources, he concludes that there cannot be infinite economic growth. This is a law of nature, and humans are part of that nature and cannot escape this law. Since existing development cannot be separated from economic growth, development cannot be sustainable (sustainable indefinitely). This type of analysis leads to the conclusion that the sustainability of development or growth is an illusion.

N. Georgescu-Roegen, in his epistemological reconstruction of economic sciences, observes that modern economic thought is modelled by a mechanistic epistemology. He compares the economic process to a mechanical model governed by the principles of conservation and maximization. Motion and transformations are understood in a linear and reversible way. However, the system is not closed, and it does not behave reversibly[343]. To support his understanding, he invokes the law of entropy, which states that a closed system (any system) evolves qualitatively in an irreversible manner. More precisely, the degree of chaos, disorder, or the quantity of matter-energy useless to humans constantly and irreversibly increases. The measure of this chaos, disorder, or matter-energy useless to humans is entropy. Energy with low entropy is useful or free, while energy with high entropy is useless[344].

On the basis of the theory of entropy, the concept of *degrowth* (fr. *Décroissance*) emerged, suggesting that every human or organism action, and even all natural

342 The second law of thermodynamics, known as the law of entropy, states that mass-energy can only be transformed in one direction, meaning only from a useful state to a useless one. In general terms, this law asserts that everything tends towards chaos and decay. Entropy is a measure of the extent to which useful energy in any subsystem of the universe changes into a useless form. If order is restored in one subsystem, it is at the expense of disorder in the surrounding natural environment. Entropy refutes the theory that science and technology create a more orderly world. When energy becomes useless, the term "heat death" is used. When matter becomes useless, the term "chaos of matter" is used. The result in both cases is entropy. Energy always flows from a more concentrated state to a less concentrated one. Bertrand Russell explains this phenomenon as follows: "Whenever there is a concentration of energy in one region and very little in a neighboring one, energy tends to move from one region to the other until the amount of energy in both regions is equalized. This process can be described as a tendency toward democracy." Quated in: J. Rifkin, T. Howard, *Entropia. Nowy światopogląd*, Katowice 2008, p. 18, 55.

343 S. Leyens, *Du développement durable à la décroissance, aller et retour*, „Les Carnets du développement durable" 2010, no. 1, p. 17.

344 *Ibidem.*

processes, can only lead to a deficit for the entire system[345]. S. Leyens clearly points out that the concept of degrowth "is more of an awakening of conscience and cannot rationally replace SD"[346]. This researcher makes a comparison of the main assumptions, concluding ultimately that despite similarities, the use of these concepts is different[347]. Degrowth does not mean stopping growth (some call it the anti-growth concept), but rather reducing the production of current types of goods *per capita*. Following the creator of entropy, N. Georgescu-Roegen, degrowth aims to reduce the production of current goods per capita, but not necessarily to reduce or stop development[348]. On the other hand, S. Latouche indicates that the idea of degrowth has a dual origin. Degrowth emerged on one hand as an expression of growing ecological awareness and, on the other hand, from the criticism of technology and development. The reasons for developing an alternative vision of development in the form of degrowth are twofold. The first is the failure of development policy in Third World countries at the end of World War II. The second is the harmful impact of human activity in Western societies on the natural environment (the Western model of unlimited growth).

Degrowth is presented as a radical change capable of providing answers to the problems caused by the system of unlimited growth[349]. However, some authors, such as F.-D. Vivien, place the degrowth movement in the category of "all economic activities [emphasizing] social issues arising from the problem of sustainable development"[350]. On the other hand, S. Leyens disagrees, stating that degrowth should not be reduced merely to a program of actions, specifically proposals for rebuilding a society that escapes the obsession with possession and production. According to him, this characteristic (social issues) is less significant in the degrowth concept and arises more from concerns, providing a response rather than focusing on it[351]. In his view, degrowth is not primarily about successful and just development (or, as in the concept of SD, about its sustainability), but primarily about care (not about development or technological criticism) and awareness of the ecological crisis. The social program infused with ecological awareness is secondary; it is a way and a response to the ecological problem, not an end in itself. Both social issues and the growth of inequalities within and between

345 *Ibidem*, p. 19.
346 *Ibidem*, p. 7.
347 *Ibidem*.
348 *Ibidem*, p. 10.
349 *Ibidem*, p. 12.
350 F.-D. Vivien, *Le développement soutenable*, Paris 2005, p. 83.
351 S. Leyens, *Du développement durable…*, p. 13.

states, especially on the North-South axis, take a back seat in the degrowth concept compared to ecological issues. The criticism of the Western economic model is invoked in its context as the main culprit for the ecological crisis.

Supporters of entropy emphasize that both rich and poor countries are currently grappling with analogous problems. The same inexorable force of decay and chaos operates everywhere on our planet. This happens because everything functions within the framework of an existing "worldview that is collapsing and dying before our eyes, contaminating everything it brought to life"[352]. Therefore, degrowth is not just about reducing growth but, above all, about changing the worldview.

Degrowth, more than any other concept, imposes the necessity of limitations, also taking into account the element of time. There is no other way to change the course of physical reality, but we have an impact on the rate at which the entropy process will progress. And here, it seems that the concept of SD is one of the main ones that can reduce or limit this entropy speed. The starting point is the transition from a colonial to a climatic existence, which means the most significant change our species will have to undergo. The world is currently at a crossroads[353].

S. Leyens compared the content of the SD concept with degrowth, emphasizing that the latter movement "is not a change in the direction of development but a reflection on the responsibility for the degradation of free energy resources and robbing future generations, in which reducing growth and limiting the exploitation of natural resources will disappear, even if done"[354]. However, this disappearance can be extended over time. In this context, the researcher raises the question of the extent to which we should limit or curb the depletion of accumulated energy, which would disappear anyway, no matter what we do. This question seems to be aligned with the SD concept.

Currently, for most entropists, it is important to choose the concept of "sustainable degrowth," which means directly referring to the SD concept but going further by indicating the need for changes at various levels. In the preface to the book *Entropy: A New World View* by J. Rifkin and T. Howard, translated into Polish in 2008 by J. Bożek, a clear guideline is given on how humanity should think and act in the context of the law of entropy: "We must, I repeat, we must start living and thinking globally. Empathize and co-create the world with the poor people of the South and protect tropical forests. Choose wise politicians and not agree to «development» at any cost that brings profits to the few. We must become civic,

352 *Ibidem*, p. 16.
353 F.-D. Vivien, *Le développement soutenable*, p. 88.
354 S. Leyens, *Du développement durable…*, p. 27.

social, entrepreneurial… for a good change that preserves resources for future generations, in the spirit of intergenerational justice, and stops the degradation of both people and Earth"[355]. J. Rifkin emphasizes the growing role of institutions that expand because they are forced to mitigate crises and control the increasing socio-economic disorder, trying to maintain the maximum flow of energy. However, he points out that only in a climatic structure can we slow down the process of complexity and centralization. By minimizing the flow of energy, we slow down the entropy process (although it cannot be completely stopped), thus slowing down disorder"[356]. The smaller the entropy process, the more institutions responsible for the transformation of energy by the social organism can also be maintained in a state of slowed growth (post-growth). Climatic existence favors small, decentralized institutions, while colonizing existence favors large and centralized institutions[357]. By minimizing the consumption of non-renewable resources and utilizing natural resources only at a rate at which they can replenish, it is possible to minimize the deficit between consumption in society and "production" in nature[358]. The faster processing of natural resources by developed countries results in less remaining in the "nature warehouse" for other countries and future generations. The consequence is that natural resources are depleted more quickly, creating increasing amounts of waste and greater disorder. However, it must be realized that the reserves of untapped non-renewable resources are primarily located in Southern countries. These resources are their last "bargaining chip" in the competition for a more equitable distribution of wealth between industrialized and developing countries. Maghreb or Mashreq countries are already playing this game to their advantage. Cartel agreements control the conditions and flow of oil exports. For many people in the South, slogans about the era of limits, slowing development, or establishing a degrowth economic policy are seen as another attempt by Western countries to maintain poorer nations in a servile international position. In this context, T.C. Kurien, who spoke on behalf of the poor at the World Council of Churches in 1979, pointed out that "we have no right to impose on poorer countries how they should conduct their economic development if we ourselves do not show not so much the will as the readiness for great sacrifices in the name of humanity."[359]. Such sacrifices have been made in Europe and worldwide since the mid-1990s, with the most recent expression being the climate conference signed

355 J. RiLin, T. Howard, *Entropia…*, pp. 8–9.
356 *Ibidem*, p. 114.
357 *Ibidem*, p. 115.
358 *Ibidem*, p. 164.
359 *Ibidem*, p. 236.

in Paris in December 2015[360]. However, nations with high energy consumption must demonstrate not only the will but also concrete actions[361].

The justification for the validity of the entropy theory can be found in reality by invoking the phenomenon of the "Arab revolution," known as the "Arab Spring," which occurred in 2011 in one of the Maghreb countries and then "spilled over" in the form of a domino effect to the other neighbouring countries on the southern flank of the Mediterranean Sea Basin (MSB). J. Rifkin observes that "history shows that whenever the energy of society (material goods) is concentrated in the hands of a few individuals or institutions to such an extent that the rest of society suffers such a great energy deficit that it threatens its survival, the society either disintegrates or resorts to revolution – or both possibilities arise simultaneously"[362]. Without a fundamental redistribution of wealth not only between the North and the South but also at the local, regional, and national levels, any discussions about reducing the energy flow and the need to respect limitations would not yield proper results. In a low-entropy society, "less means more," where society rejects material consumption, and frugal energy management becomes the paramount task. In this context, many points of convergence can be found between the concept of post-growth and degrowth and the SD society. In both, every global citizen ceases to be a passenger on their individual journey titled "the time in which they live" but takes the driver's seat, becoming the driver. If someone dares to become a passenger again at any point in their life, the rest should make them aware of it and help them return to the shared helm toward the survival of life on Earth,

---

360 195 countries adopted the first-ever universal, legally binding global climate agreement in history. The main goal of the agreement was to limit global warming to below 2°C. The European Union (EU) played a crucial role in this context and emphasized during the conference in Paris that it would continue to support climate-protective actions, leading to emission reductions and building resilience to the effects of climate change in developing countries. Developed countries committed to providing $100 billion annually for this purpose by the year 2020.

361 On June 1, 2017, D. Trump withdrew from the Paris Agreement, starting the stage of negotiations that may end with the signing of a new agreement, but "on terms that would be fair for American companies and their workers, their nations, their taxpayers" See more : https://www.forbes.pl/wiadomosci/donald-trump-wypowiada-paryskie-porozu-mienie-klimatyczne/3n5ek53 (30.08.2018). In turn, the first decision of the new president, Joe Biden, was to return to the climate agreement, i.e. reverse Trump's decision. See more details: https://businessinsider.com.pl/wiadomosci/pierwsza-decyzja-bidena-usa-wracaja-do-paryskiego-porozumienia-klimatycznego/bye0sdz (18.12.2020).

362 J. Rifkin, T. Howard, *Entropia*..., p. 242.

following the principle of responsibility. Mahatma Gandhi believed that the essence of civilization does not lie in multiplying desires but in consciously and voluntarily renouncing them[363]. Certainly, this is not a call for extreme asceticism but a moral and spiritual necessity for the sharing of wealth so that everyone, regardless of geographic location, can lead a dignified life. A citizen of a low-entropy culture leads a frugal and simple life, giving up exclusive indulgences for the benefit of others. This can be translated into today's still-consumerist lifestyle of societies that are well aware of the need for change: to, first and foremost, minimize the number of cars in households, ideally having just one; and then, to replace this one low-entropy means of transportation – with a bicycle.

* * *

Based on the comparison of theoretical approaches in the form of a table (see more in table 6), it can be observed at first glance that these schools do not have a uniform approach to Sustainable Development (SD). While all definitions of SD adopted by economic analyses fulfill the general formulations of development outlined in the Brundtland Report, they differ fundamentally in how they satisfy the needs of current generations without compromising the developmental capacities of future generations.

Taking into account Table 6, one can notice many similarities and differences in the interpretation of what SD is and how it should be achieved. However, the criterion of the probability of achieving SD is noteworthy, where four approaches acknowledge the possibility of achieving SD goals without changing the growth mode (it will happen spontaneously or with the intervention of the state or through institutional changes). On the other hand, two other perspectives say something completely different, that development cannot be sustainable without changing the growth mode (the American school and the entropic approach)[364].

Moreover, economists address social issues minimally: four approaches (neoclassical model and three versions of ecological economics) ignore the social dimension of SD, arguing that growth will benefit everyone if competition is not disrupted. In this context, it can be strongly stated that it is not a coincidence that the theory of three pillars (humanistic approach) has become most widely spread in other social science disciplines.

---

363 *Ibidem*, p. 257.

364 G. Destais, *Les theorizations économiques du développement durable. Propositions de décryptage critique, Colloque international Pancophone*, „Le développement durable: débats et controverse" 15–16 décembre 2011, Université Blaise Pascal, Clermont-Ferrand, p. 10.

*Table 6: Sustainability in economic theories*

| Theories | Sustainability, its conditions | Nature | Substitut-ability | SD probability | Society | Normative implications |
|---|---|---|---|---|---|---|
| Neoclassical school | Maintaining total capital to continue growth | Man being outside; eco limitation; appropriation of ownership of natural resources | Strong belief in progress | SD is possible without changing the growth model, Growth is good for the environment | No social component; Growth will benefit everyone if competition is not distorted | SD will be introduced spontaneously if the market is allowed to operate freely |
| London School (ecological economics) | Reconciling nature conservation with economic growth | The economy creates negative external impacts on nature | Weak | SD is possible without changing the growth model Growth is good for the environment | As above | Public intervention is necessary to internalize externalities[365] |
| Industrial ecology (ecological economics) | The evolution of an industrial system that copies nature | The functioning of nature is a model for the economy | Weak | The economy will, as it were, spontaneously function in the same way as nature | As above | SD implies other institutions and the change will be regulated by enterprises themselves |

(*Continued*)

365 Environmental or externalities are not sufficiently integrated into the market system, leading to "market failure" in the sense of inefficient market equilibrium. "Internalization" of externalities aims to restore the efficiency and optimality of equilibrium allocation. Quoted from: H. Wiesmeth, *Environmental Economics. Theory and Policy in Equilibrium*, Berlin–Heidelberg 2012, p. 77.

*Table 6: (Continued)*

| Theories | Sustainability, its conditions | Nature | Substitut-ability | SD probability | Society | Normative implications |
|---|---|---|---|---|---|---|
| American School (ecological economics) | Preserving nature's capital | Natural capital sets constraints on the economy | Towards moderate or even strong | Degrowth requirement | As above | The need for environmental standards |
| Scientific controversies | Just like the London school | Radical uncertainty | Uncertainty | SD is possible without changing the way of growth | Actors' play in the face of uncertainty | Public intervention is needed |
| Convention-alistic moral controversies | The use of rhetorical tools in acting, which creates new compromises that then become the norm | Moral controversies regarding man's relationship to nature | Weak? | Necessary specification of democratic content and debates | Actors play to determine the right ways of relating to nature | The institution-alization of conflict at the heart of the public choice process results in the development of negotiations |
| Humanistic approach (three-dimensional) | Profitable, equitable and livable development, normative conditions defined at the intersection of three pillars (economic, social, environmental) | Constraint for the economy | Towards moderate or even strong | SD is made possible by institutional change | SD should be fair and implemented in a healthy environment | It covers various institutions |

| Theories | Sustainability, its conditions | Nature | Substitutability | SD probability | Society | Normative implications |
|---|---|---|---|---|---|---|
| Historical and institutional approach | A historically dated compromise between the centers of economic power and the forces that impose the demands of justice and nature conservation | The role of nature defenders in selecting the topics of SD | There is no hypothesis about this | There is no talk about this | Recognizing that society has an influence on the definition of SD | Open analysis in the normative dimension |
| Entropic approach | The economy follows the principle of entropy (sustainable degrowth) | The end of the approach: man is the "lord and owner of nature" | Weak | Development that implies growth cannot be sustainable (sustainability). Degrowth is an ecological requirement | Social conflict is an inherent part of man's struggle for survival, in the search for just degrowth | Degrowth implies different institutions |

Source: por. G. Destais, *Les théorizsations économiques du développement durable. Propositions de décryptage critique, Colloque international Pancophone*, „Le développement durable: débats et controverse" 15–16 décembre 2011, Université Blaise Pascal, Clermont-Ferrand, p. 9.

*Table 7: Classification of analysis types according to their normative impact*

| **Normative perspectives** | **Towards sustainable development (SD)** | | | | | For post-growth or no growth |
|---|---|---|---|---|---|---|
| | **SD does not involve changes in growth** | | **SD involves other institutions** | | | |
| | SD will be imposed by force | Public interventions are a necessity | Changes will be spontaneous | Institutional changes will be necessary | Non-normative analyses | |
| **Economic analyses** | Neo-classical approach | London school | Ecological economics (industrial ecology) | Humanities issues (three pillars) | Environmental conventions (controversial world) | American school |
| | | Scientific controversies in an uncertain world | | | Historical and institute analyses | Entropy |

Source: G. Destais, *Les théorisations économiques du développement durable. Propositions de décryptage critique, Colloque international Pancophone*, „Le développement durable: débats et controverse" 15–16 décembre 2011, Université Blaise Pascal, Clermont-Ferrand, p. 11.

Ultimately, the way economists deal with Sustainable Development (SD) seems far from the apparent consensus initiated in the Brundtland Report. Contrary to what many people think, incorporating the social dimension of SD is not considered necessary by all economists. However, in practice, the analysis of economic theories (approaches) reveals a strong division between theories that only concern the relationship between the economy and the environment and those that address all aspects of social life. Another significant distinction can be made between normative approaches (which define what SD should be and how it should be implemented) and descriptive approaches (which aim to highlight the challenges associated with the advent of SD). In terms of social compromises or changes in the values regulating the foundations of SD institutions, there is no mandatory nature. Therefore, none of the economic approaches can claim to be a satisfactory theoretical response to the current challenges facing humanity. One question remains open at the end of this analysis: why are there so many conflicting theoretical approaches among economists regarding SD? The answer to this question has been provided by the analysis conducted above, allowing us to grasp the differences in the evolution of economists' theoretical approaches to SD since the emergence of these perspectives. However, this is not aimed at eliminating or removing them but rather appreciating to what extent a compromise is possible among all those who take ecological issues seriously and intend to solve them. This compromise seems to be in *statu nascendi*.

# 3. Ecological approaches to sustainable development

The analysis below of the most important ecological theoretical approaches reveals both similarities and complete contradictions with the mainstream of SD. It is essential to note that the genesis of the SD concept and its evolution can be linked to the emergence of "ecology" as a science in the 1960s, whose theories gave character and meaning to the SD concept itself.

The word "ecology" was coined by the German biologist E. Haeckel in 1866 and comes from the Greek *oikos* (home, place of life)[366]. According to biological definitions, ecology is the study of organisms in their "home"; the science of relationships between organisms (groups of organisms) and the environment; the entirety or model of relationships between organisms and their environment; the functioning of living organisms in their surroundings[367]. It clearly pertains to relationships among organisms as well as relationships between organisms and the physical and chemical properties of their habitats. In other words, ecology perceives the world around us as it is (physical, chemical, and biological), infinitely variable in time and space[368]. Here, each organism is an element of the environment for all others, meaning that it constantly reacts to the dynamics of others, modifying them. Therefore, the key term defining ecology is "interaction." Currently, ecology takes on a new dimension (becomes a science for action) and a broader meaning, as evidenced by the ideas of "political ecology," "industrial ecology," or "urban ecology." Finally, most ecological issues concern objects or questions that have a strong social dimension, such as the role of forests in climate regulation or the role of soil in sustaining agricultural production. Therefore, according to L. Abbadie, "ecology is at a crucial moment in its history. It is no longer just a discipline that fundamentally aims for cognitive goals. Now, it has

366 P. Matczak, *Problemy ekologiczne jako problemy społeczne*, Poznań 2000, p. 12.

367 *Ibidem*.

368 L. Abbadie, *L'écologie, une science pour le développement durable* [in:] *Le développement durable à découvert*, ed. A. Euzen, L. Eymard, F. Gaill, Paris 2013, pp. 46–47.

become a socially engaged science (...). It is also a science at the crossroads, drawing knowledge from many other disciplines (...). In this sense, ecology provides access to an integrated understanding of our environment and a more robust awareness of our place in the world. A challenge, even a difficulty for contemporary ecology, is to embrace this inevitable social role while simultaneously maintaining its conceptual specificity"[369].

## 3.1. Green criticism

The green alternative to SD rejects the view that capitalism and industrialization can provide human development based on equality and justice. Here, it is assumed that changes in the behavior of individuals, institutions, and organizations are a prerequisite for SD[370]. Thus, the green alternative criticizes the current world system, labeling it as the main culprit for crises such as the financial crisis, political revolutions, environmental degradation, or poverty. Therefore, for the green alternative, theoretical approaches aligning with the mainstream of SD cannot bring about the expected changes. A. Dobson, in his 2007 book *Green Political Thought*, distinguishes between two ecological positions (environmentalism and ecologism). According to him, environmentalists (greens) believe that environmental issues can be managed without fundamental social and cultural changes, while ecologists (Greens) argue the opposite, asserting that this requires a radical change in our relationships with nature, our values, and lifestyles. While "greens" acknowledge the needs of the environment, supporting the *status quo*[371]1 (advocates of SD), "Greens" representing the green radical alternative are more than skeptical about the industrial system's ability to reform itself in the right direction. They are also skeptical about the effectiveness of public policy focused solely on production patterns and technological innovations issues capable of solving the problems of global constraints.

369 *Ibidem.*

370 A. Dobson, *Environmental Citizenship: Towards Sustainable Development*, „Sustainable Development" 2007, no. 15, p. 276.

371 Por. E. Rokicka, W. Woźniak, W *kierunku zrównoważonego rozwoju. Koncepcje*, interpretacje, konteksty, Łódź 2016, pp. 133–134.

Therefore, it can be said that ecologism, once synonymous with ecology[372], is a radical branch of environmentalism. At the heart of ecologism lies the belief that there is no lasting solution to the ecological crisis without a fundamental change in the orientation of values, norms, and cultural beliefs. While eco-efficiency is the key to ecological modernization (EM), "sufficiency," "locality," and "de-commodification" are the mantras of the most active radicals in the green movement. Compared to the green radicalism of the 70s and 80s, the current movement is more practical and concrete, even if a significant part of what happens under the banners of post-growth campaigns remains purely intellectual[373]. By refusing to engage in sterile disputes – growth versus economic limitation, anthropocentrism versus ecocentrism, technology versus culture – it encourages involvement in the entire spectrum of activities within eco-efficiency, sufficiency, and de-commodification.

Green critique is a type of discourse that rejects the basic structure of industrialized society and its place for the natural environment, proposing its own different way of perceiving people, society, and how we position ourselves in this world. Within this particular discourse, many discussions and debates take place concerning how change can be achieved. Therefore, there are two categories of

372 According to the PWN dictionary, ecology is the science of the structure and functioning of nature at various levels of organization, the economy of nature. On the other hand, ecologism is a philosophical direction (second half of the 20th century) addressing issues of environmental protection and humanity's place in the world—mainly the mutual dependencies between humans and nature that decide the quality of life in a short time frame and, in the broader perspective, the conditions for the survival of human populations. Ecologism is a new trend that is still shaping, representing an ideology that has emerged from alarming signals resulting from assessments of threats to the natural environment, which are a direct consequence of human activity (opposition to the ozone hole, desertification, climate warming, loss of the quality of human existence for an increasing population worldwide, etc.).

373 http://zielonewiadomosci.pl/tematy/ekologia/wszystkie-odcienie-ekopolityki/ (18.08.2019)

green radicalism: the first is green awareness (ecologism), and the second is green politics (environmetalism)[374].

Green consciousness (ecologism) is a discourse that emphasizes stress in creating a change in the way people experience and perceive the surrounding world. Its goal is to change human consciousness: the state of being aware of the things around them. It is believed that other more tangible actions, such as politics, changing social structures and institutions, will naturally change after a change in human consciousness. The capitalist demands for the development of the ecological system are extensive and do not align with what is needed for the current economic system. According to M. Koch, "capitalist development cannot ignore the tension between the needs of the economy and the ecological system"[375].The example of the tension between economic and ecological aspects is evident in the deforestation of rainforests. "Rainforests are being cut down in some places for production purposes. (…) Our economic system and our planetary system are currently at war. Moreover, our economy is at war with many forms of life on Earth, including human life"[376].

On the other hand, green politics (environmentalism) reflects opposition to the degradation of the natural environment due to the accelerated pace of economic development (intensified in the second half of the 20th century) and the decline in the quality of human existence. However, what gives environmentalism a radical character (ecologism) is the fact that it offers an alternative to the anthropocentric

---

374 S. Konstańczyk emphasizes the fact that environmentalism is characterized by high heterogeneity, and many sciences attribute this term to themselves. Sociologists define it as a "particular sociological theory, according to which differences between human cultures should be fully explained by factors such as soil, climate, food reserves." In political science, it constitutes the ideology of politically relevant movements. In this sense, it is often a conglomerate of mutually exclusive demands, the realization of which is supposed to bring about simultaneous and desired changes in culture and the natural environment. An example is the German Green Party (established in 1979, giving rise to the formation of the European Green Party in the European Parliament in 2004, setting up an international platform integrating Green political parties), whose slogans such as "decentralization, anti-violence, participatory democracy, egalitarianism, anti-nuclearism… allowed the unification of many previously scattered pro-environmental movements". Quoted from: S. Konstańczyk, *Koncepcje ekofilozofii* [in:] *Ekorozwój i Agenda 21. Interdyscyplinarny model kształcenia*, ed. P. Pieczyński, Szczecin 2007, pp. 133 134.

375 M. Koch, *Capitalism and Climate Change – Theoretical, Discussion, Historical Development and Policy Responses*, New York 2012, p. 36.

376 N. Klein, *This changes everything*, London 2014, p. 21.

position adopted by all ideologies. It does not perceive the natural world solely as a convenient source for satisfying human needs[377]. Therefore, supporters of ecologism are not environmentalists[378]. The latter adopt a managerial approach to environmental issues, which is typical of the mainstream of SD. In contrast, the former believe that SD requires a radical change in thinking about the human-nature relationship, as well as changes at both the political and societal levels. Following A. Fragnière, ecologism can be considered a radical branch of environmentalism that uses ecology as a lever for radical criticism[379]. Environmentalism acknowledges that environmental issues can be managed without fundamental social and cultural changes, which is contrary to the stance of ecologism. Ecologism posits that only a radical change in human behavior, values, and lifestyle can save humanity from destruction and is a necessary condition. Indeed, ecologists and analysts interested in this trend converge to argue that ecologism differs from environmentalism in that the former deals with the thinking and change of what currently causes the problems that environmentalism observes and signals"[380] (see. Tab. 8).

However, supporters of both positions do not completely reject the capitalist economy. Here, the state and law serve as guarantees for the process of change, which in turn ensures the functioning of market rules resulting from political

377 See. A. Heywood, *Politologia*, Warszawa 2006, p. 76.

378 It is important to note that in recent years (since 2012), a new movement called "anti-environmentalism" has emerged in the United States, advocated by radical conservatives. It also draws support from the strong dynamics of the TEA Party, including generous donors, as well as the endorsement of all conservative media and the viral effect of the internet. "Anti-environmentalism" is not a conscious desire to harm the environment but rather, a systematic opposition to the modality and very principle of public policy intended to protect it. Its supporters, who are political activists, do not agree with the destruction of the natural environment and oppose the very idea of adopting public policies to protect it. Therefore, the US Environmental Protection Agency (EPA) and the concept of climate change are the main targets of the new crusaders. One of the main explanations for the growing "success" of this new phenomenon is the primacy of entrepreneurship over socialism. See more: Y. M. *Péréon, "L'anti-environnementalisme", nouveau théme des conservateurs américains*, "Potomac Paper" Septembre 2011, no. 8, pp. 1–34.

379 A. Fragnière, *Écologie et liberté: apports et insuffisances de l'écologie politique* [in:] *Théories et pratiques écologie: de l'écologie urbaine à l'imaginations environmentale*, ed. M. Antonioli, Paris 2013, pp. 138–139.

380 F. Flipo, *Penser l'écologie politique*, „La revue électronique en sciences de l'environnement" 2016, vol. 16, no. 1, https://journals.openedition.org/vertigo/16993 (24.03.2021).

compromise. Advocates of both trends need a powerful state to create a set of measures that will redirect consumption and production towards low-emission products, set standards, introduce environmental taxes, etc. Similarly, economists dealing with the environment must emphasize the redistributive dimension of policies, whether through taxation or the provision of public goods[381]. In the context of SD, green criticism (also known in the literature as the green alternative) advocates for the concept of constraints imposed by ecosystems and making decisions at the lowest possible level.

*Table 8: Environmentalism and ecologism*

| **Environmentalism** | **Ecologism** |
|---|---|
| • does not question the relationship dominating man over nature (anthropocentric approach)<br>• takes action for the benefit of the natural environment and the creatures living in it<br>• belief that development based on the SD concept is the solution<br>• an attempt to reconcile capitalism and ecology<br>• the belief that science and technology will solve the problems resulting from ecological crises | • tries to understand the main foundations of the eco-social crisis<br>• the assumption that man's domination over nature reflects man's domination over man (ecocentric approach)<br>• only a profound social transformation will restore the balance that has been exceeded<br>• belief in the ability of communities/ society to take care of themselves<br>• technologies provide only temporary solutions |

Source: K. Harrison, T. Boyd, *Environmentalism and ecologism* [in:] *Understanding Political Ideas Movements*, Manchester 2003, pp. 274–294.

In green criticism (alternative), the focus is on realizing the vision of "greening" the economy, creating the so-called green economy. This concept played a crucial role in the electoral success of the Greens in Europe. The "green economy"[382] is a new paradigm of development capable of responding to the crises affecting the entire world. It represents a model of ecological prosperity or an alternative to globalized capitalism by placing natural capital on the market for ecosystem services, privatizing resources, patenting living creatures, etc. This approach aims

381 P. Defeyt, *Ecologiser l'économie: une sacrée enterprise*, http://www.etopia.be/IMG/pdf/r4_defeyt_web.pdf (11.04.2021), p. 50.

382 Defined by the UN as an "environmentally friendly way of conducting economic activities," the "green economy" aims to reconcile economic growth and nature.

to regulate our relationship with the environment in a sustainable way, stimulate the creation of new jobs, thus ensuring a profitable future for capitalism. The context of the emergence of the concept of the "green economy" speaks for itself. The ecological crisis, along with the awareness of the physical constraints of irresponsible exploitation of natural resources, has taken on such a "climate" in recent years that even the most productive actors have understood the crucial importance of strategies such as "mitigation," "adaptation," and even "prediction" or "prudence". The United Nations Environment Programme (UNEP) 2011 report titled *Towards a Green Economy: Pathways to Sustainable Development and Poverty Eradication* is a true masterpiece in the global conceptualization of the "green economy." In this report, UNEP aimed to demonstrate that the greening of the economy is not a hindrance to growth but rather a new engine for development. This "green engine" is expected to create new jobs and promote poverty eradication, thereby updating the dimension of "social cohesion" within the framework of sustainable development. UNEP defines a "green economy" as an economy that improves well-being and social justice while significantly reducing environmental risks and the risk of resource scarcity[383]. The new concept of the "green economy" proposes an ecological approach to conducting business. Therefore, it is quite natural that in 2012, the World Bank, OECD, Global Green Growth Institute (GGGI), and UNEP decided to create a new joint initiative promoting the green economy: the knowledge platform on green growth. This platform calls for action (policy advice, technical assistance, etc.) at all levels to "create conditions for green investments," meaning more efficient, effective, and sensible economic systems in managing natural resources[384]. The European Union has defined its own strategy, *Europe 2020*, based on achieving "smart, sustainable, and inclusive growth." Southern countries are relatively uncertain, and in some cases even skeptical, about the concept of the "green economy," viewing it as another expression of new ecological protectionism (standards, trade barriers, etc.) from Northern countries that could harm economic entities in the South[385].

383 *Économie verte: marchandiser la planète pour la Sauer?*, „Alternatives Sud" 2012, vol. XX- 2013/1, https://www.cetri.be/Economie-verte-marchandiser-la-2993?lang=fr (12.05.2018).

384 *Ibidem*.

385 *Ibidem*.

## 3.2. Ecosocialism

Ecosocialism, also known as green socialism, combines ecology with the rich tradition of socialist thought and actions, especially those associated with Marxism. Marxism shows that the ecological crisis is rooted in the destructive capitalist system and provides ways to understand the functioning of capitalism and envision a system beyond capitalism[386], where production is driven by human needs. Regardless of what we may think of "existing socialisms" in the 20th century, eco-socialists emphatically emphasize that socialists have failed miserably in ecological terms. Therefore, eco-socialists advocate for a new kind of socialism that takes into account the place of people in the biosphere of the planet. They start from the premise that environmental degradation and social injustice stem from the same source: a world where profit is the ultimate goal.

Therefore, in the face of global threats, theorists aligned with the movement for global ecological and social changes have unearthed a potent ecological critique of capitalism rooted in the principles of historical materialism by Karl Marx[387]. This has led to the development of a comprehensive concept of socialism rooted in Marxist analysis of the metabolic rift, in the "universal metabolism of nature"[388] and its vision of shifting development toward the sustainable development of humanity. According to the American sociologist J.B. Foster, such a social and ecological transformation will require a two-stage strategy. Firstly, the struggle for radical reforms in the present that challenge the destructive logic of

386 See. J. Dowbor, *Poza kapitalizm. Nowa architektura społeczna*, Warsaw 2020.

387 See more: M. Cichoracki, *Marksowski materializm historyczny – koncepcja związku między bazą a nadbudową oraz prymatu czynników ekonomicznych*, „Filozofia Publiczna i Edukacja Demokratyczna" 2012, t. I, no. 1, pp. 133–138.

388 „The concept of "metabolic rift" originates from Karl Marx's description of a fundamental change in the relationship between the human species and the rest of nature, which developed with class societies, especially capitalism. "Metabolism" for Marx encompassed all of nature and its interconnected processes, of which humans were a part. Marx believed that capitalism severed this connection, causing an "irreparable rift in the interdependent process of social metabolism, a metabolism determined by the natural laws of life itself".

capital[389]. Secondly, building a broad movement to carry out a long, revolutionary transformation necessary for the continued development and survival of humanity[390]. Development, especially in affluent economies, must take on a new form: qualitative, collective, and cultural, emphasizing the development of a self-sustaining human being in harmony with Karl Marx's original view of socialism[391].

Ecosocialism in the West developed alongside feminism, while in the global South, it was recognized as ecology for the poor[392]. During the 1960s and 1970s, radical ecological economist K.W. Kapp and socialist biologist B. Commoner drew on Karl Marx's ideas to explain ecological contradictions. In the 1980s, the works of British sociologist T. Benton and French-Austrian social philosopher A. Gorz (representatives of the so-called New Left) initiated a new ecosocialist tradition. In the 1990s, T. Burkett (referred to as a second-stage ecosocialist) contributed to the development of a Marxist ecological concept[393], by reconstructing Karl Marx's arguments on social metabolism, leading to its reintegration with Marxist theory[394].

However, the foundation of this approach has been publications such as *Ecological Socialism: From Deep Ecology to Social Justice* by D. Pepper in 1994 and

389 Capital as a system was internally oriented towards the maximum possible accumulation and discharge of matter and energy regardless of human needs and natural constraints. According to Karl Marx, such a correlation of flows based on capitalist economy, i.e., material flows (related to use value) and flows of labor value (related to exchange value), leads to a growing contradiction between environmental resilience imperatives and economic growth. Quoted from: J.B. Foster, B. Clark, R. York, *The Ecological Rifi: Capitalism's War on the Earth*, New York 2010, pp. 207–214.

390 J.B. Foster, *Marxism and Ecology: Common Fonts of a Great Transition*, „Great Transition Initiative. Toward a Transformative Vision and Praxis" 2015, October, p. 1.

391 *Ibidem*, p. 9.

392 See more: J. Martinez-Alier, *The Environmentalism of the Poor. A study of ecological conflicts and valuation*, Northamption, Massachusetts 2002; eadem, Ecology and the Poor: *A Neglected Dimension of Latin American History* [in:] *Perspectives in Resource Management in Developing Countries*, t. II, part 1, ed. B. Thakur, New Delhi 2007, pp. 619–640.

393 A characteristic feature of the Marxist ecological theory was the emphasis on unequal ecological exchange or ecological imperialism, where one country can ecologically exploit another. This can be seen in Karl Marx's famous remark about how for over 100 years, England "indirectly exported Irish soil," weakening the long-term fertility of Irish agriculture. In recent years, Marxist theorists have expanded this analysis of ecological imperialism, perceiving it as an integral part of all attempts to address the ecological problem. Quoted from: J.B. Foster, *Marxism and Ecology...*, p. 7.

394 *Ibidem*, p. 5.

the *Ecosocialist Manifesto* by J. Kovel and M. Löwy in 2001. The ecosocialist ideology is present in many green parties worldwide, dominating, for example, in the Green Party of the United States in the West and in the People's Republic of China (PRC) in the East, where ecosocialist principles are reflected in the national strategy introduced in 2007 aiming to "build an eco-civilization." Thus, environmental protection and management have become an integral part of "socialist modernization towards a new era" both in theoretical and practical terms[395]. The significance of this ecological political philosophy in the People's Republic of China (PRC), according to Professor Q. Huan, stems from two essential reasons. Firstly, contemporary ecological challenges are not just temporary issues but are inseparably linked to the capitalist way of understanding the world. Attempts to address ecological problems within the framework of the capitalist regime, such as "green capitalism" or "ecocapitalism," are not effective. Secondly, ecosocialism is an updated version of socialism, something different from a simplified or distorted "greened" traditional socialism[396].

Both socialism and ecology appeal to qualitative values: among socialists, these values include use-value, satisfaction of needs, and social equality; among ecologists, the focus is on the protection of nature and ecological balance. In ecosocialism, both perspectives conceive the economy as "embedded" in the social or natural environment. French-Brazilian sociologist and philosopher M. Löwy argues that in ecosocialism, Marxists and ecologists have merged what once significantly differentiated them[397]: „The idea of socialism, as opposed to its miserable bureaucratic deformations, involves the production of use-values, goods necessary to satisfy human needs. For Karl Marx, the ultimate goal of technological progress is not the infinite accumulation of goods («having»), but the reduction of the working day and the accumulation of leisure time («being»). In reality, one can find material in the writings of Karl Marx and Friedrich Engels to support both interpretations. The ecological issue poses a significant challenge to renew Marxist thought at the beginning of the 21st century. This requires Marxists to undertake a deep critical revision of their traditional concept of «productive forces» and to radically break with the ideology of linear progress and the technological-economic paradigm of contemporary industrial civilization (...) Capital

395 Ch. Schickert, *W imię wizji socjalistycznej. Wywiad z Qingzhi Huanem*, „Globalny Dialog" 2019, t. IX, p. 6.

396 *Ibidem*.

397 M. Löwy, *What is Ecosocialism?*, „Capitalisme. Nature. Socialism" 2005, vol. 16, no. 2, p. 15.

threatens or destroys its own conditions, starting with the natural environment – possibilities that Marx did not adequately consider"[398].

M. Löwy, as a leading creator of contemporary ecosocialism, points to two fundamental reasons for the emergence of this movement. The first lies in the mode of production and consumption in advanced capitalist states, which is based on the logic of unlimited accumulation (of capital, profits), waste of resources, conspicuous consumption, and the accelerating destruction of the environment, ultimately leading to an ecological crisis extending across the entire planet. The second reason is the continuation of capitalist "progress" and the expansion of a civilization based on the market economy, which threatens the survival of the human species. Rationality limited by the capitalist market, with its short-term calculations of profit and loss, is in internal contradiction with ecological rationality, which takes into account the natural cycles. According to the researcher, this is not a matter of contrasting "bad" capitalists fighting against environmentalists with "good" green capitalists[399]. The same system based on ruthless competition, profitability requirements, and a race for quick profit is a destroyer of the balance of nature[400].

For eco-socialists, the market logic of profit and the logic of bureaucratic authoritarianism in the late stages of "actually existing socialism" are incompatible with the necessity of protecting the natural environment. Criticizing the ideology of dominant sectors of the labor movement, eco-socialists recognize that workers and their organizations are a necessary force for the radical transformation of the system and the establishment of a new socialist and ecological society. R. Williams, as one of the representatives of eco-socialism, alongside those mentioned earlier, sought to create ecologically rational societies based on democratic control, social equality, and the primacy of use-values over exchange-values in his works. This concept assumes collective ownership of the means of production and democratic planning, allowing society to determine the goals of investment and production, as well as the new technological structure of productive forces. By adopting a new model of strongly democratic planning, society can take control of the means of production and its own destiny. Shorter working hours and a

398 *Ibidem*, p. 17.

399 M. Löwy calls "green capitalism" an advertising trick, a label to sell goods or - at best - a local initiative equivalent to "a drop of water on the dry soil of the capitalist desert".

400 M. Löwy, *What is Ecosocialism?*, p. 18.

focus on genuine needs rather than consumerism can facilitate the prioritization of "being" over "having" and achieve a deeper sense of freedom for all[401].

For eco-socialists, the challenge for the future lies in realizing a "moral economy." Such an economy must exist in the sense that E.P. Thompson used this term[402], implying economic policies based on non-monetary and non-economic criteria. In other words, it is necessary to reintegrate the economy in an ecological, social, and political direction[403]. Partial reforms are entirely insufficient; what is needed is the replacement of micro-rationality with social and ecological macro-rationality, which demands a true civilizational change. Radical change pertains not only to production but also to consumption. The solution here is not merely to restrict the latter. The economy in the transitional period toward socialism, "re-embedded" in the social and natural environment, would be based on the democratic choice of priorities and investments by the population itself, rather than by market forces.

The exponential growth observed over decades, leading to the "common ruin of the contending classes," has led eco-socialists to develop a two-stage strategy for an ecological-social revolution. The first stage focuses on the question of what can be done now, what is realistic in the short term under current conditions. This can be considered the eco-democratic stage of the global ecological revolution,

401 M. Löwy, *Ecosocialism: A Radical Alternative* [in:] *Reflections on Socialism in the Twenty-First Century*, Facing Market Liberalism, Rising Inequalities and the Environmental Imperative, ed. C. Brundenius, Switzerland 2020, p. 199.

402 The concept of the "moral economy" is an elaboration of the ideas of the English historian E.P. Thompson, a term used in the 18th century by various authors who believed that economic and moral problems were increasingly diverging. E.P. Thompson wrote about the moral economy of the poor in the context of widespread food riots in the English countryside at the end of the 18th century. According to him, these riots were generally peaceful acts that demonstrated a common political culture based on feudal rights to "fix prices" of basic goods in the market. These peasants argued that the traditional "fair price" was more important to the community than the "free" market price. They punished large farmers who sold their surpluses at higher prices outside the village, while there were still people in the village who needed that food. In the 1970s, the concept of the "moral economy" was further developed in anthropological studies of peasant economies. The notion of a non-capitalist cultural mentality utilizing the market for its own purposes was combined by others (with the approval of E.P. Thompson) with subsistence farming and the need for life insurance in difficult times. Quoted from: N. Götz, *„Moral economy": its conceptual history and analytical prospects*, „Journal of Global Ethics" 2015, no. 11, pp. 147–162.

403 M. Löwy, *What is Ecosocialism?*, p. 19.

utilizing the maximum available means, such as emission fees and dividends, banning coal and unconventional fossil fuels, a significant shift to solar and wind energy, and other sustainable energy sources like energy efficiency. It also involves financing cuts in military expenditures, a moratorium on economic growth in affluent economies to limit carbon dioxide emissions, combined with radical redistribution and a new international process of climate negotiations based on egalitarian and ecocentric principles laid out in the World People's Conference on Climate Change and the Rights of Mother Earth in Bolivia in 2010[404] as a path towards achieving long-term goals[405]. Alongside a broad range of similar initiatives, such actions constitute a rational and realistic starting point for revolution and serve as a means of mobilizing the general public[406]. The long-term goal of systemic transformation raises the issue of the second stage of the ecological revolution or the eco-social phase. The fundamental question, of course, is the historical context in which this change can take place. The revolutionary change is intended to be carried out by a larger part of humanity, establishing more egalitarian conditions and processes for governing the global society, including necessary ecological, social, and economic planning. In the near future, the "ecological

404 Bolivia offers a paradigm strongly borrowed from the concepts of indigenous people, particularly the Aymaras, where "Mother Earth" (Pachamama) is considered a distinct entity, equal to human beings, with a set of rights that should be recognized. To emphasize this perspective, the United Nations passed a resolution in 2009 designating April 22 as the "International Mother Earth Day." The Copenhagen Summit (COP 15) in December 2009 concluded a sharp dispute initiated by Bolivia in international climate change negotiations. Since then, the Andean-Amazonian country has led a movement aiming to radically challenge the current model of addressing climate change. This challenge materialized through the World People's Conference on Climate Change and the Rights of Mother Earth held in Cochabamba from April 19 to 22, 2010, initiated by Evo Morales. The outcome was the "People's Agreement," an extensive document presenting demands and requirements towards the affluent North regarding the reduction of CO2 emissions and mitigation of climate change. This summit symbolizes sharp criticism from many countries of the international approach to combating climate change. Moreover, it is noteworthy that in August 2010, Bolivia managed to incorporate nearly 10 proposals from the Cochabamba text into the negotiated text at the subsequent summit in Cancun in November 2010 (COP 16). It is clear that there is a contradiction between domestic economic policy and foreign policy focused on environmental advocacy. Quoted from: P.-J. Brasier, *La Bolivie et le changement climatique*, „SciencesPo" 8 octobre 2010, https://www.sciencespo.fr/opalc/content/la-bolivie-et-le-changement-climatique (23.03.2021).

405 J.B. Foster, *Marxism and Ecology…*, p. 9–10.

406 *Ibidem.*

proletariat" will inevitably emerge from the combination of ecological degradation and economic difficulties already present today, especially in the lowest strata of society. Material crises affecting people's lives will become increasingly indistinguishable in terms of their diverse ecological and economic consequences (e.g., a food crisis). Such conditions will compel the working population to rebel against the system. Eco-socialists assume that the youth will demystify and radicalize as material living conditions worsen, and women will lead the fight for a more ecological global society[407].

Eco-socialism proposes a strategic alliance between the "red" and "green" - not in the narrow sense applied by politicians to social democratic and green parties, but in a broader sense between the workers' movement and the ecological movement, as well as solidarity movements with the oppressed and exploited in the Global South. Having no illusions about "ecological" capitalism does not mean refraining from the fight for immediate reforms. Some types of ecological taxes can be useful, provided they are based on egalitarian social logic (making polluters pay, not the society). The struggle to ban HCFC[408], which destroys the ozone layer, the introduction of a moratorium on genetically modified organisms, the reduction of greenhouse gas emissions, thereby prioritizing public transport over anti-social, highly polluting private cars, can be beneficial.

Certain direct demands can quickly become the driving force for convergence between social and environmental movements, labor unions, and environmental advocates, bridging the gap between the "red" and "green" factions. Among these actions, key for ecosocialists are the promotion of affordable and free public transportation (trains, subways, buses, etc.) as an alternative to the "choking" and pollution caused by private cars in cities and towns; rejection of the debt system and extreme neoliberal "structural adjustments" imposed by the International Monetary Fund and the World Bank on these countries; protection of public health from air, water, and food pollution due to the greed of large capitalist enterprises, and the reduction of working hours to address unemployment and create a society that prioritizes leisure over the accumulation of goods.

* * *

---

407 *Ibidem*, p. 11.

408 HCFC (ang. hydrochlorofluorocarbons) – are organic chemical compounds from the group of freons, derivatives of hydrocarbons, in which some hydrogen atoms are replaced by chlorine and fluorine atoms. They have been used as refrigerants but are considered to contribute to the depletion of the ozone layer, and therefore, their use is being phased out.

Ecosocialism is not a monolithic structure. E. Szoc points to the diversity of approaches within the ecosocialist movement and the numerous "tensions" between them, which may sometimes indicate deep-seated contradictions, but also, or perhaps primarily, highlight that these diverse approaches determine a specific transformative policy that goes beyond the utterance of "powerless slogans" and the resignation to small steps[409]. In reality, among ecosocialists, there is a lively debate, especially regarding short-term strategies. While all ecosocialists agree that capitalism must go, they also acknowledge that the only way to achieve this is through collaboration with larger organizations that are not socialist. They also agree on the need to pursue a series of environmental reforms, especially those that radicalize people fighting for them and bring together different branches of the environmental movement. Contemporary ecosocialism, in addition to criticizing the capitalist system, seeks to show not only why various ecosocialist initiatives are an alternative to current actions but also a real solution to the mentioned problems in all societies and finally that "another world" is indeed possible[410]. However, significant interpretative divergences within eco-socialism do not provide a chance for this ideology to become complementary.

## 3.3. Political ecology

Political ecology (PE) is a collection of ideas that emphasize the inclusion of ecological challenges in political actions and social organizations. It is a cultural movement fueled by influences from various currents (such as feminism, the Third World, pacifism, non-violence, libertarianism, self-management[411] etc.). Ecology becomes political when it demands profound transformations of the current economic and social model, as well as a revision of the relationship between humans and their environment, i.e., the natural environment[412].

---

409 E. Szoc, *Écosocialisme (s)*, „Politique revue belge d'analyse et de debat" 2020, no. 91, https://www.revuepolitique.be/ecosocialismes/ (22.03.2021).

410 Ch. Schickert, *W imię wizji...*, p. 6.

411 An example of self-management can be seen in the case of Algeria just after gaining independence in 1962. In some "vacant spaces" left by settlers (agricultural settlements and small to medium-sized enterprises), workers formed management committees to ensure continuity but, more importantly, to redirect their activities towards meeting the "needs of the people." The establishment of a centralized state and political control over labor quickly put an end to these experiments in worker self-management.

412 O. Fressard, C. Larrière, L. Schmid, *L'écologie est politique*, Paris 2013, p. 64.

Although this movement has been widespread since the 1970s[413], its roots can be traced back to the work of the geographer and diplomat G.P. Marsh, published in 1864, titled *Man and Nature*. This publication, considered the first scientific treatise (the first to assess the damage caused and present a program of reforms), showed in a scientific way how human activities could have a destructive impact on the environment. It revealed deep and dangerous interactions in the human-nature relationship: "Man has too long forgotten that the earth was given to him for usufruct alone, not for consumption, still less for profligate waste"[414]. The author paid particular attention to the Mediterranean region and highlighted clear evidence of destructive human activity in this area. Among these, he noted the extinction of species, soil erosion, revolutionary changes in Mediterranean oceanography due to projects like the construction of the Suez Canal, and the transformation of wild and unregulated areas into intensively utilized and urbanized spaces[415]. At the same time, he emphasized that destructive processes, whether organic or inorganic, were largely cyclical or repeatable, such as earthquakes or volcanic eruptions. On the other hand, human impacts on the environment were long-lasting and often irreversibly transformed. G.P. Marsh defends the thesis that every rational use of natural resources must respect the natural balance, which is possible through an understanding of the laws of nature and requires caution[416].

PE is defined today according to four axes of claims that encompass inseparable yet complex connections:

- environmental quality,
- social justice,
- citizenship,
- international solidarity.

In the United States, prominent figures of the green movement include H.D. Thoreau, A. Leopold, and R. Garson. In Europe, the first person to combine the "struggle for nature with political struggle" was the libertarian geographer

413 Political ecology emerged after the events of May 1968 and the oil shocks of that time, as well as in response to the intensified reactions of certain individuals (organisms) to the destruction of the ecosystem (their environment).

414 G.P. Marsh, *Man and Nature; Physical Geography as Modified by Human Action*, New York 1869, p. 577, quoted from: D. Lowenthal, Marsh's Man and Nature at 150, „The George Wright Forum" 2015, vol. 32, no. 3, pp. 227–235.

415 *Ibidem*.

416 *Ibidem*.

É. Reclus[417]. While the goal of ecology is to study the relationship between organisms and the natural environment, political ecology is, in a sense, a result of the awareness of the anthropocentric limitations of humans. It raises issues that are essential to the anthropology of the ecological role of the human species. Political ecology aims to raise awareness of the polluting impact of humans on the environment (ecological footprint)[418], including cultural, structural, political, and social aspects. Political ecology clearly stands out from other ecological movements that typically do not consider these aspects in their reflections. This approach questions the traditional way of interaction between humans and their environment (natural environment), including in political programs. This cultural approach to the ecology of the human species – a species that uses politics to secure its future and that of its offspring – is also a social movement transforming society in a way that is more adapted to an ecological vision (global, integrating successive generations) in the face of current reality. PE takes into account the consequences of human actions in the place of residence and our actions for the environment, not only ecological but also human and social, including the negative impact on physical and mental health, on the health of others, and on future generations. It is therefore consistent with political theories and movements such as the labor movement, republican democracy, socialism, feminism, regionalism, etc.

According to many researchers, such as A. Lipietz, A. Gorz, or M. Bookchin, political ecology shows similarities to Marxism because it relies on critical and theoretical knowledge of the "existing order of things." It integrates relationships between humanity and nature, as well as relationships among people in nature. However, it goes beyond recognizing a historical balance of power between capital owners and workers, aiming to transcend this dichotomy. It is, above all, more than materialistic and progressive.

Wider scope and interdisciplinary nature of political ecology give the impression that this trend converges with many definitions. However, shared assumptions

---

417 https://www.universalis.fr/encyclopedie/mouvement-ecologiste/1-emergence-de-la-pensee-ecologiste/ (10.07.2018).

418 The Ecological Footprint is a method in which the land and sea area serve as indicators, and various consumption categories are converted into the surface area of productive land. It is an indicator that allows estimating the consumption of natural resources in relation to the Earth's capacity to regenerate them. It forms the basis for analyzing human demand for the natural resources of the biosphere. See more: M. Wackernagel, W. Rees, *Our Ecological Footprint: Reducing Human Impact on the Earth*, Gabriela Island 1996, p. 176.

in this field give it significance. R.L. Bryant and S. Bailey developed three fundamental assumptions about practicing PE:

Firstly, the costs and benefits associated with environmental changes are distributed unevenly. Environmental changes do not impact society uniformly: political, social, and economic differences result in an uneven distribution of costs and benefits.

Secondly, this unequal distribution inevitably reinforces or diminishes existing social and economic inequalities. In this assumption, PE is inherently embedded in economic policy since "every change in environmental conditions must affect the political and economic status quo".

Thirdly, the unequal distribution of costs and benefits, along with the reinforcement or diminishment of pre-existing inequalities, has political implications concerning the altered power relations that are now emerging[419].

Moreover, PE seeks to provide criticism as well as alternatives in the interaction between the environment and political, economic, and social factors. P. Robbins argues that this discipline has a "normative understanding that there is likely a better, less coercive, less exploitative, and more sustainable way of doing things"[420].

Based on these assumptions, political ecology can be used to:

- informing decision-makers and organizations about the state of environmental protection and economic and social development, thus contributing to better environmental management,
- understanding the environmental decisions that communities make in the context of their political evironment, economic pressures and social regulations,
- highlighting how unequal relations within and between societies impact the natural environment, especially in the context of state policies[421].

Therefore, PE refers to the emerging movement in response to new environmental questions and issues. However, a drawback of this approach is that it may struggle to move beyond the initial confusion, especially the elements of religiosity, romanticism, voluntarism, moral aspirations, a desire for harmony, and love for people and animals instead of the unavoidable responsibility, making it a significant cognitive issue. Reducing ecology and politics to the love of nature is historically inevitable and practically unsustainable. Advocates of this approach argue that

---

419 R.L. Bryant, S. Bailey, *Third World Political Ecology*, London 1997, p. 28.
420 P. Robbins, *Political ecology: a critical introduction*, New Jersey 2004, p. 12.
421 *Ibidem*.

"they do not have to be sentimental to take environmental politics seriously, especially its political dimension, which introduces a division among ecologists that we absolutely cannot collect in one stream, ranging from deep ecology to social ecology." PE must integrate the contradiction between nature and culture (landscape and city), limiting our technical possibilities for transforming the world, but it is a matter of building collective intelligence, not soul conversion; it is a matter of a political project, not morality[422].

It is difficult to deny the existence of political struggles within ecology, indicating a truly political dimension of ecology, far from being "neither right nor left" or allegedly apolitical in the general interest. There is a frontal opposition between different tendencies in ecology, which are largely irreconcilable, and their divergences are far from clear to everyone. In the continuity of social struggles, there is an awareness of our global solidarity as well as our boundaries, undoubtedly representing progress in understanding. The only thing that unites these different ecologists is the awareness of environmental issues, but with diagnoses that are quite distant. Following the French philosopher and ecologist J. Zinem, "political ecology is defined by an awareness of our natural environment and interdependencies, awareness of our belonging to ecosystems that we cannot destroy, awareness of our ecological footprint and the will not only to protect our living conditions but to improve the quality of life—all things that are not given and depend on political debate (…) political ecology is the affirmation of our solidarity and responsibility for the world, transforming the biosphere in a way into a living organism from which we will create a nervous system"[423].

The novelty of PE lies in safeguarding the future and the fact of collectively assuming responsibility for our actions, which corresponds quite well to what F. Hegel calls the "transition from history to projected history"[424]. In contrast to the idealism of totalitarian utopias aiming to create a new one-dimensional human (like *homo economicus* or *homo sovieticus*), political ecology must adhere to reality and act cautiously, taking people as they are, in their various dimensions, with all their contradictions, diversity, and internal tensions. It is no longer the end of history but its continuation, its endurance. Historically, political ecology corresponds to modernity, i.e., postmodernism, which integrates self-sustainability/endurance and can criticize itself, being aware of the limits

422 *Ibidem.*
423 J. Zin, *Qu'est-ce que l'écologie-politique?*, „Ecologie & politique" 2010/2, no. 40, p. 45.
424 *Ibidem.*

of techno-economic progress, its dangers, such as ecological costs, but also its global dimension[425].

PE, which combines nature with local and global culture, is also a denial of all divisions: technological, ecological, economic, political, and social spheres, despite their relative autonomy. Not because the biosphere unites us all, erasing any separation among us and making us one with the nature we have been destroying. What connects us does not eliminate what divides us. For the dominated, it is necessary to recognize actual social divisions and give them political expression. It is about understanding our interdependence and the general consequences of our actions, adapting to our environment, and preserving the conditions for life, "not cutting the branches on which we sit"[426].

Instead of talking about "the ethics of responsibility"[427], which may sound too individualistic, it would be better to talk about "collective responsibility politics" towards future generations and the consequences of our actions, considering the negative impact of our industry: pollution-related burdens, resource depletion, disruption of ecological balance (global warming, deforestation, loss of biodiversity, GMOs, etc.). Responsibility for a shared future is inherently a confirmation of our current solidarity and a political demand for human development as the development of our capabilities and effective autonomy "here and now." It's not about individual moral values but about a political project, so that the ecologists' motto "autonomy, solidarity, responsibility" is embraced[428]. J. Zin emphasizes the need to understand the dynamics of capitalism (its productivity), "before we learn how to control it or how to get out of it, in order to finally understand everything that changes our entry into the digital era"[429].

According to A. Gorz, "political ecology cannot be reduced to limiting consumption but must imply an exit from capitalist productivism and liberal laissez-faire, preserving individual autonomy and social solidarity. We also need self-employed institutions, especially communal cooperatives helping isolated workers, including immaterial workers. Similarly, guaranteed incomes, communal and local cooperatives, and local currencies together create a new production system, transferred, combining production, reproduction, and circulation (work,

---

425 *Ibidem.*

426 *Ibidem*, p. 46.

427 See more: P. Hugon, *L'éthique de la responsabilité et du risque au regard des projets de développement durable, de la responsabilité sociale de l'entreprise et des risques systémiques*, „Mondes en Développement" 2014, vol. 42, t. 4, no. 168, pp. 11–25.

428 J. Zin, *Qu'est-ce que…*, p. 47.

429 *Ibidem.*

income, trade)"[430]. If we cannot hope for an immediate exit from capitalism, we can at least exit from market totalitarianism and start removing the wage society. Political ecology should ultimately signify a more ecological (post-totalitarian) way of practicing politics: a minority democracy rooted in the local and direct community, the opposite of any majority dictatorship. This could eventually establish true cognitive democracy in the interaction between local action and global thinking.

## 3.4. Ecoanarchism

Ecoanarchism is a radical approach to green ideas within the framework of anarchism. The emphasis on anarchist ideas providing opportunities to address the ecological crisis is a common theme across various branches of anarchism today. The term "anarchism" originates from two ancient Greek words: an and arhè, which literally mean absence of authority or absence of leadership[431]. Many anarchist discourses give the impression of rejecting the idea of political power and state organization in favor of a stateless system based on voluntarily emerging associations of producers and consumers. Simultaneously, many of them advocate for the idea of society, showing themselves as ardent supporters of democratic and collective structures[432]. Moreover, concepts with anarchist roots, such as participatory democracy, decentralization, self-sufficiency, egalitarianism, and alternative technologies, are significant in discussions within the field of SD.

Ecoanarchists argue that the process of capitalist rationalization is clearly suffering from many irrationalities, with the most important being environmental problems and "boredom" in the North, coupled with a lack of resources to meet basic needs in the South. Eco-anarchism takes two forms: the first represented by social ecologists, and the second by so-called primitive anarchists. The first, as a socio-political direction, sees the fundamental source of liberation in the existence of the state and capitalism. The ideas of individual freedom, belief in the goodness of human nature, individualism, and voluntarism form the basis of this doctrine[433]. A distinctive expression of this approach is anarcho-communism, as

---

430 *Ibidem*, p. 48.

431 D.F. White, G. Kossoff, *Anarchisme, libertarisme et environnementalisme: la pensée anti-autoritaire et la quête de sociétés auto-organisées*, „Écologie & politique" 2011, no. 41, p. 146.

432 *Ibidem*.

433 E. Rokicka, W. Woźniak, *W kierunku...*, p. 138.

advocated by P. Kropotkin (who lived at the turn of the 19th and 20th centuries). According to him, only an anarchist society, based on the confederation of communities and the integration of manual and intellectual labor, as well as the decentralization and integration of agriculture and industry, will allow equal citizens to meet their needs without conflicting with nature. Organizational forms based on voluntarism, mutual aid[434] (rather than competition), and respect for all forms of life (federations of freely associating groups of producers and consumers) are intended to replace state institutions. P. Kropotkin, considering historical data but also ethnographic studies of tribal peoples like the Buryats (a Mongolian people) and the Kabyles (a Berber people living in Algeria and bordering areas of Tunisia), argued that it is not competition but mutual aid that is the norm of social organization. As a result, networks of cooperation, benefiting everyone involved, are a constant feature of human societies[435].

P. Kropotkin is convinced that the state destroys both individual and collective initiative and is a fundamental obstacle to the "development of society on the principles of equality and freedom because the state is a historical form created to obstruct such development"[436]. At the same time, he notes that the rural cultures mentioned above (such as the Kabyle people) not only owned and worked on the land together (collectively draining swamps, building roads, bridges, and defensive structures, etc.) but also developed systems of customary law guaranteed not by coercion but by the moral authority of the assembly of the people (formerly as a group of assembled individuals to discuss matters of common interest). These examples demonstrate that the principle of voluntary and direct association has over time provided the basis for a strong and creative social fabric[437]. He adds that mutual aid did not disappear from the stage with the rise of the feudal system. While the authoritarian tradition is strengthened around monarchs and barons

---

434 Mutual aid suggests that if humans were in constant opposition to each other, we wouldn't be able to create sustainable human communities. As relatively slow creatures, we might have vanished from the stage of evolution long ago. See more: P. Kropotkin, *Pomoc wzajemna jako czynnik rozwoju*, Poznań 2006, pp. 3–15, 146–194.

435 P. Kropotkine, *Mutual aid. A factor of evolution*, London 1987 (Franch edition: *L'entraide. Un facteur de l'évolution*, Montréal 2005), Quoted from: D.F. White, G. Kossoff, *Anarchisme, libertarisme...*, p. 150.

436 P. Kropotkin, *Państwo i jego rola polityczna*, Warsaw 1924, p. 3, http://www.biblioteka-cyfrowa.pl/Content/77566/Kropotkin_P_Panstwo_i_jego_rola_historyczna.pdf (7.10.2019).

437 D.F. White, G. Kossoff, *Anarchisme, libertarisme...*, p. 150.

(in the 12th century and subsequent centuries), Europe simultaneously experiences an important counter-current in the form of the "communal revolution." From this moment, we observe the slow growth of hundreds of cities with a desire to liberate themselves from the authority of power to govern themselves. These "free cities" not only experienced a highly decentralized form of local organization but also developed a new form of mutual aid, namely guilds[438], which allowed brotherly and egalitarian associations to engage in trade and craftsmanship[439]. P. Kropotkin believed that only a community, as opposed to other forms of collectives, guarantees the fullness of freedom.

While there are many ecological themes within classical anarchism, the similarities between the thinking of ecologists and anarchists have emerged relatively recently (mainly since the publication of Murray Bookchin's essay *Ecology and Revolutionary Thought* in 1965). It would not be an exaggeration to say that the ideas and works of M. Bookchin, who has been writing about ecological issues since the 1950s and has been linking these issues with revolutionary social anarchism since the 1960s, paved the way toward an ecological society, an ecology of freedom. Murray Bookchin and other representatives of social ecology place ecology and ecological solutions at the heart of anarchism and anarchist ideals, analyzing various aspects of the green movement[440].

Quoting Murray Bookchin, "both the ecologist and the anarchist place a strong emphasis on spontaneity" and "recognize that greater unity is achieved through diversification. Every expansion is created by diversifying and enriching its parts"[441]. As an ecologist, he wants to expand the scope of the ecosystem and promote free play among species, much like an anarchist aims to broaden the scope of social experiences and eliminate all obstacles in its development. Here, anarchist concerns about free development, decentralization, diversity, and spontaneity find reflection in ecological ideas and concerns. Hierarchy, centralization, the state, and the concentration of wealth inherently reduce diversity and the free development of individuals and their communities, thereby weakening the social ecosystem and the actual ecosystems in which people are a part. For M. Bookchin, the relentless growth of capitalism "at any cost"

---

438 Guild (confraternity) is the term for medieval merchant and crafts associations.
439 D.F. White, G. Kossoff, *Anarchisme, libertarisme...*, p. 151.
440 R.F. Nash, *The Rights of Nature. A history of Environmental Ethics*, London 1989, pp. 164–165.
441 *Ibidem.*

inevitably leads to the "cancer of the biosphere" and ecological ruin[442]. As he writes, "we must preserve and encourage diversity," but in modern capitalist society, "everything that is spontaneous, creative, and individualized is limited by norms, rules, and massification"[443].

Social ecologists consider it essential to attack hierarchy and capitalism rather than civilization as the main cause of ecological problems. This is one of the key points where they disagree with advocates of the second stream of anarchist ideas, known as primitivists. The latter seem to be much more critical of all aspects of modern life, with some even calling for the "end of civilization." In extreme cases, anarchist primitivists argue for a return to the "hunter-gatherer" forms of human society, completely rejecting technology. The struggle for change is thus a struggle against civilization and for the Earth, where technology should be eliminated[444]. This is a biocentric stance aiming to promote solidarity not only between humans but also between humans and the natural environment[445].

However, very few anarchists go to such extremes. Indeed, most anarchists argue that "primitivists" are not anarchists, and a return to "hunter-gatherer" societies would result in mass starvation in almost every state, thereby causing a collapse of social infrastructure. They reject "primitivism" and the claim that we can linearly return to our primitive roots, to traditions from thousands of years ago.

In addition to M. Bookchin, the works of other anarchist thinkers, such as P. Geddes, E. Howard, and C. Ward, have played a crucial role in the development of eco-anarchist thought, firmly aligning it with the mainstream of SD. These researchers focus on various aspects of the natural environment, primarily in urban gardens (public and allotment), through participation in urban planning, and in the contemporary debate on sustainable cities. In this context, M. Bookchin, in his 1965 publication *The Crisis in Our Cities*, argues for the need to return to "normal, sustainable, and controlled rhythms of human life, i.e., an environment that meets our expectations as individuals and biological

---

442 https://www.revue-ballast.fr/bookchin-ecologie-radicale-et-municipalisme-libertaire/ (20.08.2018).

443 *Ibidem*.

444 *L'En Dehors: Quotidien anarchiste individualiste*, http://endehors.net/news/civilisation-primitivisme-et-anarchisme (21.08.2018).

445 The special features of such anarchism are the promotion of veganism and animal rights (eng. *veganarchism*).

beings"[446]. While current trends in urban conglomerations are considered highly undesirable, the idea of returning to a kind of pre-industrial rural past is equally problematic. M. Bookchin argues that "we need a new kind of human community," a community that is "neither an absolute return to the past nor a suburban adaptation to the present"[447]. The way M. Bookchin encourages ecological urban planning is interesting not only because he defends medium-sized cities as potential places for ecological policy but also because he seeks to connect this environmental urbanization project with policies of ecological technology, participation, and citizenship[448].

However, the most crucial question is not whether technology can free humanity from needs but to what extent it can contribute to the humanization of society and the relationships between people and nature. Therefore, the future society must be based on ecological technologies that are both environmental restorers and, more importantly, promote personal and community autonomy"[449].

Regardless of the ongoing criticism of ecoanarchist views, they have played a significant role in inspiring debates in the field of urban sociology and urban planning (clean production, zero waste, contours of a low-carbon economy, the vision of sustainable cities, etc.). Such influences suggest that although the disappearance of anarchist and libertarian thought has long been proclaimed, the quest for self-organized, sustainable societies will draw inspiration from the philosophies of anarchists.

## 3.5. Deep ecology

The term "deep ecology" (DE) originated from the work of Norwegian philosopher Arne Naess (1912–2009) and is essentially attributed to him. This concept, born in the early 1970s, reflects disillusionment with the mainstream of Western culture permeated by consumerism and the ongoing degradation of the natural environment. The author somewhat accuses traditional ecology based on an

---

446 M. Bookchin, *Our synthetic environment*, New York 1962; *idem, Crisis in our cities*, New York–Englewood Cliffs 1965, Quoted from: D.F. White, G. Kossoff, *Anarchisme, libertarisme…*, p. 163.

447 *Ibidem*, p. 164.

448 *Ibidem.*

449 *Ibidem.*

anthropocentric vision of its past passivity, which he sees as the cause of the continued ecological crisis in the world[450].

A. Naess opposed the eco-reformist vision of environmental conservation through technology or nature management, labeling it as "shallow ecology." Therefore, it can be clearly stated that this concept is in opposition to the mainstream of deep ecology. It is a biocentric (ecocentric) approach that attributes equal value to all living beings. Deep ecology is radical in nature, reaching to the very roots of our contemporary problems. According to the creator of this philosophy, if we are to effectively counter the destruction of nature while protecting our own species, it is essential to address the deep causes of the ecological crisis, even the cultural crisis. Implementing immediate solutions (ISO requirements or the "Earth Hour" initiative) that emerge in response to environmental threats, according to the philosopher, is not a solution.

Instead, deep ecology (DE) suggests asking profound, probing questions (why do we live? which values do we truly need? etc.), which are intended to reach the very core of the problem. This process of deep questioning leads to a reassessment of the position that humans occupy in relation to other beings and the entire biosphere. The consequence of this is the adoption of a biocentric perspective, where life itself is the highest value. In other words, this approach recognizes that there is a world, life, and humans are an integral part of it, not the center of the universe, as in the anthropocentric approach. Therefore, humans are part of a larger whole organized in the form of the web of life. Interconnections and interdependence are the fundamental principles organizing reality and have ethical and moral implications for human functioning.

DE points towards a direction of development far from the materialistic or physical conception of human development and signifies a path leading to self-realization and spiritual growth. This approach represents a holistic vision that cannot be reduced to scientific knowledge, permeated with a philosophical, and even mystical, perspective[451].

The shallow (surface) ecology movement, actually one of the most powerful, and the DE movement, which is much less influential, are in conflict, trying to

450 S. Konstańczak, *Koncepcje ekofilozofii* [in:] *Ekorozwój i Agenda 21. Interdyscyplinarny model kształcenia*, ed. P. Pieczyński, Szczecin 2007, p. 130.

451 J. Blondel, *De l'utopie ecologiste au developpement durable*, „Études" 2003, vol. 399, no. 10, p. 331.

attract as many followers as possible. A. Naess characterized the two trends or tendencies in ecology, noting the merits that DE brings with it (see table 9).

*Table 9: The vision of deep ecology by emphasizing the features of two trends according to A. Naess*

| | |
|---|---|
| **Surface ecology movement** | 1. Fight against pollution and resource depletion. Central goal: health and wealth of people in developed countries. |
| **Deep ecology movement** | 2a. Rejection of the vision of humans in the environment in favor of a relational vision, a holistic view in the field (relational, total image of the field). Organisms are nodes in the network or field of the biosphere, where each supports other inherent (internal) relationships. The internal relationship between two things A and B is such that the relationship belongs to the basic definition or creates the foundation of A and B, so that in the absence of this relationship, A and B cease to be what they are. The total field model solves not only the concept of humans in the environment but any notion of things understood as compact entities in the environment—except in situations where the level of verbal exchange is superficial.<br>2b. Egalitarianism of the biosphere is a principle. Adding this clause ("principle") is necessary because every realistic practice requires, to some extent, killing, utilizing, or repressing. The field ecologist's practice leads them to deep respect and even reverence for various forms and ways of life. They acquire knowledge of the interior, a kind of knowledge that others usually reserve for their own kind and is also very limited, as it usually encompasses only a limited number of forms and ways of life. The field ecologist argues that the equal right to life and flourishing is an axiom of obvious and intuitively clear value. Limiting this axiom in humans results from anthropocentrism, whose harmful effects affect the quality of human life itself. This quality of life depends in part on deep satisfaction and pleasure and on the satisfaction we feel in close association with other forms of life. Attempting to ignore our natural interdependence and establish a division of roles between, on the one hand, the "master," and on the other hand, the "slave," has contributed to the alienation of humanity itself. |

Source: A. Naess, *The Shallow and the Deep, Long-Rang Ecology Movement.* A Summary, „Inquiry" 1973, vol. 16, pp. 95–100; quoted from: Ch. Ruelle, F. Neyrat, *Écologie=X. Une introduction*, „Labyrinthe" 2008, no. 30, p. 5.

According to C. Carré, an animator of many deep ecology workshops in France, "A. Naess uses the word 'deep' to describe experiences with ecology (what to do to make contact with nature an intimate experience), as opposed to its simple study. So, while ecology examines relationships between living systems and their environment, deep ecology relates to a sense of belonging to life"[452].

The ethics of deep ecology are based on the following assumptions:

1. The well-being and development of human and non-human forms of life on Earth have intrinsic value, regardless of the utility they may provide to humans.
2. The richness and diversity of life forms contribute to the realization of this value and are values in themselves.
3. Currently, humans excessively interfere with the Earth's ecosystem, resulting in a rapid deterioration of the natural environment.
4. Humans do not have the right to reduce the wealth and diversity of biological life, except to satisfy important human needs.
5. The flourishing of human life and culture is deemed possible only through a significant reduction in the human population. Similarly, the development of non-human life also necessitates a comparable decrease.
6. Policies need to be changed. These policies influence fundamental economic, technological, and ideological structures. The result will be a society completely different from the present one.
7. Ideological changes involve assessing the quality of life rather than adhering to ever-increasing standards of living. It's crucial to recognize the difference between "good quality" and a "race to an exceptionally high standard of living," (which could be harmful to nature)[453];
8. Acceptance of the principles of DE must therefore entail an obligation to participate in the transformation of society and promote its principles[454].

Despite attributing the precursor of Deep Ecology to Arne Naess, an understanding of the essence of deep ecological thinking can also be found in the reflections of Lynn White, an American professor of medieval history. In 1967, he published an article titled *The Historical Roots of Our Ecologic Crisis* in the journal "Science."[455]. According to Lynn White, the dualistic and hierarchical nature of the relationship between humans (seen as masters of nature) and nature, introduced by Judeo-Christianity, is the source of the current ecological crisis. In this

452 *Claire Carré interview*, http://nature-humaine.fr/wp-content/docs/dossiers/ateliers_ecologie_profonde.pdf (25.08.2018).

453 http://nature-humaine.fr/ressources/les-dossiers/ (26.08.2018).

454 S. Konstańczak, *Koncepcje ekofilozofii*, p. 130.

455 L. White, *The Historical Roots of Our Ecologie Crisis*, „Science" 1967, vol. 155, no. 3767, pp. 1203–1207.

tradition, "man is created in the image of God" and possesses a soul, unlike animals. Furthermore, the Book of Genesis introduces hierarchy between them, as all animals, and nature in general, are destined to satisfy human needs. White emphasized that in ancient times, pagan animism acted as a protective barrier for nature. Back then, people believed that trees, rivers, and animals had souls. Christianity, by destroying this paganism, paved the way for humans to exploit nature with a certain indifference. White called the triumph of Judeo-Christianity over pagan animism "the greatest psychological and cultural revolution in the history of humanity"[456]. Despite the passage of time and a kind of crisis of Christianity in industrialized Western societies, the dualistic and hierarchical attitude in the relationship between humans and nature seems to persist in the minds[457]. As seen, L. White's views somewhat stand as an alternative to SD and can be aligned (although there was no such mainstream at that time) with the radical ecological approach known as deep ecology. Additionally, to support this hypothesis, one can refer to his statement that "the ecological crisis will not be solved by further scientific advancements and technology; humans should reconsider their views and relationship with nature (getting closer to nature and realizing the inherent interdependence of living together), somehow return to a kind of paganism." Once again, science and technology must assist us, but relying solely on them indicates a narrow view of the situation"[458].

Even if L. White's thesis is highly debatable today, it is certain that the Western model of the relationship between humans and nature fundamentally differs

456 *Ibidem.*

457 In the context of recent years, a particular role in addressing climate change is played by Pope Francis, who calls for bold legislative actions and labels environmental destruction as a sin. "His voice is all the more important as there is currently no clear leader among the parties to the Paris Agreement. The Pope can be considered such a leader, and one could argue that his words are already a guidepost: 'We know that technology based on the use of highly polluting fossil fuels – especially coal, but also oil and, to a lesser degree, gas – needs to be progressively replaced'" (paragraph 165 of the Encyclical). "Unfortunately, there is very limited progress concerning climate change. Reducing greenhouse gas emissions requires honesty, courage, and responsibility, especially from the most powerful and polluting countries" (paragraph 169). "The problem is that we still lack the culture needed to confront this crisis, and it is necessary to create leadership that would point out paths while trying to meet the needs of future generations."'" (point 53). Quoted from: H. Schudy, *Wokół Szczytu Klimatycznego COP22 w Marrakeszu – Trzeźwośi i Sarmatyzm*, 30th November 2016, http://www.eko.org.pl/index_news.php?dzial=2&kat=20&art=1808 (26.08.2018).

458 *Ibidem.*

from those supported by major Asian traditions (Hinduism, Buddhism, Taoism, Confucianism, Shintoism). These traditions acknowledge the "sacred" nature or regard it as a "greater whole," of which humans are only a part. Humans should be careful not to disrupt the harmony of this whole"[459]. Similarly, Islam in its sources contains a deep motivation to respect both the natural and human-transformed environment. Nature cannot be treated purely instrumentally and utilitarianly; it requires respect and adherence to certain moral rules. In Islam, "nature is God's creation, which, with its beauty and order, reflects the goodness and wisdom of the Creator. While man is indeed the most perfect of creatures and these are for his use, it is far from the idea of their objectification and unlimited exploitation. Man should curb his greed and extravagance because true wealth awaits him only in the afterlife"[460]. Islam is far from anthropocentrism; "man is a trustee of the Earth, and he should manage it in an economical and responsible manner, treating sentient beings humanely[461]." K. Waloszczyk raises the question of how much these beautiful ideas of Islam (similarly to other religions) are implemented in practice. In the face of the ecological crisis and global challenges related to the shrinking ecosystems, the great Islamic civilization, encompassing 44 countries and over a billion people, is not untouched by these issues[462]. Even though the religion itself may not prevent environmental degradation, similar to economic underdevelopment, its influence on the quality of life and the implementation of various pro-environmental concepts, including SD, is significant.

## 3.6. Ecofeminism

While the position of women was carefully considered in the development of the SD concept[463], ecofeminists criticize this movement, aligning themselves with the radical branch of ecology.

Ecofeminism the relationships between two forms of domination: men over women and humans over nature. Although the term "ecofeminism" was

459 K. Waloszczyk, *Zielony wątek w religiach świata* [in:] *Ekorozwój i Agenda 21.* Interdyscy- plinarny model kształcenia, ed. P. Pieczyński, Szczecin 2007, pp. 85–86.

460 *Ibidem.*

461 *Ibidem.*

462 *Ibidem*, p. 86.

463 It is not a coincidence that a woman, from whom the name of the report defining the concept of SD originated, led the Brundtland Commission. Similarly, the Fourth World Conference on Women held in Beijing in 1995 marked a ten-year cycle and a period of intensive UN activity on other topics of great importance to women, including their role in SD.

introduced by the French feminist F. d'Eaubonne in 1974, the idea developed as an independent movement in the English-speaking world[464]. Many Anglo-Saxon philosophers, such as M. Mellor, C. Kupiec, V. Plumwood, A. Salleh, K. Warren, and also Hindu scholar V. Shiva, have adopted the term "ecofeminism" to emphasize the connections between the exploitation and domination of humans over nature and the exploitation and oppression of women by men[465]. This movement developed in the 1980s, placing at its center the relationships between human domination over nature and its impact on women. The aim was to ensure that women's voices were heard in environmental ethics, which had traditionally focused on the relationship between humans and nature without specifying which humans were considered[466].

In the strict sense of the term, ecofeminism advocates for a matriarchal way of life. It can be considered an alternative social movement that combines feminist ideas with environmental protection issues. Supporters of this movement blame patriarchy for oppressive behaviours towards women and, simultaneously, consider it the main cause of the destructive treatment of nature. Can we identify a parallel between the status of women and the state of the environment? This is the starting point of ecofeminist thought. Born from the intersection of various social movements – feminist, pacifist, and ecological – in the 1970s, ecofeminism focuses on the concepts of capitalism and patriarchy and aims to restore rights to women and the planet. In other words, the emergence of this concept is a result of the aforementioned dominations that have led to the ecological crisis we are currently experiencing.

Ecofeminism is not just a neologism that emphasizes a simple convergence of feminists and environmentalists. It is a very active trend with the goal of advocating for the rights of women and nature. Furthermore, women are not the only ecofeminists. The French poet Louis Aragon wrote in his work titled *Le Fou d'Elsa*[467] from 1963: „For me, a woman is the future of humanity in the sense in

---

464 K.J. Warren, *Le pouvoir et la promesse de l'écofeminisme*, „Multitudes" 2009(1), no. 36, p. 170.

465 A.-L. Gandon, *L'écoféminisme: une pensée féministe de la nature et de la société*, „Recherches feminists" 2009, vol. 22, no. 1, p. 5.

466 C. Larrère, *L'ecofeminisme: feminisme écologique ou ecologie feministe*, „Traces. Revue de Sciences humaines" 2012, no. 22, p. 105.

467 In this work, L. Aragon describes the relationship between the Muslim and Catholic worlds during the Spanish Inquisition, using the fall of Granada and the escape of Muhammad XII, – also known as Boabdil (Emir of Granada from 1482 to 1483 and 1485 to 1492), from Isabella I of Castile (queen of Aragon from 1479 to 1504).

which Marx said that man is the future of man"[468]. Can we talk about women without talking about nature?[469] In her 1990 pilot article, K.J. Warren presents the "power and promise of ecofeminism" and emphasizes the mutual interweaving of both issues: the importance of feminism for environmental ethics, and equally important, the significance of ecology for feminism[470]. This is because nature is an integral part of the women's cause. In reality, ecofeminism has developed more in the first direction: it seems to be more similar to the feminist movement within environmental ethics than to constitute a form of feminism—of an ecological kind—within many feminist tendencies[471].

Since the 1990s, ecofeminism has split into two streams: socio-economic and mystical. The socio-economic stream is represented by Vandana Shiva, who condemns both male domination over women, i.e., patriarchy, and the domination of the North over the South. Her main goal is to liberate women from socio-economic and technological influence of men, assimilate them, and connect them to nature. "We regard feminist issues as the devastation of the Earth and its beings by corporate warriors and the threat of nuclear annihilation by military warriors. It is the same masculinist mentality that would deny us the right to our own bodies and sexuality, and which depended on many systems of state rule and power to achieve its goals"[472]. Therefore, male dominance creates a system of exploitation, violence, and predation on women and nature, which, along with capitalism, becomes an "economy of plunder." This is the system that V. Shiva's ecofeminism challenges. The precursor of this movement calls for the regeneration of the economy, ecosystems, and human social life, both biological aspects (health, reproduction, food,

468 http://cafes-philo.org/2016/01/quel-est-le-role-de-la-fete/ (1.09.2018); Z.J. Zdybicka, *Człowiek – zbawcą człowieka? Uwagi o marksistowskiej teorii religii* [in:] *Wobec filozofii marksistowskiej: polskie doświadczenia*, ed. A.B. Stępień, Lublin 1990, pp. 171–200.

469 From antiquity to the Renaissance, the Earth was perceived as a living entity, more precisely as an adoptive mother carrying life within itself; even minerals were considered living entities that "grew in the belly" of the Earth and regenerated there. Quoted from: C. Merchant, *The Heath of Nature: Women, Ecology and the Scientific Revolution*, Harvard 1996, p. 78, Quoted from: C. Larrère, *L'écoféminisme…*, p. 107.

470 K.J. Warren, *The power and the promise of ecological feminism* [in:] *Environmental Philosophy. From Animal Rights to Radical Ecology*, ed. M. Zimmerman, New Jersey1990, pp. 325–345.

471 C. Larrère, *L'écoféminisme…*, p. 106.

472 A.-L. Gandon, *L'écoféminisme…*, p. 15.

etc.) and cultural and political aspects (human rights, democracy, art, etc.)[473]. According to V. Shiva, women are guardians of nature and tradition. This is especially evident in the impoverished towns of Africa, where they play a leading role in the social and solidarity economy[474]. These factors explain the strong involvement of women in the struggles of the poor concerning environmental issues in the Global South. To some extent, the fight for the natural environment can be achieved only when impoverished women maintain a certain autonomy from men. This presents an opportunity to strengthen the position of poor women and create a situation conducive to ecological awareness expressed in femininity. This is undoubtedly one of the factors explaining the significance and specificity of ecofeminism in the Global South. J. Martine, in her article on ecofeminism, notes that "in Northern countries, ecofeminists often emphasize the emotional dimension of their commitment, fear of future ecological disasters, raising the intensity of their feelings, allowing them to take action and criticize their own blindness of Western rationality leading to catastrophic consequences. Activists in the South also have this emotional expression, but according to the author, the latter are more proud of being on the «stage» as women, with their traditional female skills of resistance and organization"[475]. Against this background of differences, J. Martine also makes a distinction between feminism and ecofeminism from the North/South perspective. "Firstly, feminism in the North (and equality

---

473 J. Martine, *L'écoféminisme et les mobilisations pour l'environnement dans les pays du Sud», suivi de « Le débat sur le care dans le féminisme nord-américain et sa convergence avec l'écofémi- nisme*, „Les Possibles" 2017, no. 14, p. 2.

474 The term "social and solidarity economy" (SSE) emerged in the 1980s. Despite small differences in approaches to defining SSE, it can be considered as an economy serving a different kind of development. Today, we speak of social and solidarity economy to refer to businesses and associations that focus more on social or ecological value added than on the pursuit of financial benefits. This social utility, difficult to quantify, is at the core of the economic project of the social and solidarity economy organization. The initiative "Women at the Heart of the Social and Solidarity Economy" brings together women from all regions of the world to share feminist experiences and perspectives on the social and solidarity economy. These discussions help identify opportunities and alternatives for the future. For feminists, SSE represents a vector for the development of women's security and economic autonomy, equal access to goods and services, and fair wage distribution in society. See more: D. Fournier, *Femmes au coeur de l'économie sociale et solidaire*, Montréal 2011, http://www.reliess.org/wp-content/uploads/2011/04/Document-pr%C3%A9paratoire-Femmes-au-coeur-de-lESS.pdf (7.09.2018).

475 J. Martine, *L'écoféminisme…*, p. 2.

movements in the South) usually emphasizes the emancipation of women from traditional family roles through access to paid employment and valued careers, power in the economy. In this strategy, equal rights are the decisive requirement. In this strategy, equal rights are the decisive requirement.

Meanwhile, feminism in the South, of course, also fights for equal rights, but in peasant, indigenous, and environmental movements, it emphasizes the collective strengthening of women's positions based on their roles and rights in traditional agriculture or in sustaining the family. Secondly, feminism has recently emerged in the context of the ecological challenge to the capitalist mode of development. In this context, national production, especially family farming, can serve as a resilience function against pauperization and environmental damage. Furthermore, in the face of soil impoverishment due to capitalist agricultural practices, as well as necessary relocations, family farming is a formula for the future in the sustainable and «care for the world» economic project. In peasant agriculture, there is, however, a significant necessary share of national production, partially organized within families and partially within cooperative structures. Therefore, both in terms of strength in the social project, it is understandable that ecofeminism is not enchanted by the wage system but values forms of female autonomy in domestic work (and the solidarity economy!). In short, in the current era of the expansion and crisis of capitalism, we must listen to the diversity of achievements of both fighters' cultures, equality feminism and ecofeminism, and integrate their mutual criticism"[476].

The second stream of ecofeminism is much more esoteric and involves a number of authors drawing inspiration from religious currents. They perceive women as "beings close to Nature, speaking about Mother Earth" and aspire to beliefs that do not establish relationships of domination between women and men, as well as between humans and nature. Their goal is to transcend hierarchical and dualistic understandings of the world[477]. Even if these two streams have different approaches, their critical analyses of patriarchy, capitalism, the commodification of living beings, the green revolution, and industrial agriculture converge, leading to the same conclusion: women are the only hope for the future. Ecofeminism assumes that, in general, women are more sensitive to the beauty of nature and, consequently, to its threats. Indeed, it is hard to dispute this statement when we observe ourselves, our grandmothers, mothers, and sisters from a young age. This feminine trait leads ecofeminism to view women as almost predisposed to

476 *Ibidem*.
477 C. Larrère, *L'écoféminisme…*, p. 108.

the role of warriors fighting for environmental issues and in the name of ecology. Especially since they perform more household chores and make purchases, especially those that are eco-friendly.

Aware of the above-mentioned currents within ecofeminism and the diversity of thoughts on what it is, it is necessary to return to social ecofeminism represented by two women (M. Mies and V. Shiva), rooted in Southern countries. This perspective adds a third dominant (colonial or postcolonial) to the intersection of two dominants (women and nature). In their 1993 book titled "Ecofeminism," these feminists demonstrate that Southern countries, suffering from the legacy of colonial domination, have realized their economic potential, often deeply degrading their environment. Environmental consequences of development and globalization are increasingly burdening women. They see that their traditional activities (collecting firewood or fetching water)[478] are compromised or hindered by industrialization and the commercialization of agricultural work. At the same time, they are the target of authoritarian directives controlling demography as a major force responsible for environmental problems[479].

Ecofeminism can be interpreted as an expression of the special role of Southern women in the environmental struggle, helping to understand the contrasts and possible complementarity of ecofeminism with equality feminism, which developed in the West at the turn of the 19th and 20th centuries. J. Falquet, in her presentation at the III International Colloquium of Francophone Feminist Researchers held in Toulouse (September 17–22, 2002), drew particular attention to the contradictions inherent in the term "development," indicating that "development directions result from complex power relations and multifaceted struggles between different sectors with conflicting interests". According to the author, the analysis of social relations reveals three main oppositions that can be associated with class exploitation, racism, and gender. "Indeed, we can consider that 'development' is the result of the historical evolution of capital/labor relations in each society. Simultaneously, development is also a product of the system of international relations marked by colonization and imperialism, power relations between East and West, and especially North and South. The third perspective – often

---

478 Many women's movements in southern countries give a political dimension to these indigenous actions and fight against environmental degradation, seeking greater social justice and democracy.

479 C. Larrère, *L'écoféminisme…*, p. 109.

neglected – ultimately shows development as a result of the evolution of gender relations and the sexual division of labor"[480].

On the other hand, the French feminist and professor at École Polytechnique in Paris, E. Badinter, the author of the 2010 publication titled *Conflict. Woman and Mother*, is decidedly opposed to the radical ecofeminist movement[481]. She identifies what she sees as the "sanctification of motherhood and radical ecology" in the environmental movement as a threat to women's rights. According to her, feminism has deviated from the path of emancipation and paradoxically pushes women back into the home, children, and kitchen. E. Badinter questions the idea of maternal instinct altogether and fights against the pressure on women to be perfect mothers—or even mothers at all. She argues that today's expectations for mothers—emphasis on natural, domestic, environmentally friendly child-rearing—regress women in cultural and intellectual development[482]. In the book that sparked a lively discussion both in France and among feminists worldwide, E. Badinter notes that "feminism forgets about its real achievements, gets bogged down in sterile considerations about the differences between women and men, instead of striving for full equality, it tends to conflict genders, reinforce stereotypes, etc."[483].

It is worth noting the activities of a group of feminists gathered around the so-called Maria'M Group, which is based on strong ideals of an original and unique approach to interreligious dialogue among feminists (between Catholic and Muslim feminists). They anchor their commitment to equality and social justice within their traditional religions while simultaneously reflecting on transforming it into feminist activism[484]. A notable expression of the activities of these feminists, who can be termed ecofeminists, is their presence at the World Social Forum organized in 2016 in Montreal, where feminists from Arab countries were also present. A significant example is the statement made by an Algerian feminist and doctoral student at the Faculty of Law at the University of Montreal, S. Amor, who provides many observations regarding the convergence of Catholic and Islamic religions in terms of what women are fighting for in both cultures and around the world: "Both Islam and feminism have a similar project: transforming social relations to establish equality and social justice (…) Ecofeminism allowed me to verbalize the triple domination that I reject: the domination of men over women, the domination of

480 The speech was published in: J. Falquet, *Femmes, féminisme et "développement": une analyse critique des politiques des institutions internationals* [in:] *Regards de femmes sur la globalization. Approches critiques*, ed. J. Bisilliat, Paris 2003, pp. 75–112.

481 E. Badinter, *Konflikt. Kobieta i matka*, Warsaw 2013.

482 *Ibidem*.

483 *Ibidem*.

484 http://cjf.qc.ca/vivre-ensemble/mariam/ (28.08.2018).

humans over nature, and colonial and post-colonial domination (…) Spiritual ecofeminism allows me to reconcile my faith with a kind of feminism focused on social justice and the preservation of the nature in which I live (…) Environmental awareness is evidence of the existence of God, of whom women and men are a part.

A change in our relationship with nature is necessary when we witness the ecological crisis with our own eyes…due to the domination of nature (…) The diversity of people (in terms of species, colors, languages) is part of the divine plan of "mutual knowledge." This places relationships on a cooperative level rather than a competitive one (…) Such a concept promotes the abandonment of the spirit of domination and exploitation and the adoption of muhsin behavior, which is the ethics of maintaining emotional bonds. Therefore, interactions should be characterized by building relationships of kindness and tolerance towards others (…) My faith and spiritual ecofeminism, in which I place myself, converge at the point of social justice. Because justice is a condition for equality, which aligns with ecofeminism, involving the combination of earth protection and equitable resource distribution (…) As a result, faith and ecofeminism lead to social responsibility. This manifests in everyday actions (refusing products from companies that pollute the natural environment or exploit children…). The power of purchasing should be utilized as a lever of resistance to bring about social changes, to eliminate poverty and inequalities"[485].

* * *

P. de Plunkett, in the journal "L'Éthique écologique," points out that "ecology is neither a sect nor a dream. Its domain is realism and the common good in a new form. It constitutes a terrain for dialogue and actions between believers and non-believers, proposing a lifestyle whose genetic code is close to the Gospel"[486].

Following J. Blondel (retired member of the French National Center for Scientific Research – CNRS), these "multiple forms of ecology and the confusion associated with using the same word for different practices, and even ideologies, are a sign that Kantian distinctions between knowledge and thought, freedom and subordination, meaning and knowledge do not resolve the problem of the ultimate relationships that people have with nature"[487].

---

485 S. Amor, *Un féminisme islamique en dialogue: une chance pour le féminisme et un approfondissement de la foi*, „Webzine" 2016, vol. 24, no. 83, http://cjf.qc.ca/vivre-ensemble/webzine/article/un-feminisme-islamique-en-dialogue-une-chance-pour-le-feminisme-et-un-approfon-dissement-de-la-foi/(1.09.2018).

486 P. de Plunkett, *L'écologie radicale: intéressante, utile et même nécessaire*, „L'Éthique écologique" 2008, no. 42, http://www.libertepolitique.com/La-revue/La-revue-Liberte-Politique/L-ethique-ecologique (1.09.2018).

487 J. Blondel, *De l'utopie…*, p. 332.

# 4. A sociological approach to sustainable development

*When I talk about sustainable development, my goal is not nature itself but the interests of humanity, manifested in the sustainability of nature.*

R. Passet[488]

Because sociology is defined as the science of social phenomena, the inherent focus on analyzing the sources of social systems as a reality sui generis has led this science to neglect natural phenomena. Even today, there is a tendency to separate natural sciences and social sciences, assigning each its proper domain – the former to nature and the latter to society. However, an increasing number of researchers and scientists are incorporating environmental issues, realizing the inevitable interrelation between what is social and what is environmental. In doing so, they break away from the previous neglect of nature in the realm of sociological research. It becomes challenging to remain "blind" to the biophysical realities within which societies develop.

The aim of this chapter is to analyze the sociological perspective on SD, which has long been neglected not only in the ongoing discourses between economists and ecologists but also disregarded by sociologists themselves. The first subsection is an attempt to grasp the social pillar of SD, emphasizing its multidimensionality concerning the scope and role of the entities involved in it. The characteristics and essence of this pillar indicate the urgent need to investigate social phenomena and processes, the analysis of which can influence the evolution of existing theoretical frameworks and prompt new interpretations. The second subsection, in turn, reflects a revival of the theoretical debate among sociologists through issues within the scope of the social dimension of SD, materialized by the emergence of the environmental sociology trend.

488 R. Passet, F.-D. Vivien, *René Passet...*, p. 416.

## 4.1. The essence of the social dimension of sustainable development

Despite the fact that the concept of Sustainable Development (SD) from the very beginning included content aspiring to "establish harmony between people and between people and nature" (as stated in the Brundtland report)[489], the social dimension is a weak pillar of sustainable development. Often neglected or forgotten, it is fundamental in its interactions with the other two spheres: the economic sphere and the environmental protection sphere. Hence, the development of theoretical approaches to this dimension of the concept, which we are experiencing, is not so much a complement to the remaining perceptions (economists and ecologists) regarding the future of sustainable development but a parallel foundation in understanding the essence of the SD concept.

In this context, the question arises as to whether the notion of progress or human development is closely linked to the improvement of living conditions (and thus a certain quality of life) and work, which, in turn, are a prerequisite for the growing awareness of ecosystem needs. Human labor is at the heart of the social dimension of SD, and social elements directly or indirectly derived from the contents of the Brundtland concept must be considered in "theoretical" approaches. This is a condition for economic development and environmental respect not leading to the exploitation of certain categories of workers or, at the international level, certain nations. This is the originality of the SD concept. Following R. Brazillier, one can ask how to reconcile what appears contradictory at first glance[490].

The social dimension of SD finds itself between an ecocentric approach (whose main goal is the protection of all living beings) and an anthropocentric approach (whose primary objective is human well-being). In this context, it is important to ask how to find harmony between society and the environment. Harmony

489 Own translation based on Rapport de Brundtland (CMED 1988).

490 R. Bazillier, *Le travail, grand oublié du développement durable*, Paris 2011, pp. 11–13.

among people is approached through the theory of negotiation[491], which focuses on human relationships and is based on conflict resolution between actors for the ultimate goal of reaching a consensus (in the form of an agreement between the actors)[492]. On the other hand, harmony between people and nature can be observed through conservative (preservative) policies, which primarily focus their efforts on nature, sometimes at the expense of the actors[493].

The social pillar of SD is a complex concept encompassing many social categories (such as social cohesion, social institutions, lifestyle, and quality of life, justice), for which there is no consensus and common definition. There have been few theoretical debates in this area, as discussions (between economists and ecologists) on topics falling within the scope of sociologists took place outside the latter. French researchers L. Sébastien and Ch. Brodhag encourage the development of a socio-centric approach to the social dimension of SD. It means placing humans at the heart of the issues and reflections on the relationships between people, as well as what relates to humans and their environment (natural

491 See more: A. Flanders, *Éléments pour une théorie de la négociation collective*, „Sociologie du travail" 1968, no. 1, pp. 13–35, https://www.persee.fr/doc/sotra_0038-0296_1968_num_10_1_1376#sotra_0038-0296_1968_num_10_1_T1_0033_0000 (9.08.2021); I.W. Zartman, *Concevoir la théorie de la négociation en tant qu'approche de résolution de conflits économiques*, „Revue Francaise de Gestion" 2004, no. 153, pp. 15–27, https://www.cairn.info/ revue-francaise-de-gestion-2004-6-page-15.htm (11.08.2021).

492 The shape of the final negotiation outcome and the scope of agreements are largely determined by fundamental concepts of fairness and justice. Achieving a fair agreement is often more important than obtaining the best agreement. Fairness and justice are the primary motivating forces in all human decision-making processes, including negotiations. The goal of negotiations is to build a common ground leading to long-term trust, often involving third parties, the so-called neutral side, to extract issues from emotions and maintain the focus of the involved parties. See more: I.W. Zartman, D. Druckman, D. Pruitt, *Negotiation as a Search for Justice*, „International Negotiation" 1996, no. 1(1), pp. 79–80.

493 See more: L. Sébastien, Ch. Brodhag, *À la recherche de la dimension sociale du développement durable*, „Les dimensions Humanie et sociale du Développement Durable" 2004, no. 3, https://journals.openedition.org/developpementdurable/1133 (12.08.2021).

environment). Analyzing "social cohesion"[494], reveals a crucial element in realizing the assumptions of the SD concept. Therefore, it is not surprising that many development strategies of countries and international organizations refer to its definition set by the Council of Europe in 1997 as "one of the most important needs of a wider Europe and (…) an essential complement to the promotion of human rights and dignity"[495]. The focus of various international relations actors on "social cohesion" signifies a response to changes in society that increase the risk of inequality and instability. This social category thus considers interactions between different social entities and the extent to which they manage to ensure

494 "Social cohesion" is a term that emerged only in the 1990s (coined by British sociologist R. Pahl), but its roots can be traced back to É. Durkheim's work on the concept of "solidarity," as well as later works by J. Rawls on "justice" and N. Elias and his concept of "bonds." Social cohesion is a multidimensional term, leading to the development of two discourses in approaching this idea. In a narrow interpretation, social cohesion means "reducing differences in individuals' access to work and reducing poverty, thus reducing social inequalities and social exclusion." As a result, the main focus of research related to this term is the issues of unemployment, poverty, and social exclusion. A broader understanding of this term refers to the relationship between social cohesion and quality of life. In this sense, social cohesion means "the ability of society to provide prosperity to all its members while simultaneously minimizing internal differentiation and avoiding polarization." Therefore, taking into account these two discourses, the essence of "social cohesion" is the improvement of quality of life by creating a sense of community in society. See more: E. Jastrzębska, *Spójnośi społeczna w kontekście społecznej odpowiedzialności przedsiębiorstw. Definiowanie, pomiar i dobre praktyki biznesu*, „Optimum. Studia Ekonomiczne" 2017, no 4(88), pp. 115–118. However, it is worth noting that in recent years, a new definition of social cohesion has emerged (created by X. Fonseca, S. Lukosch, F. Brazier): it is "a continuous process of developing prosperity, a sense of belonging, and voluntary social participation of members of society, while simultaneously developing communities that tolerate and promote diversity of values and cultures, and at the same time ensure equal rights and opportunities in society." This definition emphasizes the role of multiculturalism, the value of tolerance that embellishes the construction of cohesion for resilient societies of the future, and links the factor of "sense of belonging" with resilient societies as one of the factors correlated with social mechanisms of inclusion and the development of systems built with the market in mind. Quoated from: X. Fonseca, S. Lukosch, F. Brazier, *Social cohesion revisited: a new definition and how to characterize it*, „Innovation: The European Journal of Social Science Research" 2019, vol. 32, no. 2, https://www.tandfonline.com/doi/full/10.1080/13511610.2018.1497480 (12.08.2021).

495 *Metodological guide on social cohesion policy*, Council of Europe, April 2013, p. 15, http:// www.coe.int/t/dg3/socialpolicies/socialcohesiondev/source/GUIDE_en.pdf (14.08.2021).

well-being for everyone[496]. This concept is gaining importance in the quest for "balance" in society[497], which, in turn, addresses the needs of individuals in terms of personal development and a sense of belonging. It combines individual freedom with social justice, including a fair distribution of resources, economic efficiency, pluralism, and shared principles for peaceful conflict resolution[498].

Alongside "social cohesion," the term sustainable communities[499] is increasingly appearing in the policies of individual countries or international organizations (e.g., the EU). Despite various definitions, it is usually referred to as communities that are planned, built, and modified to promote sustainable living where people want to live and work now and in the future[500]. These communities prioritize safety, environmental sensitivity, and social inclusion[501]. The essence of these sustainable communities, similar to the concept of SD itself, is sustainability. In the social context, this can be understood as the "ability of society itself or its manifestation as a local community to self-sustain and regenerate the functioning of that society at an acceptable level"[502]. This is related to the aforementioned

---

496 *Ibidem.*

497 "Social equilibrium" is a theoretical state of balance in a social system that refers both to internal balance among interconnected social phenomena and to the external relationship the system maintains with its environment. It is the tendency of a social system, when disrupted, to return to its original state because after any small change in a social element, changes occur in other related elements that work towards reducing the initial disturbance. American sociologist T. Parsons postulated that all social systems have a tendency to approach a state of equilibrium, although no specific system will achieve a state of perfect balance. For T. Parsons, a fully balanced society served more as a theoretical reference point than a description of an actual system. Quoted from: *Encyclopaedia Britannica*, https://www.britannica.com/ topic/social-equilibrium (14.08.2021).

498 *Metodological guide…*, p. 15.

499 https://sustain.org/about/what-is-a-sustainable-community/ (20.08.2021).

500 The concept of sustainable communities was first introduced in a UK government report by the then Deputy Prime Minister J. Prescott in a £38 billion economic, social, and environmental plan. In the document titled *Sustainable Communities: Building for the future*, the government outlined how it planned to address ("step-by-step change") the need for more affordable housing, especially in the south-east of England, and improve the quality of both urban and rural neighbourhoods in line with the concept of SD.

501 See more: M. Raco, *Sustainable Development, Rolled-out Neoliberalism and Sustainable Comminities*, „Antipode" 2005, vol. 37, no. 2, pp. 324–347.

502 N. Dempsey, *Does quality of the built environment affect social cohesion?*, „Urban Design and Planning" 2008, no. 161, pp. 105–114.

"social cohesion" and "social capital"[503] as concepts that encompass social networks, norms of reciprocity, and features of social organization and integration resulting from social behaviors[504].

The construction of such *sustainable communities* requires knowledge and planning skills but also "broad general skills" such as community management, communication, risk-taking, leadership, and partnership cooperation. It is noteworthy that the term "sustainable communities," which emerged from discourses on sustainable development and originally referred to improving the environment (natural surroundings) in which people live, has ultimately been applied to urban areas[505]. Sustainable (equitable) cities have become the driving force behind contemporary social transformation. Most researchers agree that adapting urban forms is one way to reconcile the inevitability of the development of large urban agglomerations with its social and environmental repercussions. Therefore, various ideas (debates continue) are emerging on how to build cities based on the concept of *sustainable communities.* Regardless of the ideas on how to organize cities in line with the concept of SD, the key to their establishment is compromise as a condition for effectively addressing social dilemmas. Cities are also places where many social problems occur simultaneously: unemployment, segregation, or poverty. These entities, therefore, clearly fall within the social dimension of SD, and their activities at the local level can play a significant role in implementing both local SD strategies and those at the supranational level (EU) focused on smart, sustainable development, preventing social exclusion.

However, the crucial aspect in the analysis of the social sense of the sustainable development concept is not only considering the level of activity of social actors

---

503 "Social capital" is a term dating back to the 1970s (Pierre Bourdieu is credited as the term's originator, later popularized by James Coleman). It refers to the capital (as an element of the process of social production and life) whose value is based on the mutual relationships and trust among individuals, allowing them to achieve more economic and social benefits. See more: M. Klimowicz, *Kapitał społeczny. Zagadnienia metodologiczne* [in:] *Kapitał społeczny – interpretacje, impresje, operacjonalizacja*, ed. M. Klimowicz, W. Bokajło, Warszawa 2010, pp. 43–52.

504 N. Dempsey, *Does quality…*

505 This concept gains particular significance in the face of rapid global urbanization, and ensuring a better quality of life in so-called sustainable or balanced cities becomes a key challenge. See a more in-depth analysis of the connections between the built environment and people's subjective perception of well-being: K. Mouratidis, *Urban planning and quality of life: A review of pathways linking the built environment to subjective well-being*, „Cities" 2021, vol. 115, https://www.sciencedirect.com/science/article/pii/ S0264275121001293?via%3Dihub (13.08.2021).

and their problems (the proximity of actors to local issues in organized territorial spaces, whether smaller or larger) but also examining the "quality of life." This is the biggest challenge and a category that has become part of the subject of analysis for sociologists, economists, psychologists, and even political scientists[506]. Measured using economic indicators such as HDI, the quality of life depends on socioeconomic factors, both objective (e.g., health) and subjective (e.g., happiness). Research on the quality of life began to be developed in the 1970s. (back then used to refer to "well-being" - M. Durand and Y. Harf)[507], was coined to describe and measure the impact of various conditions on people's daily lives, taking into account to varying degrees the emotional aspect and social functions rather than purely physical conditions. The complexity of this concept arises from the fact that humans live in a triple environment, which forms the conceptual framework for the quality of life. Following J. Sztumski, "people live in a specific natural environment, where they find their place and obtain the means to exist. Coexisting individuals co-create in the natural environment another environment shaping their existence, i.e., the social environment (…), where structures and rules of their functioning emerge, allowing for better adaptation to the existing conditions determined by the natural environment, but also for their transformation due to the development of human needs". People, by refining tools and using them, bring about transformations in the natural environment. Moreover, through this process, they develop, creating successive civilizations, which also has an impact on their social environment"[508]. Despite the ambiguities surrounding this concept, researchers agree that "quality of life" is synonymous with well-being, mental health, and life satisfaction, which are often, though not always, conditioned by one's social status.

Although the main goal of humans is to achieve prosperity, it is not easy to precisely determine which elements to place in the social sphere. The quality of work and income levels may seem closer to the economic dimension of the SD concept. Their relationships with the environment, as well as the environment's connection with the economy, are more challenging to express. One could argue that environmental challenges are largely social problems, and these are a function of human behavior[509].

506 J. Sztumski, *Jakośi życia jako kategoria socjologiczno-społeczna*, „Studia Ekonomiczne" 2014, no 179, p. 21.

507 M. Durand, Y. Harf, *La qualité de vie. Mouvement écologique – Mouvement ouvrier*, Paris 1977, p. 257, Quoted from: D. Bley, N. Vernazza-Licht, *Villes et qualité de vie* [in:] *Ville et environnement*, ed. E. Dorier-Apprill, Paris 2006, p. 110.

508 J. Sztumski, Jakośi życia…, p. 23.

509 S. Torjman, *The Social Dimension of Sustainable Development*, Ottawa 2000, p. 2.

Another component directly derived from the content of the SD concept that fits into the social dimension of SD is the "ability of future generations to meet their own needs." This statement encompasses not only the material and non-material definition of "needs"[510], but also the element of equality inherent in intergenerational relations and the necessity of passing on the accumulated capital (economic, human, environmental) available to the present generation to future generations. Therefore, the "capabilities" or "possibilities" of a given society determine the subsequent elements for sociological investigations within the framework of the SD concept. To achieve a certain level of development (well-being), we must "act" correctly (do and be), perform a series of actions, and possess various qualities (such as being healthy, socially recognized, respected, having the ability to participate in collective decisions, etc.). These successes can only happen when there is the capability to "do" things and achieve desired states. Amartya Sen advocates for "capabilities equality," achievable through the internal and instrumental role of democracy. According to him, human development is a moral imperative that should be realized within a democratic framework because only such a system provides people with the opportunities to assert their rights and entitlements to life. This way of thinking certainly influenced the shaping of the main assumptions of the SD mainstream, such as civic participation (see Chapter 1). Capabilities (possibilities) according to Amartya Sen are a kind of freedom, for example, the freedom to achieve material things in accordance with and to the extent that the individual sets for themselves. In this approach, the focus is not only on what individuals possess but also on their ability to use their possessions to choose their own lifestyle[511].

---

510 The creator of the most famous definition and classification of needs is considered to be Abraham Maslow and his "hierarchy of needs." Maslow's idea was fully expressed in his 1954 book titled "Motivation and Personality." The hierarchy of needs, often represented as a pyramid, remains a popular framework in sociological research and psychology education. Maslow classified needs into a hierarchy, ranging from the most basic (physiological, safety) to higher-level needs (belonging and love, esteem, and self-actualization). Over time, this hierarchy has been revised, and contemporary scholars prefer to think of these levels as continuously overlapping rather than strictly sequential. Another definition of needs was presented by the Finnish sociologist Erik Allardt in 1972. Based on survey research *Scandinavian Welfare Survey*, he proposed a conceptualization built on three pillars defining human needs: "to have," "to be," and "to love." According to Allardt, the human "being" cannot be limited solely to material possessions, and "to live" does not mean only "to have" but primarily "to be" and "to love." See more: E. Allardt, *Dimensions of Welfare in a Comparative Scandinavian Study*,„Acta Sociologica" 1976, vol. 19, no. 3, pp. 227–239.

511 É. Monnet, *La théorie des „capabilités" d'Amartya Sen face au problème du relativisme*, „Tracés. Revue de Science humaines" 2007, no. 12, p. 103.

The interpretation of the Brundtland concept emphasized further elements within the social dimension of the SD concept. The category of "poverty" comes to the forefront. This phenomenon is one of the key challenges facing the world, as the United Nations already stated in 1994, describing it as "the greatest threat to political stability, social cohesion, and environmental health on the planet"[512]. Low incomes are associated with a poorer state of health, which is particularly impactful for individuals living in poverty. The longer someone lives without adequate income, the faster the risk to their health increases. The risk applies to both the individual affected, influencing their ability to maintain employment in the future and participate in society, and to the state due to the increased costs associated with supporting individuals in need.

Despite attempts to combat this phenomenon, reflected in North-South relations, the gap continues to deepen on various levels. In the face of successive versions of the SARS-CoV-2/COVID-19 pandemic, the prospects in this regard are not optimistic[513]. "Poverty" is a complex phenomenon, as it relates not only to material shortages but is associated with various social concepts concerning organizational and collective response capabilities, such as lack of employment and access to education or healthcare[514]. It also involves a lack of access to natural resources[515], sources of funding, or the inability to make decisions[516]. Conducting qualitative research to deepen our understanding of the various dimensions of this phenomenon is key to better informing and, consequently, creating more effective strategies to combat it. It is important to note that poverty entails inequalities,

512 *Human Development Report (UNDP) 1994*, https://www.undp.org/publications/human-development-report-1994#modal-publication-download (13.08.2021).

513 See more: A. Tinson, *Living in poverty was bad for your health long before COVID-19*, 25 July 2020, https://www.health.org.uk/publications/long-reads/living-in-poverty-was-bad-for-your-health-long-before-COVID-19 (13.08.2021).

514 A. Koffi, *Les contradictions des politiques de ciblage dans les projets de lutte contre la pauvreté dans l'ouest montagneux ivoirien*, DEA 2009, http://www.memoireonline.com/09/11/4823/m_Les-contradictions-des-politiques-de-ciblagedans-les-projets-de-lutte--contre-la-pauvrete-dans-lou31.html (16.08.2021).

515 For more information explaining the negative correlation between natural resource dependence and poverty, see: F.J. Zimmerman, M.R. Carter, *Asset smoothing, consumption smoothing and the reproduction of inequality under risk and subsistence constraints*, „Journal of Development Economics" 2003, vol. 71, no. 2, pp. 233–260.

516 See more: J. Sheehy-Skeffington, J. Rea, *How poverty affects people's decision-making processes*, „Joseph Rowntree Foundation – Inspiring Social Change" February 2017; A. Adamković, *Consequences of Poverty on Economic Decision-Making: Assessing the Verisimilitude of the Cognitive Mechanism*, „Front. Psychol." 13 February 2020, https://www.frontiersin.org/articles/10.3389/fpsyg.2020.00171/full (16.08.2020).

and these inequalities further lead to psychosocial stress, which over time can result in deteriorating health and increased mortality[517]. Therefore, an increase in inequality, regardless of its cause, generates social tensions, potentially leading to social revolutions. All these situations impact the reduction and even the halt of growth, resulting in the blockage of all forms of development. In this context, the key role in improving or counteracting these negative phenomena is played by the construction of civil society. This process is particularly significant in the context of implementing the Rio Declaration of 1992, where the Principle 10 of SD emphasizes that "the best way to address environmental issues is to ensure the participation of all interested citizens at the appropriate level"[518]. The formulation, concise and unambiguous by directly mentioning the "environment" and all "citizens," still seems relatively effective. Moreover, Principle 10 is not only a confirmation of the principle itself but also specifies ways of its implementation, indicating that "each individual shall have appropriate access to information held by public authorities." Additionally, it emphasizes that "States shall facilitate and encourage public awareness and participation" and that "effective access to judicial and administrative proceedings must be provided"[519]. Taking "citizenship" into account in research on SD means considering not only straightforward normative institutional frameworks but also the social condition that corresponds to certain forms of coexistence in a group (such as the culture of deliberation) and certain forms of articulating social relations characteristic of contemporary societies (such as identity fragmentation)[520]. Participation is a two-way communication (power - social entities) aimed at making more effective decisions with strong social support. The basis of a sustainable society is the construction of a civil society that encourages original solutions to shape more cohesive communities, which, incidentally, aligns with one of the main streams of thinking about SD (see Chapter 1).

Following S. Torjman, crucial importance in reducing poverty and inequality worldwide lies in supporting education, which is considered a fundamental

---

517 V. Murali, F. Oyebode, *Poverty, social inequality and mental health*, „Advances in Psychiatric Treatment" 2004, vol. 10, no. 3, pp. 216–224.

518 *Déclaration de Rio sur l'environnement et le développement principes de gestion des fôrets, Rio de Janeiro*, Brésil 3–14 Juin 1992, https://www.un.org/french/events/rio92/rio-fp.htm (16.08.2021).

519 *Ibidem.*

520 R. Nabli, Entrepreneurs, *État et citoyenneté. Le cas de la Tunisie*, „Revue algérienne d'an- thropologie et de sciences sociales" 2010, no. 50, pp. 39–40.

form of social investment[521]. Nowadays, the development prospects of countries or regions are increasingly determined by intellectual potential and knowledge associated with the greatest achievements of modern science. Shaping appropriate civic attitudes in line with the concept of Sustainable Development is a task for the entire education and educational system. Only then will knowledge about the threats and challenges of modern civilization allow for solving problems that we already know are not just the proclamation of "crazy scientists" interpreting data they came to study in their own, self-known way (see more in the IPCC 2021 Report)[522].

The examination of the content of the SD concept shows that the social dimension of RS has been quite clearly specified: "striving for SD requires a social system capable of finding solutions to tensions arising from the persistence of unsustainable development (…). SD involves concern for social justice between generations, which should extend to the present generation." Further in the report, it is stated: "We are capable of improving our techniques and our social organization in such a way as to embark on the path of a new era of economic growth"[523]. However, when it comes to methods of improvement or changes in social organization, it is difficult to find any mention in the report.

Next to "capabilities," one of the complementary criteria highlighted in the social dimension directly emphasized in the Brundtland concept is "justice." In the UNDP report from 2011, Sustainable Development and Justice: A Better Future for All, the need for greater efforts towards the just development of humanity was underscored by addressing gender inequalities and equalizing opportunities for marginalized communities[524]. If capabilities cannot be increased, then justice is limited among individuals of the same generation. When there is no reinforcement of capabilities, vulnerability to risks (poverty and exclusion) increases. In such cases, the transmission of capabilities between generations is weakened, creating a loss for the next generation, meaning intergenerational justice is no longer respected. We can draw conclusions from these proposals and create a definition for the social scope of Sustainable Development. "Development is sustainable in social terms if public policies (encompassing ecological, economic,

521 S. Torjman, *Community-Based Poverty Reduction*, Ottawa 1998, pp. 4–5.

522 See more: *Sixth Assessment Report (AR6)*, Climate Change…

523 Own translation based on Rapport de Brundtland (CMED 1988).

524 *Human Development report 2011. Sustainability and Equity: A Better Future for All*, http://hdr.undp.org/sites/default/files/reports/271/hdr_2011_en_complete (17.08.2021).

and social issues) do not cause social dysfunctions that may question the ability to improve well-being for both the current and future society"[525].

An inherent element of the definition of Sustainable Development is "intragenerational and intergenerational solidarity." While the former relates to the distribution of well-being or its conditions within the same generation, the latter seeks methods for determining well-being in the future and for future generations. In this context, the concept of the social dimension of SD suggests that "public policies" should create conditions for improving the well-being of both the current generation and future generations. New mechanisms must be developed at the heart of public policies to avoid severe social crises[526].

* * *

SD is necessarily "focused on people who care about the planet (…), guided by values of equal rights and social justice; it requires proactive states and efficiently functioning institutions, and will only become a reality with the involvement of citizens who take matters into their own hands"[527]. To be socially sustainable, development must fulfill promises of material well-being, encompassing good health, education, and access to essential goods and services for a decent life. Accompanying this will be social, cultural, and political achievements that can give individuals a sense of security, dignity, and the ability to be part of a community through recognition and representation. All these conditions are inseparably linked to environmental resources necessary for sustaining life, health, and well-being[528].

The perspective on social sustainability involves not only concern for social issues and problems but also the recognition and understanding of how social

525 *Ibidem*, p. 83.

526 J.L. Dubois, F.R. Metieu, *La dimension sociale du développement durable: reduction de la pauvreté ou durabilité sociale?* [in:] *Développement durable? Doctrines, pratiques, évaluations*, ed. M. Jean-Yves, L. Guillaume, Paris 2002, p. 92.

527 UNRISD, *Les facteurs sociaux du développement durable*, Au dèla de 2015, „Synthèse" 2014, no. 4, p. 1.

528 *Ibidem*.

factors[529] impact the outcomes of development. Experts from the United Nations Research Institute for Social Development (UNRISD) highlighted the importance of social structures, institutions, and agencies in determining social, economic, political, and environmental outcomes. They also emphasize the complex interactions among various determinants of development, synergies between policies and programs in different areas, and the need for coherence and coordination between sectors, various actors, and levels—local, national, and global[530].

* * *

The social dimension of SD presents a wide range of actors and complex determinants of their behavior that influence the achievement of any sustainable development goal. Due to the fact that power structures, inequalities, knowledge and beliefs, social norms, and management methods impact individual or collective

529 Among these factors are: 1. Appropriate social policy – it plays a crucial role not only in reducing poverty but also in promoting economic development and social inclusion. It can be significant in ensuring "equality of access" to goods, services, and resources essential for SD. 2. Social reproduction and care economy are the foundation of a vibrant and sustainable society and economy. This involves invisible and mostly unpaid caregiving work for children, the sick, and the elderly. It encompasses responsibilities that, in the majority of households, fall on women. However, this is an issue that is still often overlooked despite the considerable attention given to gender equality and the conditions of women in development programs. 3. Equality of opportunities – in the face of developmental environmental inequalities, there is currently a tendency for development initiatives to work towards equal opportunities through projects aimed at leveling the initial conditions faced by individuals or groups (equal access to healthcare or education). 4. Employment-based economic policies – to focus economic policy on employment, it is necessary to coordinate a range of macroeconomic, sectoral, and social policies, including employment policies. For it to be sustainable, job creation and overall economic policy must also be "green." The "green economy" has emerged as an approach to SD that benefits everyone, as it creates jobs, stimulates growth, and simultaneously limits the negative impact on the environment. 5. Social and Solidarity Economy – this concept is often illustrated by ideas such as food sovereignty, *buen vivir*, and happiness, which aim to defend values and lifestyles associated with discrete consumption, living in harmony with the environment and others, responding to a deep sense of belonging. 6. Participation and Responsibility – participatory mechanisms must enable groups in unfavorable situations to voice their concerns, assert their rights, mobilize collectively, and participate in decisions that affect them. On the other hand, public and private institutions should be responsible for engaging society in greater activity and providing legal and physical avenues for expressing them.

530 UNRISD, *Les facteurs sociaux…*, p. 2.

behaviors, predicting the outcome of these interactions is challenging. Therefore, for policies to be in line with SD, it is necessary to consider, in both theoretical considerations and attempts at application, the three pillars on which SD is based. Additionally, it is crucial to ensure that they are coherent and flexible. Coherence, in this context, means that progress in one area does not pose threats in another. It can be said that SD encompasses many social categories explicitly or implicitly derived from the concept, and appropriately defining and considering them in the development strategies of nations can influence the process of more effectively solving complex social problems. Therefore, SD should be viewed as a "complex lens" applicable to the world, requiring comprehensive and more sophisticated solutions than those applied so far. However, it should be emphasized that these recommendations stem from interpretations of the concept, which researchers, societies, nations, states, and organizations may undertake in their own way. Therefore, there is not one but many variations of SD, but each of them should take into account the three spheres that form its framework. Crucial in this regard is the consideration of the diversity of political, economic, and cultural systems to collaboratively work out compromises, creating the foundations for a strong partnership.

Therefore, in the face of one's own observations and following S. Torjman, the identification of priority areas fitting into the social pillar of SD manifests in two aspects. Firstly, priority areas of this dimension are directly and indirectly derived (somewhat hidden) from the Brundtland concept itself and rooted (embedded) in the principles underlying the concept of SD[531]. Secondly, the main guidelines stem from the conclusions outlined in key international documents[532], and the focus on issues such as poverty, social exclusion, peace and security, human rights, health, and respect for cultural diversity is an expression of warnings from international organizations in the face of the rapid increase in these problems.

## 4.2. Environmental sociology

Key role in the context of SD was played by *environmental sociology (fr. Sociologie environnementale)*. It emerged as a mainstream sociology in the 1970s, following the media coverage of the Meadows report in 1972. This report helped highlight the high degree of dependence of human societies on their environment, and thus, on the natural environment. American sociologists R. Dunlap and

---

531 More on the principles of SD: K. Stachurska-Szczesiak, *Rozwój samopodtrzymujący…*, s. 93–114.

532 S. Torjman, *The Social Dimension…*, p. 2.

W. Catton are considered precursors of this trend. They argued that the oil crisis of 1973 underscored the failure of sociologists to consider the potential impact of environmental limits and constraints on humanity[533]. Thus, they propose a paradigm shift in sociology: moving from the old Human Exemptionalism Paradigm (HEP) – which characterized sociology's worldview by believing that humans are exempt from environmental constraints due to their powerful inventive capacity, to the *New Ecological Paradigm* (NEP). The latter paradigm aligns with the limitations of nature, seeking to understand how resource scarcity and environmental constraints shape social phenomena. It is based on several assumptions:

- firstly, humans are one of many species, all of which are interdependently involved in biotic communities that shape social life,
- secondly, the entanglement of causes, effects and feedbacks in the natural world has many unintended consequences that differ from the intentions of human action,
- thirdly, the world is a finite reality, so there are powerful physical and biological barriers that limit economic growth, social progress and other social phenomena[534].

Environmental sociology departs from the paradigm of the autonomy of social reality shaped by the French philosopher and precursor of modern sociology, É. Durkheim. Durkheim treated sociology as the analysis of social facts in relation only to other social facts[535]. Hence, research in environmental sociology is considered to have demonstrated the openness of the sociological paradigm, allowing for the consideration of the environment mainly through the study of the social consequences of natural phenomena. On the other hand, without replacing the sociological artifact, the environment enables this discipline to redefine its place in the entire scientific system. In the early 1990s, R.E. Dunlap created a model titled "Major Causes of Environmental Problems," which reflects his anthropocentric thinking about environmental sociology[536] (see figure 4).

---

533 M. Szuba, *Gouverner dans un monde fini: des limites globales au rationnement individuel, sociologie environnementale du projet britannique de politique de Carte carbone (1996–2010)*, Université Panthéon-Sorbonne – Paris I, 2014, (rozprawa doktorska), https://tel.archives-ou- vertes.fr/tel-01794527/document (27.08.2021), p. 10.

534 *Ibidem*, p. 11.

535 A. Papaux, D. Bourg, *Dictionnaire de la pensée écologique*, Paris 2015, pp. 943–946.

536 J.M. Jermier, *Exploring Deep Subjectivity in Sociology and Organizational Studies*, „Organization & Environment" 2008, vol. 21, no. 4, pp. 460–470.

*Figure 4: R. E. Dunlup's model.*

The main environmental problems include:

- population (P.R. Ehrlich)[537] →
- technologies (B. Commoner)[538] →
- culture system (L.A. White)[539] → Environmental problems
- social system (A. Schnaiberg)[540] →
- personality system (Pogo comic)[541] →

Source: R.E. Dunlop, *From environmental to ecological problems* [in:] *The Sociology of the Environment*, M. Redclift, G. Woodgate, Cheltenham 1995, pp. 89–118.

---

537 The author of *The Population Bomb* is Paul R. Ehrlich. This book, published in 1968, addressed the issues of overpopulation and expressed concerns about a potential massive famine in the 1970s and 1980s due to the rapid growth of the world's population. Ehrlich called for immediate political actions aimed at controlling population growth. See. P.R. Ehrlich, A.H. Ehrlich, The *Population Bomb Revisited*, „Electronic Journal of Sustainable Development" 2009, vol. 1, pp. 63–71.

538 The author of *The Closing Circle*, published in 1971, is Barry Commoner. In this book, he suggested that the American economy should undergo restructuring to adapt to the uncompromising laws of ecology. Commoner argued that modern industrial technology and intensive fuel production pose a threat to humanity as a whole. He criticized the capitalist system, attributing the environmental crisis to it. The book was successful in drawing attention to how little people were aware of the impact of their behaviors, habits, and lifestyle on the natural environment. See. B. Commoner, *Zamykający się krąg*, Warszawa 1974, p. 390.

539 L.A. White, in his works *The Science of Culture* (1949) and *The Evolution of Culture* (1959), conceptualized culture as a thermodynamic system devoid of determinism, where technology and energy play a crucial role. According to his theory, humans, in order to survive and develop, adapt to nature by utilizing the surplus of accumulated energy. See. G.B. Pepper, Leslie A. *White's Theory of Cultural Evolution*, „The American Cath- olic Sociological Review" 1960, vol. 21, no. 4, pp. 319–330. W 1967 r. L.A. White, in his research while searching for an ecological crisis, concluded that Christianity, being the most anthropocentric religion in the world (establishing relationships of human dominance over the rest of creation), is the primary driving force behind ecological catastrophes. Thus, Western culture has a detrimental impact on the natural environment.

540 A.Schnaiberg, an American sociologist, made his contribution to environmental sociology. His publication "The Environment: From Surplus to Scarcity" from 1980 represents one of the early contemporary sociological approaches to understanding environmental issues. His concept of the Treadmill of Production (TOP) arose from

R.E. Dunlap demonstrates that environmental problems are associated with technical, demographic, cultural, social, and personal factors, connecting each of them to the individual. The model by R.E. Dunlap was somewhat modified in 1996 by Canadian environmental sociologist J.-G. Vaillancourt. He asserts that to address environmental issues, action should be based on five types of strategies: reducing the population, implementing gentler technologies, changing the social system, raising awareness of human values, and altering behaviors (both individual and collective)[542] (see Figure 5).

*Figure 5: J. G. Vaillancourt's model.*

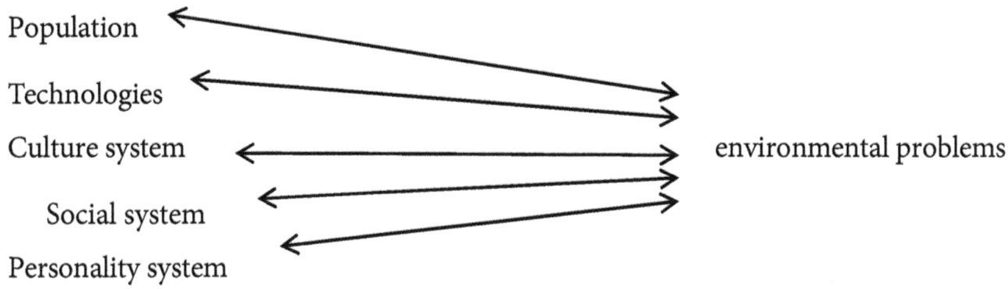


Source: J.G. Vaillancourt, *Sociologie de l'environnement: de l'écologie humaine à l'écosociologie* [in:] *La recherché sociale en environnement: nouveaux paradigms*, ed. R. Tessier, J.G. Vaillancourt, Montréal 1996, p. 31.

---

two observations. Firstly, there was a significant change in the impact of production processes on ecosystems in the second half of the 20th century. Secondly, societal and political responses to these production processes were quite variable and unstable. The underlying idea of this theory is that humans are dependent on a constant flow of energy from nature, and each of us is in a continuous state of interaction with the surrounding world. See. A. Schnaiberg, D.N. Pellow, A. Weinberg, *The Treadmill of Production and the Environmental State*, New York 2000, pp. 1–10. The reference in R.E. Dunlap's model to A. Schnaiberg's social system resembled the idea that socio-economic models of production and consumption have consistently favored low-cost systems (both economically and socially) but exert strong pressure on the ecosystem.

541 The personality system refers to the comic strip Pogo (which ran from 1948 to 1975) created by W. Kelly. The slogan associated with this character is "We have met the enemy and He is us." By referencing this slogan, R.E. Dunlap reminds us that individual human behaviors are one of the main factors contributing to the ecological crisis, http://www.thisdayinquotes.com/2011/04/we-have-met-enemy--and-he-is-us.html (9.09.2019).

542 J.G. Vaillancourt, *Sociologie de l'environnement: de l'écologie humaine à l'écosociologie* [in:] *La recherché sociale en environnement: nouveaux paradigms*, ed. R. Tessier, J.G. Vaillancourt, Montréal 1996, pp. 19–47.

According to J.G. Vaillancourt's model, it would be necessary to act on each of these variables simultaneously to limit the impact of societies on the environment. Only this reciprocity allows for the comprehensive explanation of environmental sociology: it cannot be limited solely to the content of society's impact on the natural environment, but must also consider the social aspects of natural phenomena. The use of the term "nature" here is significant because the interaction between society and nature encompasses the concept of the environment. Therefore, it is justified to question the significance of E.R. Dunlap's model described above, which integrates only social and human pressures on nature, thus proposing a partial sociology of the environment, excluding the weight of the impact of natural determinants on society.

P. Boudes, a French researcher, further reflected on the possibility of opening sociology to the environment, meaning phenomena that are not entirely socio-cultural and include elements of ecological logic, including "sustainable" or "ecological" lifestyles, etc.[543] P. Boudes drew inspiration from the work of French sociologist M. Jollivet from 1992[544], who formulated a model of mutual relations between the ecosystem and the sociosystem. M. Jollivet considered it necessary to analyze these interactions to understand how humans affect the biosphere and how the biosphere affects humans. In M. Jollivet's model, science and reality are divided into two units: natural and social sciences in one unit, and natural and social reality in the other unit. P. Boudes notes that in M. Jollivet's model, each science functions with each reality, but the model leaves empty spaces (fields). (see table 10).

*Table 10: M. Jollivet's model*

| Reality / Science | Environmental | Social |
|---|---|---|
| **The science of nature** | (A) The study of nature's actions on nature | |
| **Social studies** | | (B) The study of society's actions on society |

Source: P. Boudes, *Apports croisés de la sociologie de l'environnement et de l'analyse des modes de vie. Contextes et perspectives* [in:] *Consommer autrement. La reforme écologiques des modes de vie*, ed. M. Dobré, S. Juan, Paris 2009, p. 10.

543 P. Boudes, *Apports croisés de la sociologie de l'environnement et de l'analyse des modes de vie. Contextes et perspectives* [in:] *Consommer autrement.* La reforme écologiques des modes de vie, ed. M. Dobré, S. Juan, Paris 2009, pp. 10–11.

544 M. Jollivet, *Ecosystème et système sociaux* [in:] *Rapport final du séminaire environnement et société*, Berne 1992, p. 58

Although these two terms (ecosystem and sociosystem) refer to two scientific disciplines (ecology and sociology), studying their relationship is necessary to address the issue of human impact on nature. P. Boudes complements the model of M. Jollivet by filling in previous gaps (see table 11).

*Table 11: M. Jollivet's model supplemented by P. Boudes*

| Reality / Science | Environmental | Social |
|---|---|---|
| **The science of nature** | (A) Study of the activities of nature on nature | (C) Action research society to nature |
| **Social studies** | (D) The study of nature's effects on society | (B) Study of society's actions on society |

Source: P. Boudes, *Apports croisés de la sociologie de l'environnement et de l'analyse des modes de vie. Contextes et perspectives* [in:] *Consommer autrement. La reforme écologiques des modes de vie*, ed. M. Dobré, S. Juan, Paris 2009, p. 10.

P. Boudes also proposes a dynamic approach to the aforementioned model, in which one can locate the sciences: ecology (E), environmental sociology (F), and the mutual interactions of nature and society (G) (tab. 12).

*Table 12: Dynamic approach to P. Boudes' model/Representations of all sciences*

| Action → / On ↓ | Nature (biophysical reality) | | Society (social reality) |
|---|---|---|---|
| **Nature (biophysical reality)** | (A) Natural sciences | (E) | (C) The science of society's action on nature |
| | | (G) | |
| **Society (social reality)** | (D) The study of the effects of nature on society | (F) | (B) Social studies |

Source: P. Boudes, *Apports croisés de la sociologie de l'environnement et de l'analyse des modes de vie. Contextes et perspectives* [in:] *Consommer autrement. La reforme écologiques des modes de vie*, ed. M. Dobré, S. Juan, Paris 2009, p. 11.

This diagram indicates that ecology is both the science of nature that seeks to understand the impact of society on nature and the science of the actions of societies on nature. In turn, environmental sociology is a social science that integrates the analysis of natural actions and their impact on society. Point G is the central point of this model, signifying a departure from the traditional division between natural and social sciences (integrating both the realities of the natural world and the world of society)[545].

In light of the above, the goal of environmental sociology is to pose new questions, describe, and analyze emerging from the awareness of the mutual connections between these sciences. Within the research scope of environmental sociology lies the analysis of individuals' and communities' lifestyles. Routine use of space requires the analysis of the daily functioning paths of people (considering ways in which children go to school, how people travel using transportation means, etc.). This expands the research focus of this rapidly developing science beyond the analysis of the "purely social product," as elements such as transportation usage or people's health force researchers to also consider non-social factors in these analyses. P. Boudes emphasizes this point: "Failure to consider non-social factors in sociology poses threats to the science itself because other sciences begin to take into account various aspects of social phenomena. This opens up room for discussion, and in social matters, no one other than a sociologist has greater knowledge to explain these phenomena to other researchers"[546].

Therefore, the interest in the causes and consequences of social natural phenomena is the main contribution of environmental sociology to general sociology. Furthermore, the increasing importance of natural environmental elements in sociological research is also a result of the scope of this natural environment, which is inseparably linked to globalization processes. The environment is a vector of globalization, so globalizing sociology must more consciously participate in the global environment in its sociological analyses. The development of effective social responses to global environmental crises depends to a large extent on understanding how human-induced environmental changes are deeply embedded in global social, political, and economic relationships, as well as in epistemic structures[547].

The growing involvement of civil society in discussions about improving the state of the natural environment provides a basis for the development of environmental sociology as a separate scientific discipline. This discipline should direct its conceptual and empirical energy in many strategic areas, starting with a deeper theoretical integration of socio-economic aspects. However, this approach is not

545 P. Boudes, *Apports croisés...*, p. 11.

546 *Ibidem*, p. 14.

547 R. Hanuza-DeLay, D.J. Davidson, *The Environment and a Globalizing Sociology*, „Canadian Journal of Sociology/Cahiers Canadiens de Socjologie" 2008, no. 33(3), p. 634.

without challenges because "the environmental crisis imposes a range of social costs that manifest themselves in a complex system of economic, political, epistemological, and ecological processes"[548]. One of the challenges for sociology is the integration of previously independent research methods, including processes of global economic stratification, global distribution of environmental threats, global diversity in environmental decision-making, and paradigms in which social-ecological interaction is perceived[549].

* * *

In summarizing the considerations regarding the theoretical approaches to SD, it is noteworthy that despite their diversity, where the starting point has been the need to protect the natural environment, the perspectives of economists align with the mainstream of SD. However, this does not imply the elimination of further problems or a clear consensus on the concept of SD. Even with the passage of time, philosopher of science E. Nagel's words from 1961 remain significant in this context: "It is widely emphasized that in the field of social sciences, there is almost never complete unanimity, often found among representatives of the natural sciences, regarding established facts, satisfactory explanations of those facts, and the correctness of rational research methods. Social sciences often give the impression of being a battleground for constantly conflicting schools, so that even issues that have long been the subject of intensive research remain unresolved in the field of science"[550]. The lack of unanimity in the field of sciences regarding SD does not undermine this idea; on the contrary, its practical application paradoxically stimulates researchers and theorists to further in-depth analysis in the pursuit of identifying elements that could be labeled as the theory of SD.

548 *Ibidem*, p. 646.

549 *Ibidem*.

550 E. Nagel, *Struktura nauki. Zagadnienia logiki wyjaśnień naukowych*, Warszawa 1970, p. 385, quoted from: R. Bartkowiak, *Ekonomia rozwoju*, pp. 111–112.

# Conclusion

The world is at a critical turning point. This turning point will not come immediately. We are certainly in the middle of this process, which will take decades. In the face of the civilizational crisis posed by the coronavirus pandemic, we should emphasize what unites humanity rather than what divides it, both at the national, European, and global levels[551]. This is, therefore, a time to make real choices. We can try to continue our activities by pursuing the conventional paradigm of economic growth that has dominated economic policy since the end of World War II. Alternatively, we can strive for an ecological version of this model, which brings about "green growth," or choose the path of a radical departure from the mainstream, which does not consider growth as the real goal but aims for sustainable human well-being[552].

In this context, there is currently no more important issue than understanding how to perceive the problems facing humanity today and how to think (in order to act later) to address these problems. The main goal of this publication was to analyze the reasoning perspectives (of economists, ecologists, sociologists) on the concept of SD. The research tasks focused on two issues: 1) Explanation of the origin and evolution of the *sustainable development* concept, focusing on the analysis of thought processes (arising in various scientific disciplines) that led to the materialization of the concept itself (Brundtland Report, 1987) and its goals that set the framework for today's "Transforming Our World by 2030" plan"; 2) Identification of theoretical approaches that have influenced the clarification of the SD concept, as well as those that may play a significant role in the process of understanding what the concept entails and the possibilities it holds for human development.

The conducted research provides a basis for formulating the following conclusions. **Firstly,** the implementation of the SD concept and the examination of its effects have revived the need to revisit theoretical approaches that not only provide access to theoretical knowledge in the field of self-sustaining development but also create opportunities for seeking common scientific solutions leading to more effective application of the concept in the future. **Secondly**, the rapid change in reality caused by SARS-CoV-2/COVID-19, which serves as evidence of the

551 See. L. Dowbor, *Poza kapitalizm...*

552 R. Costanza, H. Daly (et al.), *Building Sustainable and Desirable Economy-in-Society-in-Nature*, Canberra 2013, p. 73.

ecological crisis facing humanity, creates an urgent need for the triangulation of perspectives representing various scientific disciplines. This breaks down the traditional division between social and natural sciences and forms the nucleus of an interdisciplinary "science of SD"[553]. Integrating theories that combine the strengths of various disciplines is an excellent way to create a better foundation for decision-making in the field of SD. Hence, SD requires a thorough change in our thinking, values, and actions. For this reason, theoretical approaches to the concept of sustainable development should be incorporated into all levels of education. Otherwise, as P. Martens points out, sustainable development will be a fiction[554]. **Thirdly,** in the midst of economic and ecological perspectives illustrating ways of thinking about the relationship between humans and nature, the sociological perspective of the concept of sustainable development emerges and develops strongly. This is evidenced by the recent small chapter that specifically considers the theoretical approaches of researchers in this scientific discipline.

Furthermore, by establishing a typology of theoretical perspectives within the concept of SD, it can be said that none of them (except perhaps the historical-institutional approach) provides a satisfactory theoretical answer to the current challenges facing humanity. Therefore, the analysis and clarification of perspectives on what SD is, sometimes visibly contradictory (mainstream and radical streams), aimed not only to highlight similarities and differences (which proved useful from a methodological dimension of scientific research and the use of the comparative method) but also allowed to identify a space for compromise among all those who take the mentioned crisis seriously and seek to overcome it. It can also be said that the apparent "enthusiasm" for the concept of SD, which emerged in the early 21st century, is now facing a crisis in its practical implementation, not fully coping with the injustice of the prevailing development model. Knowledge and awareness of these issues at the conceptual level can become a driving force for even closer integration of research and risk analysis, creating a core knowledge base to respond to global changes.

553 "Science of SD" should consider both practical and theoretical considerations, applying an interventionist approach aimed at breaking down barriers between traditional sciences. However, overcoming barriers due to the complexity of problems in a globalized world must not only concern the level of science but also the geographical scale, meaning going beyond the common view by considering both local and global perspectives.

554 See more: P. Martens, *Sustainability: science or fiction?*, „Sustainability: Science, Practice & Policy" 2006, vol. 2, no. 1, p. 36.

"Sustainable? Durable? Balanced? Long-term? Regardless of the translation, the essence of the concept of sustainable development contained in the Brundtland report is a question that has occupied not only public opinion but also the scientific community for many years. This applies to all disciplines that collectively provide elements for observing, understanding, modeling, and better predicting the future brought about by global change[555]. It has been almost 50 years since the Club of Rome called on the world to consider limiting economic growth. Over 30 years separate us from the Brundtland report, which urged current generations to meet their needs without compromising the ability of future generations to meet theirs. During this time, the term *sustainable development* has become a popular slogan in 21st-century development discourse. However, despite its ubiquity and immense popularity over the years, the concept of SD itself still seems unclear, as many people question what it means and what implications it holds for the theory and practice of development. This concept has attracted widespread attention that other development concepts lack, and it appears to remain a pervasive development paradigm for a long time to come[556]. Despite the dissemination of literature on the practice of sustainable development (SD), as indicated by the research of L. Shi, L. Han, F. Yang, L. Gao, it is no longer sufficient in the context of the dynamic changes in our surrounding reality. Explaining issues related to SD problems requires more than just better data and information about the principles and pillars of SD; we (decision-makers, the academic community, citizens) also need a better understanding of these connections and their implications for future human actions.

This publication is a response to the urgent need for a better understanding (highlighting key perspectives aligning with the three pillars of the SD concept). By presenting an image composed of three distinct elements and demonstrating a connected way of thinking about what the concept is, the process of constructing a "SD theory" creates an opportunity for a perspective on the sustainability[557] of

---

555 See A. Fuchs, *Préface* [in:] *Le développement durable à découvert*, ed. A. Euzen, L. Eymard, F. Gaill, Paris 2013, p. 15.

556 J. Mensah, *Sustainable development: Meaning, history, principles, pillars, and implications for human action: Literature review*, „Cogent Social Sciences" 2019, no. 5; https://www. tandfonline.com/doi/pdf/10.1080/23311886.2019.1653531 (24.07.2020).

557 However, it is important to distinguish between sustainability and sustainable development (RS - Rozwój Samopodtrzymujący in Polish). The term "sustainability" should be considered as the goal or endpoint of the process called sustainable development. Sustainability refers to a state, while sustainable development is the process of achieving that state. Quoted from: *ibidem*, p. 6.

humanity's development. The aim of this monograph was also to reduce the number of questions and uncertainties regarding the understanding of SD issues, thus contributing to the SD discourse by further explaining the paradigm and its implications for human thinking and actions in pursuit of the SD goals outlined in Agenda 2030.

The adopted hypothesis has been positively verified. There is no doubt that the dynamics of changes in the reality of international relations influence the process of convergence and even merging of different perspectives on the SD concept, thereby creating opportunities for the establishment of a truly interdisciplinary science in the future, providing a picture of complex issues and "recipes" for solving them. A significant challenge is transitioning to a better world in a peaceful and positive manner.

In conclusion, one can refer to one of the main precursors of ecological economics, R. Constanza, who states that "there is no way to predict the exact path for transitioning to a better world as outlined by the Agenda 2030 today, but painting a «picture» of a possible endpoint, which is sustainable development, and some milestones along the way will help make this choice and journey a more realistic option"[558].

558 R. Costanza, H. Daly (et. al.), *Building Sustainable...*, p. 73.

# List of Tables

# List of Figures

# Bibliography

## Documents and reports

*Commission on Growth and Development. The Growth Report: Strategies for Sustained Growth and Inclusive Development*, World Bank, Washington 2008.

*Déclaration de Rio sur l'environnement et le développement principes de gestion des fôrets*, Rio de Janeiro, Brésil 3–14 Juin 1992, https://www.un.org/french/events/rio92/ rio-fp.htm.

*Enseignement scientifique. Classe terminale, enseignement commun, voie generale, Conseil Supérieur des Programmes*, Mai 2019.

*European Governance* (*European Governance a White Paper*), Commission of the European Communities, Brussels 2001.

*Human Development report 2011. Sustainability and Equity: A Better Future for All*, http://hdr.undp.org/sites/default/files/reports/271/hdr_2011_en_complete.

*Human Development Report*, UNDP 1994.

*Metodological guide on social cohesion policy*, Council of Europe, April 2013.

*Rapport CGDD. Les filières industrielles stratégiques de l'économie verte: enjeux et perspectives*, „References" Marc 2013.

*PNUE: Vers une* économie *verte: pour un développement durable et une* éradication de la pauvreté–Synthèse à l'intention des décideurs, Rapport PNUE 2011.

*Sixth Assessment Report (AR6), Climate Change. The Physical Science Basis*, https://www.ipcc.ch/report/ar6/wg1/.

UNRISD, *Les facteurs sociaux du développement durable*, Au dèla de 2015, „Synthèse" 2014, no. 4.

## Encyclopedias and dictionaries

https://www.universalis.fr/encyclopedie/mouvement-ecologiste/1-emergence-de-la-pensee-ecologiste/.

Papaux A., Bourg D., *Dictionnaire de la pensée* écologique, Paris 2015. Podsiad A., *Słownik terminów i pojęi filozoficznych*, Warszawa 2000.

## Books and articles

Abbadie L., *L'écologie, une science pour le développement durable* [in:] *Le développement durable à découvert*, ed. A. Euzen, L. Eymard, F. Gaill, Paris 2013.

Abdelmalki L., Mundler P., *Économie de l'environnement et du développement durable*, Paris 2010.

Allardt E., *Dimensions of Welfare in a Comparative Scandinavian Study*, „Acta Sociologica" 1976, vol. 19, no. 3.

Anderson T.L., Shaw J.S., *Is Free-Market Environmentalism, „Mainstream?"*, „The Social Studies" 2000, vol. 91, no. 5.

Badinter E., *Konflikt. Kobieta i matka*, Warszawa 2013. Bartkowiak R., *Ekonomia rozwoju*, Warszawa 2013.

Bartyzel J., *Geneza i próba systematyki głównych nurtów libertarianizmu* [in:] *Libertarianizm – teoria, praktyka, interpretacje*, ed. W. Bulira, W. Gogłoza, Lublin 2010.

Bauman Z., *Kryzys państwa narodowego we współczesnej Europie*, „Przegląd Zachodni" 1994, nr 4.

Baumgärtner S., Becker Ch., Faber M., Manstetten R., *Relative and absolute scarcity of nature. Assessing the roles of economics and ecology for biodiversity conversation*, „Ecological Economics" 2006, no. 59(4).

Baxter B., *Ecologism. An Introduction*, Georgetown 2000.

Bazillier R., *Le travail, grand oublié du développement durable*, Paris 2011.

Béal V., *La modernisationé cologique: Quelle théorie pour quel changement social?* [in:] *Guide des humanités environnementales*, ed. A. Choné, I. Hajek, P. Hamman, Lille 2016.Beck U., *Ponowne odkrycie polityki: przyczynek do teorii modernizacji refleksywnej* [in:] *Modernizacja refleksyjna. Polityka, tradycja i estetyka w porządku społecznym nowo- czesności*, ed. U. Beck, A. Giddens, S. Lash, Warszawa 2009.

Bellamy Foster J., *Marxism and Ecology: Common Fonts of a Great Transition*, „Great Transition Initiative. Toward a Transformative Vision and Praxis" 2015, October.

Bertrand E., Destais Ch., *Le „théorème de Coase", uneréflexion sur les fondements microéconomiques de l'intervention publique*, „Reflets et Perspectives de la vie économique" 2002/2, v. XLI.

Bessy Ch., Favereau O., *Institutions et économie des conventions*, „Cahiers d'économie politique" 2003/1, no. 44.

Billaudot B., Destais G., *Les analyses de la durabilité enéconomie. Fondements théorétique et implications normatives*, Grenoble 2009.

Blaug M., *Economic Theory in retrospect*, Cambridge 1985.

Bley D., Vernazza-Licht N., *Villes et qualité de vie* [in:] *Ville et environnement*, ed. E. Dorier-Apprill, Paris 2006.

Blondel J., *De l'utopie écologiste au développement durable*, „Études" 2003, vol. 399, no. 10.

Blowers A., *Power, Participation and Partnership. The limits of co-operative environmental management* [in:] *Co-operative Environmental Governance. Public-Private Agreements as a Policy Strategy*, ed. P. Glasbergen, Dordrecht 1998.

Boisvert V., Carnoye L., Petitimber R., *La durabilité forte: enjeux* épistémologiques *et politiques, de l'économie écologique aux autres sciences sociales*, „Développement durable et territoires" 2019, vol. 10, no. 1.

Boisvert V., *Des limites de la mise en marché de l'environnement. Des services écosystémiques aux „banques de conservation"*, „Écologie & politique" 2016, no. 52.

Boudes P., *Apports croisés de la sociologie de l'environnement et de l'analyse des modes de vie. Contextes et perspectives* [in:] *Consommer autrement. La reforme écologiques des modes de vie*, red. M. Dobré, S. Juan, Paris 2009.

Boudes P., *Changement social et écologie: où en est la modernisation écologique?*, „Sociologos. Revue de l'association française de sociologie" 2017, no. 12.

Boyer R., *Les institutions dans la théorie de la régulation*, „CEPREMAP" 2003, no. 8. Brandenburg M., Gruchmann T., Oelze N., *Sustainable Supply Chain Management – A Conceptual Framework and Future Research Perspectives*, „Sustainability" 2019, no. 11(24).

Bresson M., *La participation: un concept constamment réinventé*, „Sociologos" 2014, no. 9.

Bryant R.L., Bailey S., *Third World Political Ecology*, London 1997.

Buclet N., *Écologie industrielle et économie circulaire: définition et principes* [in:] *Économie circulaire et écosystèmes portuaires*, ed. Y. Alix, N. Mat, J. Cerceau, Paris 2015.

Buttel F.H., *Ecological Modernization as Social Theory*, „Geoforum" 2000, no. 31(1). Buttel F.H., *Environmental Sociology and the Explanation of Environmental Reform*, „Organization and Environment" 2003, vol. 16, no. 3.

Cichoracki M., *Marksowski materializm historyczny – koncepcja związku między bazą a nadbudową oraz prymatu czynników ekonomicznych*, „Filozofia Publiczna i Edukacja Demokratyczna" 2012, v. 1, no 1.

Combe H., *La gouvernance, une impérieuse nécessité pour le développement durable*, „Développement durable et territories" 2015, vol. 6, no. 2.

Commoner B., *Zamykający się krąg*, Warszawa 1974.

Constanza R., Alperovitz G., Daly H.E., Farley J., Franco C., Jackson T., Kubiszewski I., Schor J., Victor P., *Building a Sustainable and Desirable Economy – in Society-in-Nature*, New York 2012.

Costanza R., d'Arge R., Groot R. de, Farber S., Grasso M., Hannon B., Limburg K., Naeem S., O'Neill R., Paruelo J., Raskin R., Sutton P., Van Den Belt M., *The value of the world's ecosystem services and natural capital*, „Nature" 1997, no. 387.

Costanza R., Daly H.E. (et al.), *Building Sustainable and Desirable Economy-in-Society-in-Nature*, Canberra 2013.

Costanza R., Daly H.E., *Toward an ecological economics*, „Ecological Modelling" 1987, no. 38.

Costanza R., Daly L., Fioramonti I., Giovannini E., Kubiszewski I. (et al.), *Modelling and measuring sustainable wellbeing in connection with the UN Sustainable Development Goals*, „Ecological Economics" 2016, no. 130.

Costanza R., Erickson J.D., Farley J., Kubiszewski I., *Sustainable Wellbeing Futures: A Research and Action Agenda for Ecological Economics*, Cheltenham 2020.

Crowley K., *Jobs and environment: the „double dividend" of ecological modernisation?*, „International Journal of Social Economics" 1999, vol. 26, no. 7–9.

Daly H.E., *A further critique of growth economics*, „Ecological Economics" 2013, no. 88. Daly H.E., Farley J., *Ecological Economics. Principles and Applications*, Washington 2011. Daly H.E., *On Economics as a Life Science*, „Journal of Political Economy" 1968, no. 76. Daly H.E., *Steady-State Economics. Second Edition with New Essays*, Washington 1990. Daly H.E., *Steady-State Economics. The Economics of Biophysical Equilibrium and Moral Growth*, San Francisco 1977.

Daly H.E., *The Economics of the Steady State*, „American Economic Review" 1974, no. 64(2).

Décaillot M., *Favoriser l'émergence de l'économie equitable*, „Variations. Revue internationale de théorie critique" 2007, no. 9/10.

Dempsey N., *Does quality of the built environment affect social cohesion?*, „Urban Design and Planning" 2008, no. 161.

Dermine-Brullot S., Junqua G., Zuindeau B., *Écologie industrielle et terrotoriale à l'heure de la transition écologique et sociale de l'économie*, „Revue d'Économie Régionale & Urbaine" 2017, no. 5.

Destais G., *Les théorisations économiques du développement durable. Proposition de décryptage critique*, Colloque international francophone, „Le développement durable: débats et controversies", 15 et 16 décembre Clermont-Ferrand 2011.

Dietz S., Hope Ch., Patmore N., *Some economics of „dangerous" climate change: reflections on the Stern Review*, „Global Environmental Change" 2008, vol. 17, no. 3–4.

Dobson A., *Environmental Citizenship: Towards Sustainable Development*, „Sustainable Development" 2007, no. 15.

Dowbor J., *Poza kapitalizm. Nowa architektura społeczna*, Warszawa 2020.

Dubois J.L., Metieu F.R., *La dimension sociale du développement durable: reduction de la pauvreté ou durabilité sociale?* [in:] *Développement durable? Doctrines, pratiques,* évaluations, ed. M. Jean-Yves, L. Guillaume, Paris 2002.

Dunlop R.E., *From environmental to ecological problems* [in:] *The Sociology of the Environment*, M. Redclift, G. Woodgate, Cheltenham 1995.

Dupuy J.P., *Convention et common knowledge*, „Revue économique" 1989, vol. 40, no. 2. Dyduch J., *Wykorzystanie analizy kosztów i korzyści oceny projektów inwestycyjnych*, „Managerial Economics" 2011, no 10.

Ehrlich P.R., Ehrlich A.H., *The Population Bomb Revisited, „Electronic Journal of Sustainable Development"* 2009, vol. 1.

Erkman S., *Vers une écologie industrielle*, Paris 1998.

Falque M., *Les droits de propriété dans la problématique*, „La revue foncière" 2018, no. 22

Falquet J., *Femmes, féminisme et „développement": uneanalyse critique des politiques des institutions internationals* [in:] *Regards de femmes sur la globalization. Approches critiques*, ed. J. Bisilliat, Paris 2003.

Farley J., Burke M., Flomenhoh G., Kelly B., Forrest Murray D., Posner S., Putman M., Scanlan A., Witham A., *Monetary and Fiscal Policies for a Finite Planet*, „Sustainability" 2013, no. 5.

Favereau O., *Marchés internes, marchés externes*, „Revue économique" 1989, vol. 40, no. 2.

Fitoussi J.-P., Laurent E., *La nouvelle* écologie *politique. Économie et développement humain*, Paris 2008.

Flanders A., *Éléments pour une théorie de la négociation collective*, „Sociologie du travail" 1968, no. 1.

Flipo F., *Penser l'écologie politique*, „La revue électronique en sciences de l'environnement" 2016, vol. 16, no. 1.

Fonseca X., Lukosch S., Brazier F., *Social cohesion revisited: a new definition and how to characterize it*, „Innovation: The European Journal of Social Science Research" 2019, vol. 32, no. 2.

Foster J.B., Clark B., York R., *The Ecological Rifi: Capitalism's War on the Earth*, New York 2010.

Foster J.F., *The Theory of Institutional Adjustment*, „Journal of Economic Issues" 1981, vol. 15, no. 4.

Fragnière A., *Écologie et liberté: apports et insuffisances de l'écologie politique* [in:] *Théories et pratiques écologie: de l'écologie urbaine à l'imaginations environmentale*, red. M. Antonioli, Paris 2013.

Fraser N., *Can society be commodities all the way down? Polanyian reflections on capitalist crisis*, „FMSH-WP" 2012, no. 18.

Fressard O., Larrière C., Schmid L., *L'écologie est politique*, Paris 2013.

Frosch R., Gallopoulos N., *Strategies for Manufacturing*, „Scientist American" 1989, vol. 261, no. 3.

Fuchs A., *Préface* [in:] *Le développement durable à découvert*, red. A. Euzen, L. Eymard, F. Gaill, Paris 2013.

Gandon A.-L., *L'écoféminisme: une pensée féministe de la nature et de la société*, „Recherches feminists" 2009, vol. 22, no. 1.

Gendron C., *Le développement durable comme compromis. La modernisation écologique de l'économie à l'ère de la mondialisation*, Québec 2006.

Godard O., *Le développement durable: paysage intellectuel*, „Natures, Sciences, Sociétés" 1994, vol. 2, no. 4.

Godard O., *Sustainable development and the process of justifying choices in a controversial universe* [in:] *Sustainable Development: Concepts, Rationalities and Strategies*, ed. S. Faucheux, M. O'Connor, J. der Straaten, „Environment Series" 1998.

Godard O., *Une approche méta-économique*, Paris 2015.

Gowdy J., Erickson J., *Ecological economics at a crossroads*, „Ecological Economics" 2005, no. 53.

Gowdy J., Erickson J.D., *The approach of ecological economics*, „Cambridge Journal of Economics" 2005, no. 29.

Hansen K., *Visions of Environmentalism* [in:] *Free Market Environmentalism for the Next Generation*, ed. T.L. Anderson, D.R. Leal, New York 2015.

Hanuza-DeLay R., Davidson D.J., *The Environment and a Globalizing Sociology*, „Canadian Journal of Sociology/Cahiers Canadiens de Sociologie" 2008, no. 33(3).

Hopster J., *The Speciesism Debate: Intuition, Method, and Empirical Advances*, „Animals (Basel)" 2019, no. 9.

Hourcade J.Ch., Salles J.M., Théry D., *Ecological economics and scientific controversies. Lessons Pom some recent policy making in the EEC*, „Ecological Economics" 1992, vol. 6, no. 3.

Huber J., *The lost Innocence of Ecology: New Technologies & Superindustrial Development*, Frankfurt 1982.

Huber J., *The Rainbow Society: Ecology & Social Policy*, Frankfurt 1985.

Huckle J., Wals A.E.J., *The UN Decade of Education for Sustainable Development: business as usual in the end*, „Environmental Education Research" 2015, no. 3, vol. 21.

Hugon P., *L'éthique de la responsabilité et durisque au regard des projets de développement durable, de la responsabilité sociale de l'entreprise et des risques systémiques*, „Mondes en Développement" 2014, vol. 42, v. 4, no. 168.

Jänicke M., *Ecological Modernization – a Paradise of Feasibility but no General Solution* [in:] *The Ecological Modernization Capacity of Japan and Germany. Comparing Nuclear Energy, Renewables, Automobility and Rare Earth Policy*, ed. L. Mez, L. Okamura, H. Weidner, Berlin–Tokyo 2020.

Jastrzębska E., *Spójnośi społeczna w kontekście społecznej odpowiedzialności przedsiębiorstw. Definiowanie, pomiar i dobre praktyki biznesu*, „Optimum. Studia Ekonomiczne" 2017, no 4(88).

Jermier J.M., *Exploring Deep Subjectivity in Sociology and Organizational Studies*, „Organization & Environment" 2008, vol. 21, no 4.

Jollivet M., *Ecosystème et système sociaux* [in:] *Rapport final du séminaire environnement et société*, UNESCO, Berne 1992.

Junne G., Komen J., Tomeï F., *Dematerialisation of production: Impact on raw material exports of developing countries*, „Third World Quarterly" 1989, no. 11(2).

Kates R.W., Clark W.C., Corell R., Hall J.M. (et al.), *Sustainability Science*, „Science" 2001, vol. 292, no. 5517.

Klarin T., *The Concept of Sustainable Development: From its Beginning to the Contemporary Issues*, „Zagreb International Review of Economics & Business" 2018, vol. 21, no. 1.

Klein N., *This changes everything*, London 2014.

Klimowicz M., *Kapitał społeczny. Zagadnienia metodologiczne* [in:] *Kapitał społeczny – interpretacje, impresje, operacjonalizacja*, red. M. Klimowicz, W. Bokajło, Warszawa 2010.

Koch M., *Capitalism and Climate Change – Theoretical, Discussion, Historical Development and Policy Responses*, New York 2012.

Konstańczak S., *Koncepcje ekofilozofii* [in:] *Ekorozwój i Agenda 21. Interdyscyplinarny model kształcenia*, ed. P. Pieczyński, Szczecin 2007.

Kotzé L.J., *Human rights and the environment in the Anthropocene*, „The Anthropocene Review" 2014, vol. 1(3).

Kronenberg J., *Zrównoważona produkcja* [in:] *Wyzwania zrównoważonego rozwoju w Polsce*, ed. J. Kronenberg, T. Bergier, Kraków 2010.

Kropotkin P., *Mutual aid. A factor of evolution*, London 1987 (edycja francuska: *L'entraide. Un facteur de l'évolution*, Montréal 2005).

Kropotkin P., *Pomoc wzajemna jako czynnik rozwoju*, Poznań 2006.

Krotoszyński M., *Refleksyjnośi a badania nad sprawiedliwością transakcyjną*, „Archiwum Filozofii Prawa i Filozofii Społecznej" 2015, no 2(11).

Kulawik J., *Regulacje środowiskowe i innowacje a konkurencyjnośi*, „Zagadnienia Ekonomiki Rolnej" 2016, no 1(346).

Lalucq A., *Comment l'économie est venue à l'écologie*, „Alternatives Economiques" 2013, no. 061.

Lalucq A., *Economistes et écologie: des physiocrates à Stiglitz*, „Alternatives économiques" 2013, vol. 2, no. 58.

Langhelle O., *Why Ecological Modernization and Sustainable Development Should Not Be Conflated*, „Journal of Environmental Policy & Planning" 2000, no. 2.

Larrère, *L'écoféminisme: féminisme* écologique *ou* écologie *féministe*, „Tracés. Revue de Sciences humaines" 2012, no. 22.

Laurent É., *La transitionjuste. Unnouvelâge de l'économie et de l'environnement*, „Revue de l'OFCE" 2020, no. 165.

Leyens S., *Du développement durable à la décroissance, aller et retour*, „Les Carnets du développement durable" 2010, no. 1.

Limon M., *Human rights and climate change: Constructing a case for politic alaction*, „Harvard Environmental Law Review" 2009, no. 33.

Lipietz A., *Écologie politique régulationniste ou économie de l'environnement?* [in:] *Théorie de la régulation: l'état des savoirs*, red. R. Boyer, Y. Saillard, Paris 1995.

Lissowski G., *Społeczne aspekty analizy kosztów i korzyści*, „Decyzje" 2015, no 23.
Lowenthal D., *Marsh's Man and Nature at 150*, „The George Wright Forum" 2015, vol. 32, no. 3.

Löwy M., *Ecosocialism: A Radical Alternative* [in:] *Reflections on Socialism in the Twenty-First Century, Facing Market Liberalism, Rising Inequalities and the Environmental Imperative*, ed. C. Brundenius, Switzerland 2020.

Löwy M., *What is Ecosocialism?*, „Capitalisme. Nature. Socialism" 2005, vol. 16, no. 2. Maillefert M., Rousseau S., Zuindeau B., *Lectures hétérodoxes du développement durable*, „Développement durable et territories" 2010, vol. 1, no. 3.

Martens P., *Sustainability: science or fiction?*, „Sustainability: Science, Practice & Policy" 2006, vol. 2, no. 1.

Martine J., *L'écoféminisme et les mobilisations pour l'environnement dans les pays du Sud », suivi de « Le débat sur le care dans le féminisme nord-américain et sa convergence avec l'écoféminisme*, „Les Possibles" 2017, no. 14.

Martinez-Alier J., *Ecology and the Poor: A Neglected Dimension of Latin American History* [in:] *Perspectives in Resource Management in Developing Countries*, v. II, part 1, ed. B. Thakur, New Delhi 2007.

Martinez-Alier J., *The Environmentalism of the Poor. A study of ecological conflicts and valuation*, Northamption, Massachusetts 2002.

Matczak P., *Problemy ekologiczne jako problemy społeczne*, Poznań 2000.

Merchant C., *The Heath of Nature: Women, Ecology and the Scientific Revolution*, Harvard 1996.

Miller L.M., *Two notions of conventions: an experimental analysis*, „Journal of Institutional Economics" 2008, vol. 4, no. 3.

Mol A.P.J., Sonnenfeld D.A., *Ecological modernization around the world: an introduction*, „Environmental Politics" 2000, vol. 9, no. 1.

Monnet É., *La théorie des „capabilités" d'Amartya Sen face au problème du relativisme*, „Tracés. Revue de Science humaines" 2007, no. 12.

Mouratidis K., *Urban planning and quality of life: A review of pathways linking the built environment to subjective well-being*, „Cities" 2021, vol. 115.

Murali V., Oyebode F., *Poverty, social in equality and mental health*, „Advances in Psychiatric Treatment" 2004, vol. 10, ni. 3.

Nabli R., *Entrepreneurs, État et citoyenneté. Le cas de la Tunisie*, „Revue algérienne d'anthropologie et de sciencessociales" 2010, no. 50.

Nagel E., *Struktura nauki. Zagadnienia logiki wyjaśnień naukowych*, Warszawa 1970. Norgaard R.B., *Sustainable development: A co-evolutionary view*, „Futures" 1988, vol. 20, no. 6.

Norgaard R.B., *The case for methodological pluralism*, „Ecological Economics" 1989, vol. 1, no. 1.

Novy A., *Trwale dziedzictwo Karla Polanyiego*, „Globalny Dialog" 2019, v. IX.

Ostrom E., *Governing the commons. The Evolution of Institutions for Collective Action*, Cambridge 1990.

Ouariachi T., Li Ch.-Y., Elving W.J.L., *Gamification Approaches for Education and Engagement on Pro-Environmental Behaviors: Searching for Best Practices*, „Sustainability" 3 June 2020. *Państwo w czasach zmiany*, ed. M. Pietraś, I. Hofman, S. Michałowski, Lublin 2018. Passet R., *L'économique et le vivant*, Paris 1979.

Passet R., Vivien F.-D., *René Passet: la quête d'une bioéconomie transdisciplinaire*, „Natures Sciences Sociétés" 2011/4, vol. 19.

Payre E., *L'écologie industrielle: une stratégie conciliant les dimensions économique et environnemental du développement durable?*, Paris 2008.

Pearce D., Atkinson G., Hamilton K., *The measurement of sustainability development* [in:] *Theory and Implementation of Economic Models for Sustainable Development*, ed. J.C.J.M. von den Bergh, M.W. HoLes, „Economy & Environment" 1998, vol. 15.

Pearce D.W., Atkinson G.D., *Capital theory and the measurement of sustainable development: an indicator of „weak" sustainability*, „Ecological Economics" 1993, vol. 8, no. 2.

Pearce D.W., Markandya A., Barbier E., *Blueprint for a Green Economy*, London 1989. Péréon Y.M., *„L'anti-environnementalisme", nouveau théme des conservateurs américains*, „Potomac Paper" 2011, no. 8.

Pęciak R., *Geneza podejścia regulacyjnego we Pancuskiej teorii ekonomicznej*, „Prace Naukowe Uniwersytetu Ekonomicznego we Wrocławiu – Ekonomia" 2015, no 401.

Pęciak R., *Problemy kapitalizmu we Pancuskiej teorii regulacji*, „Studia Ekonomiczne. Zeszyty Naukowe Uniwersytetu Ekonomicznego w Katowicach" 2014, no 176.

Pieczyński P., *Szczyt Ziemi w Rio* [in:] *Ekorozwój i Agenda 21. Interdyscyplinarny model kształcenia*, ed. P. Pieczyński, Szczecin 2007.

Pietraś M., *Bezpieczeństwo ekologiczne w Europie. Studium politologiczne*, Lublin 2000. Piontek W., *Gospodarowanie odpadami komunalnymi jako czynnik wzrostu gospodarczego*, Białystok 2015.

Pleszczyński J., *Ewolucyjna teoria poznania a kognitywistyka*, „Roczniki Filozoficzne" 2006, no 2, v. LIV.

Porter M.E., Linde van der C., *Towards a new conception of the environment-competitiveness relationship*, „Journal of Economic Perspectives" 1995, vol. 9, no. 4.

Postel N., *L'économie des conventions. Une approche instrumentale de la rationalité individuelle?*, „Revue économique" 1998, vol. 49, no. 6.

Poza-Vilches de M.F., Gutiérrez-Pérez J., López-Alcarria A., *Participation and Sustainable Development* [in:] *Encyclopedia of Sustainability in Higher Education*, ed. W. Leal Filho, Hamburg 2019.

Queinnec E., *Réguler l'écologie au moyen de la liberté: Bref plaidoyer en faveur de „l'écolibéralisme"*, „Journal des libertes.fr", Été 2019, no. 5.

Raco M., *Sustainable Development, Rolled-out Neoliberalism and Sustainable Comminities*, „Antipode" 2005, vol. 37, no. 2.

Rifkin J., Howard T., *Entropia. Nowy światopogląd, Katowice 2008. Robbins P., Political ecology: a critical introduction*, New Jersey 2004.

Rockström J., Steffen W., Noone K., Persson A., Chapin F.S., Lambin E., Lenton T.M., Scheffer M., Folke C., Schellnhuber H., Nykvist B., Wit de C.A., Hughes T., Leeuw van der S., Rodhe H., Sörlin S., Snyder P.K., Costanza R., Svedin U., Falkenmark M., Karlberg L., Corell R.W., Fabry V.J., Hansen J., Walker B., Liverman D., Richardson K., Crutzen P., Foley J., *Planetary boundaries: exploring the safe operating space for humanity*, „Ecology and Society" 2009, vol. 14, no. 2.

Rogall H., *Ekonomia zrównoważonego rozwoju – potrzeba reformy tradycyjnej ekonomii* [in:] *Ekonomia zrównoważonego rozwoju. Zarys problemów badawczych i dydaktyki*, ed. B. Poskrobko, Białystok 2010.

Rokicka E., Woźniak W., *W kierunku zrównoważonego rozwoju. Koncepcje, interpretacje, konteksty*, Łódź 2016.

Rothbard M.N., *The Ethics of Liberty*, New York 2003.

Rudolf W., *Koncepcja Governance i jej zastosowanie – od instytucji międzynarodowych do niższych szczebli władzy*, „Acta Universitatis Lodziensis. Folia Oeconomica" 2010, no 245.

Ruelle Ch., Neyrat F., Écologie=X. *Une introduction*, „Labyrinthe" 2008, no. 30.

Sandmo A., *The Early History of Environmental Economics*, „Review of Environmental Economics and Policy" 2015, vol. 9, no. 1.

Schickert Ch., *W imię wizji socjalistycznej. Wywiad z Qingzhi Huanem*, „Globalny Dialog" 2019, v. IX.

Schimanek T., *Partycypacja obywatelska w społeczności lokalnej*, Warszawa 2015.

Schnaiberg, A., Pellow D.N., Weinberg A., *The Treadmill of Production and the Environmental State*, New York 2000.

Scotto d'Apollonia L., *Les controverses climatiques: une analyse socioépistémique. Sociologie*, Montpellier 2014.

Sheehy-Skeffington J., Rea J., *How poverty affects people's decision-making processes*, „Joseph Rowntree Foundation – Inspiring Social Change" February 2017.

Shi L., Han L., Yang F., Gao L., *The Evolution of Sustainable Development Theory: Types, Goals, and Research Prospects*, „Sustainability" 2019, no. 11(7158).

Smith T., *The case against Pee market environmentalism*, „Journal of Agricultural and Environmental Ethics" 1995, no. 8(2).

Söderbaum P., *Positional Analysis: A Multidimensional and Democracy-Oriented Approach to Decision-Making and Sustainability*, „Sustainability" 2020, no. 12.

Söderbaum P., *Toward sustainable development: Pom neoclassical monopoly to democracy – oriented economics*, „Real-World Economics Review" 2019, no. 87.

Solow R.M., *An Almost Practical Step toward Sustainability*, „Resources Policy" 1993, vol. 19, no. 3.

Spash C.L., *Social Ecological Economics. Understanding the Past to See the Future*, „American Journal of Economics and Sociology" 2011, vol. 70, no. 2.

Spash C.L., Villena H.G., *Exploring the Approach of Institutional Economics to the Environment*, Cambridge 1999.

Stachurska-Szczesiak K., *Rozwój samopodtrzymujący w polityce Unii Europejskiej wobec państw Maghrebu*, Lublin 2019.

Stern N., *The Economics of Climate Change*, Cambridge 2007.

Sztumski J., *Jakośi życia jako kategoria socjologiczno-społeczna*, „Studia Ekonomiczne" 2014, no 179.

Śmiech S., *Ekonomiczne teorie wyceny surowców energetycznych* [in:] *Modelowanie i prognozowanie cen surowców energetycznych*, ed. M. Papież, S. Śmiech, Warszawa 2015.

Świstak A., *Opodatkowanie wydobycia surowców naturalnych w Polsce*, Warszawa 2018. Taniguchi K., Nakano E., *Citizenship Education for Sustainable Development: Theoretical and Practical Approaches for Project ESICS*, „International Journal of Information and Education Technology" 2017, no. 10, vol. 7.

Thierry C., Arnaud D., *Convention et institution*, „Document de travail" 1995, no. 4, Université de Reims.

Tibbs H., *Industrial Ecology: An Environmental Agenda for Industry*, „Technical Report" 1993, January.

Torjman S., *Community-Based Poverty Reduction*, Ottawa 1998.

Torjman S., *The Social Dimension of Sustainable Development*, Ottawa May 2000.

Tyburski W., *Wprowadzenie* [in:] *Zasady kształtowania postaw sprzyjających wdrażaniu zrównoważonego rozwoju*, ed. W. Tyburski, Toruń 2011.

Vaillancourt J.G., *Sociologie de l'environnement: de l'écologie humaine à l'écosociologie* [in:] *La recherché sociale en environnement: nouveaux paradigms*, ed. R. Tessier, J.G. Vaillancourt, Montréal 1996.

Verchère A., *Le développement durable en question: analyses économiques autour d'un improbable compromis entre acceptions optimiste et pessimiste du rapport de l'Homme à la Nature*, „L'Actualité économique" 2011, vol. 87, no. 3.

Verger Y., *L'économie stationnaire du point de vue de la production jointe: le cas des bioénergies. Écologie politique vs écologie industrielle, quelles stratégies pour le développement durable?*, Clermont-Ferrand Mars 2013.

Vivien F.-D., *Le développement soutenable*, Paris 2005.

Vivien F.-D., *Le développement soutenable: un objet* économique *controversé* [in:] *Stratégies de développement durable. Développement, environnement ou justice sociales?*, ed. A. de Heering, S. Leyens, Namur 2010.

Voget-Kleschin L., *Large-Scale Land Acquisition: Evaluating its Environmental Aspects Against the Background of Strong Sustainability*, „Journal of Agricultural and Environmental Ethics" 2013, no. 26.

Wackernagel M., Rees W., *Our Ecological Footprint: Reducing Human Impact on the Earth*, Gabriela Island 1996.

Walkowski M., *Przyczyny powstania globalnego kryzysu finansowego 2008+. Analiza i porównanie wybranych opinii*, „Przegląd Strategiczny" 2013, no 2.

Waloszczyk K., *Zielony wątek w religiach świata* [in:] *Ekorozwój i Agenda 21. Interdyscy-plinarny model kształcenia*, ed. P. Pieczyński, Szczecin 2007.

Warren K.J., *Le pouvoir et la promesse de l'écoféminisme*, „Multitudes" 2009(1), no. 36. Warren K.J., *The power and the promise of ecological feminism* [in:] *Environmental Philosophy. From Animal Rights to Radical Ecology*, red. M. Zimmerman, New Jersey 1990.

Weisz H., Clark E., *Society-Nature Coevolution: Interdisciplinary Concept for Sustainability*, „Geografiska Annaler: Series B, Human Geography" 2011, no. 93(4).

White L., *The Historical Roots of Our Ecologie Crisis*, „Science" 1967, vol. 155, no. 3767. Zajdel M., *Wybrane teorie rozwoju regionalnego oraz lokalnego a rynek pracy*, „Studia Prawno-Ekonomiczne" 2011, v. LXXXIII.

Zanden Van J.L., *Tracing the beginning of the Kuznets curve: western Europe during the early modern period*, „The Economic History Review" 1995, vol. 48, no. 4.

Zartman I.W., *Concevoir la théorie de la négociation en tant qu'approche de résolution de conflits économiques*, „Revue Francaise de Gestion" 2004, no. 153.

Zdybicka Z.J., *Człowiek – zbawcą człowieka? Uwagi o marksistowskiej teorii religii* [in:] *Wobec filozofii marksistowskiej: polskie doświadczenia*, red. A.B. Stępień, Lublin 1990. Zhang L., Mol A.P.J., Sonnenfeld D., *The interpretation of ecological modernisation in China*, „Environmental Politics" 2007, vol. 16, no. 4.

Zhou B., Ma Q., Wu J., Hu G., Mao D., Zeng X., Guo J., Fang X., Liu Y., Lyu L., *Sustainability science revisited: Recent advances and new opportunities*, „Chinese J. Appl. Ecol" 2019, no. 30.

Zimmerman F.J., Carter M.R., *Asset smoothing, consumption smoothing and the reproduction of inequality under risk and subsistence constraints*, „Journal of Development Economics" 2003, vol. 71, no. 2.

Zin J., *Qu'est-ce que l'écologie-politique?*, „Ecologie & politique" 2010/2, no. 40.

Zrałek J., *Ekonomia ekologiczna. Rewizja teorii ekonomii w świetle koncepcji zrównoważonego rozwoju gospodarczego*, „Studia Ekonomiczne. Zeszyty Naukowe Uniwersytetu Ekonomicznego w Katowicach – Ekonomia 7" 2016, no 303.

## Materials from the Internet

Adamković A., *Consequences of Poverty on Economic Decision-Making: Assessing the Verisimilitude of the Cognitive Mechanism*, „Front. Psychol." 13 February 2020, https://www.frontiersin.org/articles/10.3389/fpsyg.2020.00171/full.

Amor S., *Un féminisme islamique en dialogue: une chance pour le féminisme et un approfondissement de la foi*, „Webzine" August 2016, vol. 24, no 83, http://cjf.qc.ca/vivre-ensemble/webzine/article/un-feminisme-islamique-en-dialogue-une-chance-pour-le-feminisme-et-un-approfondissement-de-la-foi/.

Anderson M., *Economics, Steady State*, https://umaine.edu/soe/wp-content/uploads/sites/199/2013/01/Economics-Steady-State.pdf.

Brasier P.-J., *La Bolivie et le changement climatique*, „SciencesPo" 8 octobre 2010, https://www.sciencespo.fr/opalc/content/la-bolivie-et-le-changement-climatique.

Defeyt P., *Ecologiser l'économie: une sacrée enterprise*, http://www.etopia.be/IMG/pdf/ r4_defeyt_web.pdf.

de Plunkett P., *L'écologie radicale: intéressante, utile et même nécessaire*, „L'Éthique écologique" 2008, no. 42, http://www.libertepolitique.com/La-revue/La-revue-Liberte-Politique/L-ethique-ecologique.

*Économie verte: marchandiser la planète pour la Sauer?*, „Alternatives Sud" 2012, vol. XX-2013/1, https://www.cetri.be/Economie-verte-marchandiser-la-2993?lang=fr. Figuière C., Chebbi A., Écologie *Industrielle (EI) et Économie Circulaire (EC). Concurrentes ou complémentaires?*, XXXIIèmes journées du développement ATM 2016, Colloque: „Catastrophes, vulnérabilités et résiliences dans les pays en développement", Université Lille, 1–3 Juin 2016, https://halshs.archives-ouvertes.fr/halshs-01564030/document.

Fournier D., *Femmes au coeur de l'économie sociale et solidaire*, Montréal 2011, http://www.reliess.org/wp-content/uploads/2011/04/Document-pr%C3%A9paratoire-Femmes-au-coeur-de-lESS.pdf.

*From System Shock to System Change – time to transform. The Future for Sustainability*, Forum for the Future, London–New York–Singapore–Mumbai 2020.

Hurard M., *La participation citoyenne au développement durable à l'échelle locale en Europe*, http://www.pourlasolidarite.eu/sites/default/files/publications/files/working_paper_-_participation_citoyenne_26.08.11_0.pdf.

*James O'Connor second contradiction of capitalism*, https://libcom.org/blog/james-ocon-nors-second-contradiction-capitalism-25042014

Koffi A., *Les contradictions des politiques de ciblagedans les projets de lutte contre la pauvreté dans l'ouest montagneux ivoirien*, DEA 2009, http://www. memoireonline.com/09/11/4823/m_Les-contradictions-des-politiques-de-ciblagedans-les-projets-de-lutte-contre-la-pauvrete-dans-lou31.html.

Kropotkin P., *Państwo i jego rola polityczna*, Warszawa 1924, http://www.biblioteka-cyfrowa.pl/Content/77566/Kropotkin_P_Panstwo_i_jego_rola_historyczna.pdf. *L'En Dehors: Quotidien anarchiste individualiste*, http://endehors.net/news/civilisation-primitivisme-et-anarchisme.

Lepage H., *Pourquoi la propriété*, Paris 1985, https://www.icrei.fr/en/2019/10/02/did-you-say-freedom/

Linhardt D., *Didier Raoult, ou la controverse scientifique dans le temps de l'urgence*, 27 mars 2020, https://www.ehess.fr/fr/carnet/coronavirus/didier-raoult-ou-controverse-scientifique-dans-temps-lurgence.

Michnowski L., *Jak żyi?, Ekorozwój albo…*, Białystok 1995, http://www.psl.org.pl/kte/ books.htm.

Munongo V., *Un nouveau courant de pensées pour le développement durable*, 21 avril 2020, https://isnad-africa.org/2020/04/21/un-nouveau-courant-de-pensees-pour-le-developpement-durable/.

Pizer W.A., Kopp R., *Calculating the Cost of Environmental Regulation*, Resources for the Future: Discussion Paper: 03–06, https://media.rff.org/documents/RFF-DP-03-06.pdf.

*Rezolucja Zgromadzenia Ogólnego A/RES/70/1. Agenda na rzecz Zrównoważonego Rozwoju 2030*, http://www.un.org.pl/agenda-2030-rezolucja

Rothbard M.N., *O nową wolnośi. Manifest libertariański*, (1973), polskie tłumaczenie: W. Falkowski 2004, https://mises.pl/pliki/upload/Rothbard_manifest_libertari-anski.pdf.

Schudy H., *Wokół Szczytu Klimatycznego COP22 w Marrakeszu – Trzeźwośi i Sarmatyzm*, http://www.eko.org.pl/index_news.php?dzial=2&kat=20&art=1808.

Sinaï A., *L'économie écologique déploie ses propositions*, https://www.actu-environnement.com/ae/news/economie-ecologique-robert-costanza-18443.php4.

Szoc E., *Écosocialisme (s)*, „Politique revue belge d'analyse et de debat" 2020, no. 91, https://www.revuepolitique.be/ecosocialismes/.

Szuba M., *Gouverner dans un monde fini: des limites globales au rationnement individuel, sociologie environnementale du projet britannique de politique de Carte carbone (1996–2010)*, Université Panthéon-Sorbonne – Paris I,

2014 (rozprawa doktorska), https://tel.archives-ouvertes.fr/tel-01794527/document.

Theys J., *Après le „développement durable", la „modernisation* écologique"?, https://www.nss-journal.org/articles/nss/pdf/2000/01/nss20000801p13.pdf.

Tinson A., *Living in poverty was bad for your health long before COVID-19*, 25 July 2020, https://www.health.org.uk/publications/long-reads/living-in-poverty-was-bad-for-your-health-long-before-COVID-19.

## Internet sources

http://cafes-philo.org/2016/01/quel-est-le-role-de-la-fete/.http://cjf.qc.ca/vivre-en-semble/mariam/.

http://coin.wne.uw.edu.pl/tzylicz/0904AURA.pdf.

http://nature-humaine.fr/ressources/les-dossiers/.

http://nature-humaine.fr/wp-content/docs/dossiers/ateliers_ecologie_profonde.pdf.

http://www.econlib.org/library/Enc/FreeMarketEnvironmentalism.html.

http://www.oeconomia.net/private/colloqueddiufm/06.colloquedd-destais.pdf.

http://zielonewiadomosci.pl/tematy/ekologia/wszystkie-odcienie-ekopolityki/.

https://businessinsider.com.pl/wiadomosci/pierwsza-decyzja-bidena-usa-wra-caja-do paryskiego-porozumienia-klimatycznego/bye0sdz.

https://conventions.hypotheses.org/the-economics-of-convention.

https://ec.europa.eu/eurostat/documents/3217494/5704439/865-FR-FR.PDF/c99a8ad6–23bf-4bdf-9021-bfdcda583857.

https://institut-economie-circulaire.fr/.

https://is4ie.org/about/history.

https://isnad-africa.org/2020/04/21/un-nouveau-courant-de-pensees-pour-le-developpement-durable/.

https://mises.pl/wp-content/uploads/2012/05/Huerta-de-Soto-kilka-dodat-kowych-refleksji-na-temat-kryzysu.pdf.

https://theconversation.com/de-la-controverse-scientifique-au-debat-de-soci-ete-112039.

https://wiadomosci.radiozet.pl/Swiat/Zamieszki-w-Paryzu.-Protest-zoltych-kamizelek.

https://www.alternatives-economiques.fr/schema-trois-spheres-de-rene-pas-set-0103201366859.html.

https://www.economiecirculaire.org/static/h/du-concept-a-la-pratique.html.

https://www.ehess.fr/fr/carnet/coronavirus/didier-raoult-ou-controverse-scienti-fique-dans-temps-lurgence.

https://www.enseignementsup-recherche.gouv.fr/cid86688/strategie-nationale-de-recherche-france-europe-2020.html.

https://www.erudit.org/fr/revues/ae/2011-v87-n3-ae0112/1009279ar.pdf.

https://www.fondsfmoq.com/leconomie-ecologique-un-courant-digne-dinteret/.

https://www.forbes.pl/wiadomosci/donald-trump-wypowiada-paryskie-porozumienie-klimatyczne/3n5ek53.

https://www.icrei.fr/en/about_us/.

https://www.lemonde.fr/idees/article/2020/03/25/didier-raoult-le-medecin-peut-et-doit-reflechir-comme-un-medecin-et-non-pas-comme-un-methodologiste_6034436_3232.html.

https://www.nature.com/news/development-time-to-leave-gdp-behind-1.14499.

https://www.perc.org/.

https://www.polsoz.fu-berlin.de/en/polwiss/forschung/systeme/ffu/index.html.

https://www.revue-ballast.fr/bookchin-ecologie-radicale-et-municipalisme-libertaire/.

https://www.rff.org/.

https://www.telerama.fr/idees/climat-pesticides-ogm-les-scientifiques-font-le-buzz-ok-dom,136680.php.

https://www.thefuturescentre.org/fos/.

https://www.vie-publique.fr/parole-dexpert/271086-terre-climat-quest-ce-que-lan-thropocene-ere-geologique.

**Studies in Politics, Security and Society**

Edited by Stanisław Sulowski

| | |
|---|---|
| Vol. 1 | Robert Wiszniowski (ed.): Challenges to Representative Democracy. A European Perspective. 2015. |
| Vol. 2 | Jarosław Szymanek: Theory of Political Representation. 2015. |
| Vol. 3 | Alojzy Z. Nowak (ed.): Global Financial Turbulence in the Euro Area. Polish Perspective. 2015. |
| Vol. 4 | Jolanta Itrich-Drabarek: The Civil Service in Poland. Theory and Experience. 2015. |
| Vol. 5 | Agnieszka Rothert: Power of Imagination. Education, Innovations and Democracy. 2016. |
| Vol. 6 | Zbysław Dobrowolski: Combating Corruption and Other Organizational Pathologies. 2017. |
| Vol. 7 | Vito Breda: The Objectivity of Judicial Decisions. A Comparative Analysis of Nine Jurisdictions. 2017. |
| Vol. 8 | Anna Sroka: Accountability and democracy in Poland and Spain. 2017. |
| Vol. 9 | Anna Sroka / Fanny Castro-Rial Garrone / Rubén Darío Torres Kumbrián (eds.): Radicalism and Terrorism in the 21st Century. Implications for Security. 2017. |
| Vol. 10 | Filip Pierzchalski: Political Leadership in Morphogenetic Perspective. 2017. |
| Vol. 11 | Alina Petra Marinescu: The Discursive Dimension of Employee Engagement and Disengagement. Accounts of keeping and leaving jobs in present-day Bucharest organizations. 2017. |
| Vol. 12 | Jacek Giedrojć: Competition, Coordination, Social Order. Responsible Business, Civil Society, and Government in an Open Society. 2017. |
| Vol. 13 | Filip Ilkowski: Capitalist Imperialism in Contemporary Theoretical Frameworks. 2017. |
| Vol. 14 | Leszek Leszczyński / Adam Szot (eds.): Discretionary Power of Public Administration. Its Scope and Control. 2017. |
| Vol. 15 | Tadeusz Klementewicz: Understanding Politics. Theory, Procedures, Narratives. 2017. |
| Vol. 16 | Tomasz Bichta: Political Systems of the Former Yugoslavia. 2018 |
| Vol. 17 | Miroslav Palárik / Alena Mikulášová / Martin Hetényi / Róbert Arpáš: The City and Region Against the Backdrop of Totalitarianism. 2018 |
| Vol. 18 | Jolanta Itrich-Drabarek / Stanisław Mazur / Justyna Wiśniewska-Grzelak (eds.): The Transformations of the Civil Service in Poland in Comparison with International Experience. 2018. |
| Vol. 19 | Jerzy Juchnowski / R. Jan Sielezin / Ewa Maj: The Image of "White" and "Red" Russia in the Polish Political Thought of the 19th and 20th Century. Analogies and Parallels. 2018. |
| Vol. 20 | Roman Kuźniar: Europe in the International Order. 2018. |
| Vol. 21 | Piotr Jaroszyński: Europe - the Clash of Civilisations. 2018. |
| Vol. 22 | Stanisław Filipowicz: Truth and the Will to Illusion. 2018. |
| Vol. 23 | Andrzej Szeptycki: Contemporary Relations between Poland and Ukraine. The "Strategic Partnership" and the Limits Thereof. 2019. |

Vol. 24 Sylwester Gardocki / Rafał Ożarowski / Rafał Ulatowski (eds.): The Islamic World in International Relations. 2019.

Vol. 25 Jacek Zaleśny (ed.): Constitutional Courts in Post-Soviet States. Between the Model of a State of Law and Its Local Application. 2019.

Vol. 26 Andrzej Antoszewski / Przemysław Żukiewicz / Mateusz Zieliński / Katarzyna. Domagała: Formation of Government Coalition in Westminster Democracies. Towards a Network Approach. 2020.

Vol. 27 Joanna Osiejewicz: Global Governance of Oil and Gas Resources in the International Legal Perspective. 2020.

Vol. 28 Anita Oberda-Monkiewicz: Poland-Mexico towards a Strategic Partnership. 2020.

Vol. 29 Bartosz Czepil / Wojciech Opioła: Ethnic diversity and local governance quality. The case of Opole Province in Poland. 2020.

Vol. 30 Adam Szymański / Jakub Wódka / Wojciech Ufel / Amanda Dziubińska: Between Fair and Rigged. Elections as a Key Determinant of the 'Borderline Political Regime' - Turkey in Comparative Perspective. 2020.

Vol. 31 Tomasz Grzegorz Grosse (ed.): Fuel for Dominance. On the Economic Bases of Geopolitical Supremacy. 2020.

Vol. 32 Dariusz Jarosz / Maria Pasztor: From Subjection to Independence. Post-World War II Polish-Italian Relations. 2020.

Vol. 33 Paweł Sekuła: Chernobyl Liquidators. The Unknown Story. With the Testimony of the President of Latvia. 2020.

Vol. 34 Kamil Glinka (ed.): Urban Policy System in Strategic Perspective: From V4 to Ukraine. 2020.

Vol. 35 Paweł Lesiński: At the Origins of German Liberalism: the State in the Thought of Robert von Mohl. 2020.

Vol. 36 Jana Popovicsová (ed.): Reflexions about a Cultural and Social Phenomenon: Identity. 2020.

Vol. 37 Agnes Bernek: Geopolitics of Central and Eastern Europe in the 21st Century. From the Buffer Zone to the Gateway Zone. 2021.

Vol. 38 Marek Antoni Musioł: The European Union as a Post-Lisbon Regional Security Complex. 2021.

Vol. 39 Alina Petra Marinescu: Manipulation in the Disclosure of the Securitate Files. The Case of Mona Muscă. 2021

Vol. 40 Jiří Zákravský: Cycling Diplomacy. Undemocratic Regimes and ProfessionalRoad Cycling Teams Sponsorship. 2021.

Vol. 41 Mirosław Karwat / Filip Pierzchalski / Marcin Tobiasz (eds.): Constituents of Political Theory. Selected Articles of the Warsaw School of Political Theory. 2021.

Vol. 42 Angieszka Bieńczyk-Missala: Preventing Mass Human-Rights Violations and Atrocity Crimes. 2021.

Vol. 43 Jan Garlicki: Political Participation Capital. 2021.

Vol. 44 Mirosław Karwat: Theory of Provocation. In Light of Political Science. 2022.

Vol. 45 Anna Sroka / Piotr Potejko / Rubén Darío Torres Kumbrián (eds.): Migration and Border Security. Global Perspectives. 2021.

Vol. 46 Stanisław Sulowski / Tomasz Słomka (eds.): The Political System of Poland. Tradition and Contemporaneity. 2022.

Vol. 47 Ewelina Kancik-Kołtun / Josef Smolík (eds.): New Political Parties in the Party Systems of the Czech Republic. 2022.

Vol. 48 Ewa Feder-Sempach: Economic Populism in British and American Political Discourse. A Comparative Analysis of Boris Johnson's and Donald Trump's Speeches. 2022.

Vol. 49 Katarzyna Kołodziejczyk (ed.): The EU Towards the Global South During the COVID-19 Pandemic. 2022.

Vol. 50 Silvia Amato: Public Undertakings of Nuclear Waste Storage. The Role of the Government in the Dissemination of Public Knowledge. 2022.

Vol. 51 Agnieszka Cholewińska-Nielsen: Evolving Humanitarianism. The Work of the International Red Cross and Red Crescent Movement. 2022.

Vol. 52 Josef Smolik / Ewelina Kancik-Kołtun: New Political Parties in the Party System of Poland. 2023.

Vol. 53 Rafał Wiśniewski / Elżbieta Szyszlak / Radosław Zenderowski (eds.): Cultural Security. Theory – Selected Aspects – Case Studies. 2023.

Vol. 54 Filip Pierzchalski: Political Leadership: Structure – Consciousness – Emotions. 2023.

Vol. 55 Łukasz Zamęcki / Li-Jiuan Chen-Rabich (eds.): The Democratisation Process of Poland and Taiwan: Comparative Perspective. 2023.

Vol. 56 Marcin Gajek: Refusing to be Forgotten: Southern Conservatism and the Political Thought of M. E. Bradford. 2023.

Vol. 57 Sulowski Stanisław (ed.): Security Challenges at the Dawn of a New International Order. 2023.

Vol. 58 Alicja Z. Nowak / Kinga Anna Gajda (eds.): University and War in Ukraine. 2023.

Vol. 59 Bernard Wiśniewski / Paulina Polko (eds.): Contemporary Understanding of Security and Its Contexts. 2024.

Vol. 60 Aleksander Żołnierski / Dariusz Jaruga (eds.): Big Data. Post-truth and Disinformation in Politics and Economy during Times of Conflict. 2024.

Vol. 61 Mirosław Karwat / Marcin Tobiasz / Jacek Ziółkowski (eds.): Constituents of Political Theory (2). Selected Articles by the Warsaw School of Political Theory. 2025.

Vol. 62 Katarzyna Stachurska-Szczesiak: Sustainable Development. Theoretical Approaches. 2025.

www.peterlang.com

www.ingramcontent.com/pod-product-compliance
Ingram Content Group UK Ltd.
Pitfield, Milton Keynes, MK11 3LW, UK
UKHW021009120926
8556IPUK00029B/246

9 783631 930120